ABOUT TH[E AUTHOR]

Paul Mountfort is a writer, researcher and workshop presenter with a fascination for oracles (also known as divination systems), especially within Celtic and Norse tradition. He holds an M.A. in Literature, a B.A. in History, and is currently completing his doctoral dissertation on the subject of *Oracle-texts: the Western tradition*. He has written for several magazines and a variety of other media, as well as giving talks and workshops, including a set of courses at the University of Auckland's Centre for Continuing Education which are amongst the first university based courses on oracles in the world. Active in the Wiccan and Celtic pagan community, he lives with his partner and son on Waiheke Island, in Auckland's Hauraki Gulf.

To my darling Claire and son, Fintan,
for being the root, branch and flower
of my life

ogam

How to Read, Create and Shape Your Destiny Through the Celtic Oracle

paul rhys mountfort

RIDER

LONDON · SYDNEY · AUCKLAND · JOHANNESBURG

1 3 5 7 9 10 8 6 4 2

First published in 2001 by Rider,
an imprint of Ebury Press, Random House,
20 Vauxhall Bridge Road, London SW1V 2SA

Random House Australia (Pty) Limited
20 Alfred Street, Milsons Point, Sydney,
New South Wales 2061, Australia

Random House New Zealand Limited
18 Poland Road, Glenfield,
Auckland 10, New Zealand

Random House South Africa (Pty) Limited
Endulini, 5A Jubilee Road,
Parktown 2193, South Africa

The Random House Group Limited Reg. No. 954009

Papers used by Rider are natural, recyclable products
made from wood grown in sustainable forests.

Printed and bound by
Mackays of Chatham Ltd, Chatham, Kent

Illustrations by Teresa Whitty

A CIP catalogue record for this book
is available from the British Library

ISBN 0-7126-1141-X

Contents

Acknowledgements

There are always more people to thank than is fitting in an acknowledgement, for a book is a cumulative process, like growth rings on a tree. But salutations to all those whose affability, support and inspiration made the following pages possible. Close to home I would like to thank my mother and father, for long understanding where my true passions lay. I am equally indebted to my grandmother, Vivienne, a weaver, for introducing me to the mysteries of treelore from an early age. I wish her long and continued happiness! Thanks also to my extended kin, the fine members of the Feasey clan, for welcoming me into their circle. Of those friends whose camaraderie has contributed in tangible and intangible ways, Conrad and Kate, Gerard Timings, Nick Bain, Jamie Wells, Creon Upton and Cian MacFhiarais deserve special mention.

For coherence in the many references to Irish mythology, I am indebted to the celebrated collection *Irish Myths and Legends* by Lady Gregory Augusta. Specific mention to the original sources are, however, also generally given, in order to help the reader follow 'the path of Ogam' to its wellspring. To the many fine works included in the bibliography, I am equally grateful. Parts of this book began their life as a doctoral dissertation made possible by a generous grant from the University of Auckland, which I would like to acknowledge, along with my supervisor's patience over what must at times have seemed an errant topic. Sincere thanks also to the artist, Teresa Whitty, for her striking and original works, and to Nicolas Blake as the discriminating reader. Finally, a heartfelt toast to Susan Lascelles, for shepherding the manuscript to publication through the vicissitudes of the trade.

Introduction:
How to Use this Book

This book is a complete guide to Ogam divination, designed for the needs of people today, at the dawn of a new millennium. Its pages will lead you to an appreciation of the power, beauty and effectiveness of the ancient art of ogamcasting, putting in your hands the means to divine for yourself and others using the 'alphabet of the Druids'.

The fifteen-hundred-year-old Ogam alphabet is a magical and mysterious script, the Celtic equivalent of the Runes. Like the Runes, Tarot and *I Ching*, it is also used in divination, as an oracle which can teach us much about our fate and future. Unlike Tarot, whose cards depict a set of characters and situations, Ogam's twenty 'tree-letters' are all named after woodland trees. You might well ask how trees can function as an oracle system, as a set of signs, omens and auguries. The fact is that each tree in the Tree Alphabet has a set of correspondences and meanings attached to it. All the tree-letters are linked to figures or themes from Celtic mythology, and each has a unique wisdom to impart. Once they become familiar to you, you will find that the ancient tree-letters relate to your own particular circumstances, providing profound guidance and counsel.

Divination is a magical art currently undergoing a great revival. For centuries, our culture has denied and rejected the philosophy underlying divination: that so-called chance or random events can play a meaningful role in our lives. This was not the case in traditional societies, which understood, through centuries of experience, that there is a thread or pattern running through the rhythm of events. Divination is a way of tapping into this process. It utilizes 'chance' by creating meaningful systems of signs, such as the tree-letters, which the diviner draws sight unseen and interprets for their meaning. Anybody who practises divination will find that these 'random' processes actually produce results of great significance, as the Celts well knew. For Ogam is only one of a vast range of techniques used in ancient times to illuminate events in the present and chart their potential flow into the future.

Many people think of divination as mere fortune-telling. It is true that oracles can be very revealing with regard to future events. Their symbols are like the legends on a map, and we can use them to look forward to the forking pathways of 'that which is to come'. Yet in the final analysis, future-reading is less crucial to the process of consulting Ogam than is the full holistic reflection of our lives a reading provides for us. In an Ogam reading, we see mirrored in symbolic form the drives, forces, and tendencies at work within ourselves and the unique set of circumstances surrounding us. It is as much about understanding the past and being fully in the reality of the present as it is about keening the future.

Nor is divination merely a passive process of reflection. It may be likened to a diagnosis, yet it is by the same token a form of medicine in its own right. Divining is, in its highest form, a healing art that assists us in identifying and jettisoning the constricting elements of life so that we can invite in the more desirable qualities: health, happiness, success, and abundance. It is in this spirit that Ogam addresses us today.

The three sections of this book – Ogamlore, Ogamfews, and Ogamcasting – taken together present an easy and accessible approach to the art of Ogam divination. The first part, Ogamlore, goes into the history and background of the tree-alphabet and associated themes. This leads us deep into the heartland of Celtic myth and druidic lore, which will ultimately enrich your understanding of Ogam.

Some readers, however, may wish to turn straight to the next sections and begin the practical divination work. Part two, Ogamfews, presents the meanings and backgrounds of the twenty tree-letters of the original Ogam script. There are also four additional divinatory signs, known as the Four Treasures, which follow.

Finally, Ogamcasting, the third part of this book, sets out information about the theory and practice of divination. Here you will learn how to make and cast your own set of ogams. These three parts are outlined below in more detail, to enable you to best utilize the material on offer in *Ogam*.

Ogamlore

As we will see in Ogamlore, literary sources suggest that Ogam letters were traditionally carved on 'wands of yew' and used for divination, amongst other magical ritual practices now obscure to us. In the great ninth-century Irish epic of *Tochmarc Étaín* (*The Wooing of Étaín*), the hero-god Mider snatches the beautiful Étaín from King Eochaid. We are told that then: 'The king . . . sent to every part of Ireland for news of Étaín, but his messengers all came back without having been able to find her. At last, a Druid named Dallán learned, by means of ogams carved upon wands of yew, that she was hidden under Mider's *sidh* (earthen mound) of Bri Leith . . . '[1] Here we see a Druid, a member of the magician-priest caste of Celtic society, engaging in a divination rite in which Ogam is used. Indeed, Ogam formed a vital part of the pro-gramme of learning in the Druidical colleges of Ireland, along with a number of other magical and 'mantic' (divinatory) arts.

According to Irish legend, Ogma-the-Sun-Face, a god of wis-dom, learning and eloquence, invented Ogam, although we are not told exactly how. Celtic mythology furnishes no tale such as the Norse legend of Odin's quest for the Runes, yet the deep similarities suggest that a similar tradition may once have existed. The sunny attributes of Ogma indicate that he is a god of light, enlightenment and illumination, in company with other illustri-ous solar divinities such as Lugh, Mabon and the hero Cú Chulainn. Ogma's invention of the Ogam recalls a more general theme: that of a god who gifts divine knowledge through the creation of a sacred set of symbols. This myth is reminiscent of Odin's gift of the Runes to his followers, Hermes' creation of the sacred alphabets, and the invention of the trigrams of the *I Ching* by Chinese tradition's legendary folk-hero, Fu Hsi. Indeed, the god who rules over divinatory symbols and gifts them to human-kind is a cross-cultural archetype, found in many civilizations across the globe.

Ogamlore explores these areas in some depth, along with the nature, uses and variants of the Ogam script itself. Here we encounter the major form of Ogam used in contemporary divination, the Tree Alphabet. What was the purpose of its invention, what do the signs mean, and how do they take on divinatory qualities? These questions lead us into the domain of medieval manuscripts, the older Druidical learning which they echo, and the beautiful field of Celtic literature, which preserves many traces of ancient treelore. We will meet such figures as Merlin and Taliesin, together with a host of old Irish gods, along the way.

What is the relevance of this traditional material to us today? Anybody who enjoys Celtic music or the tales of Arthurian romance (with their deep Celtic echoes) will realize that the Celtic heritage is a living one. Not only is it fresh and insightful, it is still evolving. The Green Man and May Queen figures so prominent in contemporary Paganism convey the profound significance of this heritage, for they carry a deep sense of connection to the natural and divine worlds. The archetype of oneness with creation contained within these figures is returning in our times, as we strive to reconnect with the Greenworld. This is a process which goes through and beyond Druidry and links the Celtic renaissance with a much larger cultural movement.

Ogamfews

The second part of this book, Ogamfews, presents the twenty tree-letters of the ancient Ogam alphabet, along with their associations, meanings and unique wisdom. Above and beyond their basic divinatory qualities, these ogams each embody a mystery. The tree-letters correspond to mythological figures and themes from Celtic myth, legend and folklore. These themes carry and unfold for us profound lessons, teachings from the Druidic wisdom tradition.

My commentary on each ogam includes: the ogam's names, Word Ogam verses, a Visualization, its divinatory Meaning (with keywords), Natural Characteristics, Storylines (with traditional themes and tales), Folklore and Magic. A section at the beginning of Ogamfews entitled 'Guide to the Ogams' will help you in using these commentaries, as will the comments below. Remember that the art of divining with the Ogams develops with practice and experience; once grasped, it is actually a pleasantly simple and elemental technique of accessing the wisdom which lies within.

The names of the Ogam tree-letters are magical in their own right, and I have given them along with a key to their pronunciation in Gaelic. Next come the Word Ogams: cryptic kennings (puns, riddles) from the oral tradition. These little verses are obscure at first, but with time you will crack their hard outer shell and develop ideas about their relationship to the identity of the ogam concerned. Following these materials you will find a Visualization for each ogam which leads to the heart of its primary image. These images help take us beyond the written word to the intuitive and imaginative domain. They relate to the mythological characteristics associated with the tree-letter, and give us a graphic picture of that particular ogam's nature.

After the Visualization comes the most crucial part of all: a section entitled Meaning, which contains the oracle or key message of the ogam you have drawn. More than simply a prediction, it is a kind of lesson directly addressing you with guidance appropriate to the needs of the moment. Here is where the divination takes on a life of its own and acquires a personal bearing. It is suggested that you meditate on the Meaning section until its applicability to your unique circumstances 'clicks' into place. This is an intuitive rather than rational process. There is also a Reversed meaning: this occurs if the ogam appears upside-down in a reading. We can regard the reversed meaning of an ogam as its shadow side, and you should read it, even for an ogam which is not reversed. Similarly, if you draw a reversed ogam, you should still read the upright meaning.

Following the Meaning section are commentaries on the Natural Characteristics, Storylines and Folklore and Magic connected to each ogam. These background materials are there to provide you with a deeper sense of what each ogam means. You may wish to explore these over time, as certain ogams crop up again and again, and you will most likely find yourself wishing to understand their lesson more fully. The Natural Characteristics of each ogam are important, for the nature of the trees themselves help generate divinatory meanings. The Storylines also provide us with a tale or theme from Celtic myth that relates to each ogam. Finally, the brief section on Folklore and Magic sets out some of the customs and rites by which the lore of each ogam has survived, and how it may be used or celebrated today. As with the Visualization, it leads you into the all-important experiential plane.

Ogamcasting

Ogamcasting brings the art of using Ogam into the here and now. Ultimately, it leads you through the stages of choosing, making and casting your own set of ogams. First, there are sections on the wider field of Celtic Divination and on the contemporary Ogam Theory, providing you with a sense of the ancient context of ogamcasting. There is also a short section on Ogam Theory that links ogamcasting to the wider field of divinatory practice as a type of synchronistic event.

Next we move on to the Practical Work. This section gives advice regarding the making, consecration, and keeping of an ogam set, along with a traditional invocation designed to bless the act of divining. When you have followed the simple procedures outlined here, you will be ready to divine with Ogam. The following section is entitled Spreads and Castings. Set out at this point are five spreads which enable you to draw on the wisdom of the oracle. Each method has a slightly different focus, and with time you will find that some work better for certain types of enquiry than for others. In the interests of providing guidance for those unfamiliar with the art of divination – and to illuminate the unique divinatory character of Ogam – I have also included five sample readings along with the spreads. These write-ups or case studies show Ogam in motion, as it were, and give you the opportunity to observe how the ogams, and the themes they embody, play themselves out in people's lives. They also highlight how, while an oracle has a predictive dimension, the issues and solutions raised by the ogams relate to our lives on many levels: past, present and future.

Finally, there is a section entitled The Ogam Revival, which discusses the whole field of the contemporary renaissance of Ogam. My description of each of the other systems and interpretative books currently available on the market is designed to clear up some of the confusion which surrounds Ogam interpretation, for different commentators have taken quite divergent approaches. Should you choose to branch out in your Ogam Quest, this section will be an important resource.

Some have claimed that Ogam is a difficult and obscure divination system. Nothing could be further from the truth. Outlined in this book is a clear and straightforward model for Ogam divination, and with time you will find the unique identity of each tree-letter becomes established in your heart and mind. Though some carry lessons and challenges, they are guides and teachers in the great game of life. Through them, we can enter into a more profound mode of dialogue with creation and, crucially, a more fully empowered state of being.

I

Ogamlore

While I was a prisoner,
sweet inspiration filled me
and my laws were given to me
in a language without words.

Taliesin[ii]

Ogma's Invention

Irish mythology tells us that the god Ogma – one of the mythical Túatha dé Danaan of ancient Éirinn – invented the Ogam script. Ogam has twenty basic letters which are formed by notches intersecting with a crossbar, somewhat resembling branches on a tree; five extra letters were added later. Although there are lists of variant names, the main branch of Ogam letters is named after woodland trees, and forms the ancestor of the modern Irish alphabet. Each has correspondences and divinatory meanings attached to it, and as this book will show they make a wonderfully versatile and profoundly instructive divination system.

As far as the god Ogma goes, there is little in Celtic mythology to explain his invention of Ogam, though later medieval manuscripts reveal that the Ogam letters encoded all sorts of practical and esoteric information, especially of the mythological kind. Unfortunately, any tale such as that told in Norse mythology of Odin's discovery of the Runes is missing from Celtic lore. Looking at the wider, cross-cultural tradition of the god of divination does, however, provide us with some sense of what legends and conceptions may once have surrounded Ogma.

In Norse mythology the great god Odin descends the World Ash Tree, Yggdrasil, and after undergoing a sacrifice heaves up the Runes from the Well of Mimir. Mimir's Well is a symbol of its people's collective unconscious, a great spring of knowledge and insight. It is also a feminine motif relating to the mysteries of the goddess – for it is she who is, symbolically speaking, the well from which all wisdom springs. Norse myth is Celtic mythology's close cousin, but related traditions are found across the world. In Chinese legend, the folk hero Fu Hsi invented the trigrams that form the basis of the I Ching, China's great Oracle of Changes. As we read in the Ta Chuan (Great Treatise):

> When in early antiquity [Fu Hsi] ruled the world, he looked upward and contemplated the images in the heavens; he looked downwards and contemplated the patterns on earth. He contemplated the markings of birds and beasts and adaptations to the regions. He proceeded from himself and indirectly from objects. Thus he invented the eight trigrams in order to enter into connection with the virtues of the light of the gods and to regulate the conditions of all beings.[iii]

Here the hero/god creates a divination system in order to codify the wisdom of the natural world in the form of primordial signs, and these signs are there to be consulted through the act of divination. Similarly, Tarot tradition attributes the creation of its mystical images to Hermes, god of secrets and communication, and in Africa the traditional Yoruba tribal oracle, the Ise Ifa, is ruled by the god Ifa, the one who inspires the diviner in his or her interpretation of the omens.

Ogam's creator conforms to this wider archetype, though he has, of course, his own Celtic particularities. Ogma Grianaineach (of the Sun Face), also called Cermait (Honey-tongued), is a god of light and illumination, a solar divinity who offers gifts and service to humankind. A chief member of the Túatha dé Danaan (People of the Goddess Dana; the gods of ancient Ireland), he is said to have taught them writing, is named as the 'strongman of the gods', 'woodsman of the gods' and also 'shining poet'. Magical weapons are a defining feature of Celtic hero-gods, and in the ninth to tenth century *Cath Tánaiste Maige Tuired* (*The Second Battle of Moytura*) Ogma inherits a sword called Orna that boasts of its own deeds.

Irish literature does not reveal a lot more about Ogma but, supplemented by the fragmentary Continental sources, some insights of importance can be pieced together. Ogmios, Ogma's namesake in Gaul, is referred to by the Roman observer Lucian of Samosata (second century CE) as the 'Gallic Herakles', meaning Hercules – a statement that seems strange at first. After all, Ogma appears more closely related to the Roman Mercury, god of divine communication, than to the strongman Hercules. But nonetheless, as Lucian writes:

> The Celts call Herakles Ogmios in the language of their country, but the image they paint of the god is quite strange. For them he is an old man at the end of his life, with his hair receding and what hair he has being white, and with his skin being rough and sunburned . . . This old Herakles is represented as pulling along behind him a mass of men all kept together with gold and amber chains through their ears . . . The painter has perforated the god's tongue so that it appears to be pulling along the men, while the god turns smiling towards them.[iv]

The answer to this riddle is that the superhuman strength of Ogmios lies not in his club but his tongue, or put another way, in his mastery of the sacred word, whose binding character in Celtic culture is here symbolized by the chains of gold and amber. The oral tradition and poetry long held pride of place in Celtic lands and that the god governing this sphere is the strongest, most powerful of deities is therefore logical. In pre-Christian Ireland, poetry was reckoned so powerful that even kings were forced to bow to the *filid* (poets) lest they compose a biting *aer* (satire) that could not only destroy a reputation but hex and even physically blight an enemy!

Ogma's role in the creation of the Ogam points to his being particularly a god of the Druids, just as the Túatha dé Danaan in general appear to have formed the basic cast of gods and goddesses for the druidic religion in Ireland. This is reinforced by the fact that ogamlore was an essential ingredient in the syllabus of the Druidical colleges in ancient Éire, as we shall see. Apprentice Druids studied Ogam in their first three years, and present-day initiates to modern Druidry – and what is known as the Celtic Mysteries in general – often seek to emulate that programme of learning for themselves by following the 'path of Ogam'. While much of both Ogam and classical Druidry remains shrouded by the passage of the years, the chief correspondences of the Tree Ogam letters lead the explorer through the mists and into a grove of meanings that still resonates with the long-vanished lore of the Celts.

Irish saga also unambiguously states that Ogam was used in divination rituals by the Druidical orders of society. In another version of the tale of Mider and Étaín, which we met in the introduction, Ogam is consulted to locate the fair heroine Étaín: 'Codal of the Withered Breast took four rods of yew and wrote Ogams on them and through his enchantments he found out that Etain was with Midhir in Bri Leith.'[v] The use of staves or some other token (such as cards or tablets) in divination ritual is widespread across the globe. Drawing a stave, sight unseen, and reading its sign as a message from the gods is the basic formula. Today cards are more common, but the tradition continues. Through divination, using Ogam as an oracle, we can bring this ancient system alive as a practical tool to be employed in everyday life.

You can learn in Ogamcasting methods of creating your own set of 'fate-twigs' representing the original twenty letters of the Ogam

Tree Alphabet. Questions posed to the oracle can range from issues of inner truth to concerns over outer circumstances, and, as with Runes, each Ogam carries multiple levels of meaning. They are potent aids to the art of existence, and when you draw upon the magical Ogam it seems as if the great trees which are the alphabet's guardians draw near in a spirit of peace and protection.

Ogam's history, like the script itself, is full of enigmas. There is no evidence of its existence before Roman times, and as an alphabet its vowel and consonant structure appear to be related to Latin, although other outside influences have been suggested. The Celts were eclectic when it came to adopting other ways and methods, as illustrated by their decorative arts, but any 'borrowings' were at the same time thoroughly integrated into their own cultural fabric. Thus Ogam's significations are Celtic in feel despite its hybrid origins, and the style of the script is certainly peculiar to Ireland. Dating of Ogam tends to place its origin around 200–300 CE and it is generally believed to have been the creation of one man.

What makes Ogam unique is its form. Its twenty original letters fall into four *aicme* (sets of five), with the later addition of the five diphthongs. The first twenty *feda* (letters) are composed of *flesc* – a series of notches crossing a central column or line, almost like musical notation. It has often been observed that this makes the script difficult to write and goes part way to explain why Ogam appears to have had limited currency even in its land of origin. Ogam is, however, perfectly suited to being hewn in intersecting lines across a vertical column along the edge of standing stones, and this is the form by far the majority of inscriptions take. Unfortunately, the position of the *flesc* at the edge of such monuments and markers has made Ogam inscriptions vulnerable to erosion at the hands of the elements. Yet there are three-hundred odd Ogam stones preserved in the Emerald Isle, several dozen in Wales, eight in England, five in the Isle of Man and one or two in Scotland (not counting the untranslated Pictish materials).

The content of these inscriptions is usually quite mundane: they are essentially border markers. Many are also memorial stones, though attempts to link them with a cult of the dead, such as that connected to the Runes, have proved unsatisfactory. Of course, ogams inscribed on materials such as wood would long ago have vanished without trace, limiting our knowledge of the full range of forms once in use. Certainly Ogam rods carved by Druids like Codal are unlikely to have survived the ravages of the centuries! We must also distinguish between the Ogam of the inscriptions and that of the later medieval manuscripts, whose 'letters' lay on a horizontal bar and had slightly different styles of representation (such as employing dots rather than *flesc* to represent vowels). They have little to do with divination, however, and do not concern us here.

In English, Ogam letters are generally known as 'fews', but many of the Gaelic names associated with Ogam reveal a connection with the world of trees. *Feda* means 'wood', *flesc* 'twig', and the name for the consonants, *taebomnai*, means 'the side of a tree'. This is interesting, because the main variant of the Ogam script is the Tree Alphabet, with medieval sources providing lists of the tree names by which the letters were known. Whether or not the Tree Alphabet truly was the original form of Ogam, as some scholars have questioned, it is the major variant known to us. Even if the system belongs to the twilight period of paganism in Ireland, every tree-letter has deeply embedded mythological themes associated with it and taken as a whole they make a powerful and workable divinatory system. And even if discoveries in the future revise our understanding of the roots of Ogam, Tree Ogam divination is a valid way of drawing on Celtic treelore and translating its mythological elements into omens of personal significance. Its particular charm and strength is that it also leads us into rapport with the magical and regenerative energies of the Greenworld.

The Tree Alphabet

What is the basis for identifying the Ogam letters with the great trees of the forest and their remarkable body of lore? *The Ogam Tract*, a key medieval document on Ogam, leaves us in little doubt as to the author's opinion of the chief identity of each Ogam letter:

> Whence is the origin of the Ogam? Not hard. I shall speak firstly of the woods of the trees whence names have been put to the ogam

letters . . . It is from the trees of the forest that names were given to the Ogam letters metaphorically.[vi]

Ogamfews, according to the *Tract*, are named after trees, and the trees relate to these letters *metaphorically*. This is vital, for, as the remainder of Ogamlore suggests, the primary association for each ogamfew in the Tree Alphabet is a tree – but this correspondence is *metaphorical* rather than purely literal. As we will see, the trees themselves in Celtic culture each have a host of mythological associations; they are gateways to a wider wisdom tradition.

Linguistic evidence suggests that not all of the original Ogam letters were named after trees. The Tree Alphabet may, therefore, be the product of a later evolution which melded Ogam with ancient treelore into an innovative new system. Yet either way, the BethLuisFearn Tree Alphabet Ogam (named after the script's first three letters) is the variety used in Ogam divination today, and a remarkable system of correspondences it is. For convenience' sake, the script is commonly standardized as follows:

⊤	b	*beth*	said BEH	birch	*Betula pendula*
⊤⊤	l	*luis*	said LWEE	rowan	*Sorbus aucuparia*
⊤⊤⊤	f	*fearn*	said FAIR-n	alder	*Alnus glutinosa*
⊤⊤⊤⊤	s	*saille*	said SAHL-yuh	willow	*Salix* spp.
⊤⊤⊤⊤⊤	n	*nion*	said NEE-uhn	ash	*Fraxinus excelsior*
⊥	h	*húath*	said HOO-ah	hawthorn	*Crataegus* spp.
⊥⊥	d	*duir*	said DOO-r	oak	*Quercus robur*
⊥⊥⊥	t	*tinne*	said CHIN-yuh	holly	*Ilex aquifolium*
⊥⊥⊥⊥	c	*coll*	said CULL	hazel	*Corylus avellana*
⊥⊥⊥⊥⊥	q	*quert*	said KWAIRT	apple	*Malus sylvestris*
+́	m	*muin*	said MUHN	vine	*Vitis vinifera*
⫲	g	*gort*	said GORT	ivy	*Hedera helix*
⫲⫲	ng	*nGétal*	said NYEH-tl	reed/broom	*Phragmites communis*
⫲⫲⫲	ss	*straif*	said STRAHF	blackthorn	*Prunus spinosa*
⫲⫲⫲⫲	r	*ruis*	said RWEESH	elder	*Sambucus nigra*
+	a	*ailm*	said AHL-m	(silver) fir	*Pinus sylvestris* or *Abies alba*
++	o	*onn*	said UHN	gorse (furze)	*Ulex europaeus*
+++	u	*úr*	said OOR	heather	*Calluna vulgaris*
++++	e	*eadha*	said EH-yuh	aspen/poplar	*Populus tremula*
+++++	i	*idho*	said EE-yoh	yew	*Taxus baccata*

You should note that a slightly different (perhaps earlier, but less common) variation on this sequence exists, known as the BethLuisNion. Here the order of the first five letters is b, l, n, f, s rather than b, l, f, s, n. This affects the *flesc* (cross-lines) used for these letters, as ogamfews are essentially tallied by notches, producing a variation in the last three letters of the first set of five. No one knows exactly how to account for this, though one or two esoteric commentators claim that BethLuisNion is the more arcane, magical version of the script. There is, however, no real evidence for this.

The Scholar's Primer

How was Ogam originally intended to be used? There are several sources helpful to us in answering this question. Some readers may wish to explore this field themselves, in which case the *Auricept na nÉces* (*Scholar's Primer*), *De Dúilib Feda na Forfid* (*The Values of the Forfeda*) and *Lebor Ogam* (*Book of Ogam*) will be of chief interest. They derive from two medieval manuscripts, both great repositories of Celtic lore, the twelfth-century *Book of Leinster* and the *Book of Ballymote*, produced around 1391, though relevant materials are also to be found in the fifteenth-century *Yellow Book of Lecan*. These beautifully illuminated works are products of the Middle Ages but undoubtedly derive much of their content from sources older still. They take us as close as booklore may get to matters which were traditionally passed on from initiate to novitiate in the form of whispered secrets – for, as we will discover, the Druids shunned the written word.

The *Auricept na nÉces*, traditionally dated to the seventh century, is perhaps the most important of the sources. It provides lists of various Ogam scripts and their significations, along with keys to the origin and uses of the system. While obscure and confusing at times, such materials do provide us with fundamental insights into the nature of Ogam. Most illuminating of the *Auricept's* compositions is the short piece, mentioned above, called *The Ogam Tract*. It is invaluable for offering, among other things, the alphabet's primary correspondences via the Word Ogams. These lists are similar in nature to the Scandinavian Rune poems, those riddling keys to the meaning of the Runes.

The Ogam Tract

What are the place, time, person, and cause of the invention of the Ogam? Not hard. Its place the island of Ireland where the Irish live. In the time of Bres son of Elatha king of Ireland it was invented. Its person Ogma son of Elatha son of Delbaeth brother to Bres, for Bres, Ogma and Delbaeth are the three sons of Elatha son of Delbaeth there. Now Ogma, a man well-skilled in speech and in poetry, invented the Ogam. The cause of its invention, as a proof of his ingenuity, and that this speech should belong to the learned apart, to the exclusion of rustics and herdsmen . . . [vii]

So begins *The Ogam Tract*. The opening passage informs us of what we already know: that in Irish mythology Ogma, not a mere man but a figure belonging to the old gods of the Túatha dé Danaan, invented the alphabet in his role as god of speech and poetry and as a demonstration of his ingenuity – a typically Celtic concern. The last lines, together with other materials, confirm that despite 'popular' uses of Ogam (such as memorial stones), its higher mysteries were reserved for the Druidical caste of Celtic society and it was thus elevated 'to the exclusion of rustics and herdsmen'. Today, of course, Ogam divination is an art open to all.

The question-and-answer style employed in the *Tract* has been sourced by some scholars to Latin grammars, in circulation in Ireland at the time, but it was also common in the indigenous oral tradition, for much of Irish lore was couched in verbal exchanges. As we will see, such a pattern of prompts and responses was used to aid the memorization of sacred matters in magical contests presided over by Druids. Reflecting the teacher–pupil (or adept–novitiate) relationship, its presence here further argues that parts of *The Ogam Tract* are themselves based on earlier, oral learning.

The next section of the *Tract* offers some strong clues as to Ogam's wider role in the oral lore. 'Ogam from Ogma was first invented in respect to its sound *and according to its matter* [italics mine]'. Here we have reached the heart of the territory at hand, for we are being told that Ogam letters *represent not just sounds but also other additional 'matter'*. Now, the term 'matter' here means 'a body of material' – as when the Arthurian Cycle is called the

'Matter of Britain' – and refers to the set of names, significations, and mythological qualities attached to each of the ogamfews. For like Scandinavian Runes, each Ogam letter has a name (or set of names) with attendant meanings. They encode information and wisdom, and this material, as we shall see below, contains the kernels of meaning which ultimately translate into Ogam's divinatory and magical correspondences.

This is the trail, for those who wish to pursue the meaning of the Ogams to their historical sources. Of course, in this art intuition is just as vital a teacher, if not a more profound one, than 'objective facts'. Yet intuition does not suffer from having a strong foundation in the world of fact; rather, we can use historical research as the raw material from which may be refined a more profound sympathy for the magical conceptions of the pagan Celts. What is more, tradition in this sense is an ever-unfolding, growing tapestry of threads.

The Silver Branch

Why do trees – or tree-letters – carry metaphoric meaning in Celtic culture? How do earthly trees stand in the Celtic mind for a set of more magical, divinatory qualities? As Jean Markale, talking about the 'exalted and creative imagination of the Celts', expresses it, they 'saw everything on an ideographic plane'.[viii] Celtic thought works in terms of subtle associative networks of imagery to a remarkable degree and this mode of thinking is the essence of its inspiration. In his brilliant work, *Celtic Civilisation* (1975), Markale goes on to point out that this tendency to image-making and thinking in dreamlike correspondences is at the very root of the Celtic sensibility and central to its proper comprehension. We cannot understand Celtic reasoning until we undo our own logical knots and recognize, that, to the ancients, 'correspondences' in Nature were seen as manifestations of divinity within the flowing forms of the material world.

There is indeed ample evidence of a body of correspondences between the trees of the Tree Alphabet and characters or scenes from Celtic mythology and folklore. The trees of the Greenworld are the physical tokens of divine energies at work upon the Earth and as such they are the guides in our journey, initiators who arm us with correct understanding. In Irish poetry there are many descriptions of Druid and bard figures coming into the possession of divine inspiration through the medium of the great trees. The 'silver branch of poetry' is the most famous example, amply attested to, but throughout we hear of enlightenment and knowledge linked to treelore – especially that of the hazel and apple – being conferred upon the initiate. Let us look more closely at these two trees, for they are amongst the most important in the Ogam grove.

The hazel carries a vast body of lore, which is presented in more depth in the commentary on the *coll-few* (ⅢⅢ). However, the tree's intimate connection with wisdom, inspiration and poetry can be shown in a few lines. The medieval account of the origins of the Irish known as *Lebor Gabála* (*The Book of Invasions*), describes the coming the old gods of Éirinn, the Túatha dé Danaan. There we are told that they put three things above all others, the plough, the sun and the hazel tree, while in the *Dindsenchas* (*Lore of Places*) the hazels at Connla's well are described in the following terms:

> And they had a well below the sea where the nine hazels of wisdom were growing; that is, the hazels of inspiration and of the knowledge of poetry. And their leaves and their blossoms would break out in the same hour, and would fall on the well in a shower that raised a purple wave. And then the five salmon that were waiting there would eat the nuts, and their colour would come out in the red spots of their skin, and any person that would eat one of those salmon would know all wisdom and all poetry. And there were seven streams of wisdom that sprang from that well and turned back to it again; and the people of many arts have all drank from that well.[ix]

Nine hazels of wisdom sprouting from the Well Below the Sea reminds us of Norse tradition's World Tree with its mighty roots penetrating three great wells – including Mimir's Well, from which springs the wisdom of runelore. The Tree and the Well clearly belong together and in Irish myth the sacred well has many manifestations. It is further linked to the symbols of the legendary Cup of Truth and the cauldron of the mythical Welsh witch, Ceridwen (the Great Goddess). The 'people of many arts' who 'have all drunk from that well' are such figures as the Druids, bards and *ovates* (diviners).

The lore of the apple tree runs in a similar vein. As with hazel, you can find countless examples and variations of the basic theme: the apple is a tree linked to the Otherworld and its secrets, especially the gifts of poetry and associated magical arts, which are conferred in the form of a silver branch. This silver branch is usually carried by an otherworldly woman who comes from that island realm variously known as Manannán's (the sea-god's) Country, the Land of the Ever Living, the Summerland, Emain Eblach, Avallach, or Avalon, the Island of Apples. In the story of the *Immrama Bran mac Febail* (*Voyage of Bran*), best known in its eighth-century form of the *Navigatio Sancti Brendani* (*Voyage of St Brendan*), we hear that:

> One time Bran, son of Febal, was out by himself near his dun, and he heard music behind him. And it kept always after him, and at last he fell asleep with the sweetness of the sound. And when he awoke from his sleep he saw beside him a branch of silver, and it having white blossoms, and the whiteness of the silver was the same as the whiteness of the blossoms.
>
> And when he brought the branch in his hand into the royal house, and when all his people were with him they saw a woman with strange clothing standing in the house.
>
> And she began to make a song for Bran, and all the people were looking at her and listening to her, and it is what she said:
>
> 'I bring a branch of the apple-tree from Emain, from the far island around which are the shining horses of the Son of Lir . . .
>
> 'There is a white tree there with blossoms, and birds calling from them; every colour is shining there, delight is common, and music, in the Gentle-Voiced Plain, in the Silver Cloud plain to the south.'[x]

For now, it is enough to observe the relationship between this magical tree, it branches and fruit, and the most hallowed of all enclosures in early Irish belief – the otherwordly island ruled by women and sacred to the old gods. In olden times, branches of gold, silver or bronze were worn by poets as magical tools and badges of initiation to the secrets of this Otherworld, and such customs may be derived from rites of the greatest antiquity.

The Word Ogams

We have seen that the great trees are mentors and guides into a deep pool of traditional wisdom, but how do we know exactly what each tree signifies and teaches? In what forms has the tradition of Ogam interpretation been preserved? There is actually a vast body of lore surrounding each of the tree-letters, but let us begin closest to home, with the humble keys that are found in the *Book of Ballymote* and other medieval manuscripts. These materials were set down to indicate the correspondences attached to each of the Tree Alphabet fews. Similar to the Rune poems, which are used in the interpretation of the meaning of the Scandinavian runestaves, they are valuable clues to unlocking the outer doors to the secrets of the Ogam.

First comes the brief 'Elaborations' on the Ogams, which you will meet in more detail in Ogamfews. This basically consists of a set of explanatory notes attached to the names of the each ogam, preserved in the *Auricept*. By itself, this list may not appear to be the most enlightening. However, used in conjunction with the other materials drawn from the wider written sources – including the later branches of tree-wisdom found in Celtic folklore – you will find that it gives sound counsel. The Elaborations are also useful to set alongside the three *bríatharogam* or 'Word Ogams': the *Word Ogam of Morainn mac Moín*, the *Word Ogam of Cú Chulainn*, attributed to the great Irish hero, and finally the *Word Ogam of Óengus*, after Óengus, the so-called Celtic god of love. These materials give also cryptic association or kennings (puns, riddles) for each few.

The Word Ogam significations relate in some cases to the physical characteristics of the trees of the Tree Alphabet, yet often touch on the more metaphoric, mythological – and thus magical and divinatory – qualities of the each tree-letter. For example, when *duir* (oak) is described as the 'highest of bushes', we can hardly believe this to be a purely literal statement! Oak is certainly not the tallest of trees in forest lands in the British Isles, though it has long been considered the most illustrious, was a so-called chieftain tree and, as 'king of the forest', was considered the highest in status. *Beth* (the birch tree) is accompanied by this gloss in the *Word Ogam of Morainn*: 'faded trunk and fair hair, that is for birch'. This is a naturalistic enough description of the birch, perhaps. But the *Word Ogam of Morainn mac Moín* tells us that birch 'equals browed beauty, worthy of pursuit'. It is notable that the hero Diarmaid of the Fenian Cycle is famous for his beauty spot, and that he woos the wife of the ageing Finn mac Cumhail – who is constantly referred to as grey and ageing – in a burdle of birch twigs. This is no coincidence, and we can see that the Word Ogams often invoke mythological doublets for each tree – in the case of birch, its associations with the replacement of the old, grey and withered with the new and verdant.

Yet it has been suggested, by the Ogam scholar Damian McManus among others, that the Word Ogams may refer to characteristics of the Ogam letters which pre-date the Tree Alphabet. Holly, for example, is named in Gaelic *tinne*, originally derived, according to McManus, from the Old Irish words *tend* 'strong' or *tind* 'brilliant'. The Word Ogams which accompany *tinne* would thus suggest not the holly tree but a 'bar, rod of metal, ingot, mass of molten metal'. This might seem like a dead end, but looking deeper we can see that these allegedly earlier meanings are still perfectly compatible with the supposedly later tree-letters. Holly is a tree-letter of defence, linked to the ancient drama of the Oak and Holly King, and thus to weapons made by the metalworker. Furthermore, its thorns suggest the image of the sharpened sword. In fact, in every case we can see that even if the Word Ogams refer to earlier values, they still illuminate the tree-letters concerned.

Such riddling speech, full of kennings, accords perfectly with the Celtic sensibility, for as the Roman observer Diodorus Sicilus (21 BCE) put it: 'They express themselves in riddles . . . '[xi] This riddling speech is, furthermore, a feature of oracular language across the ancient world. Everybody knows that the Oracle at Delphi spoke in riddles, and the 'gnomic verses' of the Rune tradition, like the 'divinatory poems' of the *I Ching*, are often enigmatic. The Word Ogams are indeed tricky keys to Ogam interpretation, and we must ultimately go well beyond these fragments to find the fuller significance of the individual ogams. But they are a useful gateway to the 'path of Ogam', and in the next section of this book, Ogamfews, I have presented them at the beginning of my commentaries, so that when you cast the Ogam you may catch in their riddles echoes of the ancient lore of the Druids, bards and their tradition of tree wisdom.

The first of these Word Ogams, the *Word Ogam of Morainn mac Moín*, corroborates much of what is found in the Ogam Elaborations, and adds to our understanding of the meaning of the tree-letters. Morainn, its reputed author, was a great judge known for the fair and wise nature of his decisions. Now, the law of Dark Age Ireland was the Brehon law, based on the older rule of the Druids, who once formed the judiciary class. So Morainn may be taken to have been a Druid of the judiciary class. We also know Ogam is said to have been used in divining the guilt or innocence of criminals and perhaps the attribution of a Word Ogam to Morainn, whether factual or symbolic, reflects this fact. His keys will help you, too, in your judgement of the signification of the Ogamfews you draw.

The second list is known as the *Word Ogam of Cú Chulainn*. The great Cú Chulainn is best known for his role as the arch-champion of the Ulster Cycle of ancient Irish literature, revived as a symbol of Ireland's nationalist aspirations at the turn of the twentieth century. But Cú Chulainn is in essence a semi-divine character, a magically charged hero, who has solar associations, linking him to such sun-god figures as the Irish Lugh and Welsh Mabon. Legends associated with him further reveal that Cú Chulainn was a master of Ogam, using it in a ceremonial manner to thwart enemies in battle. So when you draw an ogamfew you have, in spirit, Cú Chulainn's steadfast assistance in arriving at your interpretation.

Finally, we have the *Word Ogam of Óengus*. Now Óengus mac in Og (also called the Macc Oc) is more commonly known as Aengus. He is the son of the Dagda (supreme god of Irish mythology) by the Goddess Bóann (the great Mother Goddess). Óengus comes to take his father's place as ruler of the famous *sidhe* (said 'shee', meaning burial mound) once named Bruig na Bóinde in Ireland, and the site of Europe's largest Neolithic earthen tumulus. Bruig na Bóinde, now called Newgrange, is in the Boyne Valley of County Meath, site of the Tara stone, and is the ancient

omphalos or mystical centre of ancient Ireland. The Newgrange
tumulus is aligned to the Winter Solstice sun, and has all sorts of
mythological solar associations connected with its role as a type
of sun-temple. On Midwinter's day a shaft of light penetrates its
entry passage and strikes the inner sanctum. Thus Óengus, too, is
a great and worthy guide to have with us as we walk Ogam's
paths.

You will sometimes hear Óengus described as a god of love, and
he is indeed an amorous character, who once shapeshifted into
the shape of a swan for the sake of abiding with his chosen sweetheart. However, he is more properly described as a god of beauty,
whose radiant countenance reveals him as another solar divinity.
Some commentators have noted a resemblance between him
and the Welsh god Mabon, known in Gaul as Maponos, and
indisputably associated with the sun and its light. These solar
associations connect Óengus not only with the bright figures of
Ogma (the Sun face) and Cú Chulainn (who possessed the 'hero-
light') but also the bardic figure of Taliesin – a name meaning
'radiant brow' – whom we shall meet later. Óengus' supposed
authorship of a Word Ogam would tend to reinforce a common
theme: the relationship between Ogam and divine or semi-divine
solar heroes and sages.

It must be admitted that the Word Ogams have presented
challenges to all Ogam interpreters. They cannot be used in iso-
lation to determine the divinatory character of the tree-letters
presented in Ogamfews, for many of their kennings are now
obscure to us, and often we cannot be sure if our trouble in inter-
preting them stems from our own ignorance or the medieval
texts' corruption of older, oral traditions. But they have several
virtues. Firstly, they provide further indication that the tree-
letters of the Ogam have associations which are not purely
naturalistic. How else does a blackthorn tree, for example, equal
'increasing of secrets'? Secondly, the lists give kennings on the
names and associations of the fews, and there is a subtle system of
allusion here, most likely steeped in late bardic and Druidical
lore. Their greatest value is that they intersect with what we
know of Celtic treelore – and its web of mythological significations – from elsewhere, confirming and strengthening our insight
into the central meaning of the ogams.

Other Ogam

Before leaving the technical aspects of Ogamlore, it is worth rein-
forcing the fact that there are many types of Ogam other than the
Tree Alphabet preserved in the manuscript tradition. Some of
them have lists of apparently obscure correspondences. Sow
Ogam, for example, gives these associations for the second group
of Ogamfews (h, d, t, c, q): 'Accompanying litter of a white (i.e.
milch-) sow *h*, grey *d*, black *t*, amber *c*, blue *q*'! Further variants
of Ogam from the *Tract* include River-pool Ogam, Fortress
Ogam, Bird Ogam, Colour Ogam, Man Ogam, Woman Ogam,
Agricultural Ogam, King Ogam, Water Ogam, Dog Ogam, Ox
Ogam, Cow Ogam, Blind man Ogam, Lame Ogam, Boy Ogam,
Foot Ogam, and Nose Ogam. Indeed, the sources reveal to us
over one hundred variants, some entire scripts being explained by
no more than a few cryptic words!

What is to be gathered from this hopeless mass of detail?
Whatever the gaps in the sources and possible misunderstandings
in the knowledge of the scribe(s) who set them down, one simple, unifying feature emerges from all this, and with the rest we
need not bother ourselves here. The crucial point is that the
Ogam correspondences in these various scripts are organized
quite simply *according to the first letters of what is being represented*.
For instance, the first five letters of Tree Ogam are b, l, f, s, and
n. In Fortress Ogam, the first five fortresses are Bruden /b/, Liffey
/l/, Femen /f/, Seolae /s/, and Nephin /n/; in Colour Ogam the first
five colours are *bán* (white), *liath* (grey), *flann* (red), *sodath* (fine-
coloured), and *necht* (clear). The sequence of letters is identical.

What does this tell us? Essentially, we can conclude that the
Ogam scripts of the insular (i.e. native) manuscripts were alphabetic systems that also had an encyclopaedic function. The
various scripts systematized knowledge under their subject head-
ings (rivers, colours, fortresses, etc.) in an alphabetic sequence,
thus aiding the memorization of large bodies of learning on
diverse subjects under the one system. There is no suggestion,
however, that the compartments of knowledge thus learned
relate *across* these different forms of Ogam; that, in other words,
the Bruden fortress relates in any way to the colour *bán*, other
than by virtue of their first letters. When we look for Tree Ogam

associations, therefore, we should not read too much into these independent lists. Creating magical correspondences of this kind, as some esoteric commentators have attempted to do, can lead to confusion. We should instead look to the trees themselves and their associations in Celtic treelore, divining with rods made solely of their fair wood, so to speak.

The Druids

Let us now cast our attention to a vital link in the whole chain of gold and amber that we have been following at Ogma's behest: the Druids. It is an established fact that Ogam formed part of the syllabus of learning in the bardic colleges, as will be seen below, and we can well imagine that such a codex of practical and eso-teric learning was formerly developed, utilized and preserved in ancient Druidic magic and ritual. Magic and ritual were, after all, offices sacred to the Druids. And what is known of Druidic thought and religious practice indeed deepens our appreciation of the nature and role of Ogam immeasurably.

The Druidic religion lies at the heart of the mosaic of beliefs that have come down to us in the form of Celtic folklore and the 'Faery Faith', but what is known of Druidry? There were actually three classes of Druid. As Strabo (63 BCE – 21 CE) framed it:

> Among [the Gauls] there are generally three classes to whom special honour is paid, viz. the Bards, the Uatis [Vatis] and the Druids. The Bards composed and sung odes; the Uatis attended to sacrifices and studied nature; while the Druids studied nature and moral philosophy.[xii]

Vatis (also 'ovates') means diviner, and Diodorus Siculus clarifies the role of this class of Druid when he says that 'they have sooth-sayers too of great renown who tell the future by watching the flights of birds and by observation of the entrails of victims . . .'[xiii] Sources from the wider Celtic world, including Ireland, support this tripartite division. We can add that the Druids proper were judges as well as priests, the bards were poets with shamanistic leanings, and the ovates were diviners who mastered mantic (div-inatory) techniques and were gifted with supranormal powers of prediction. Yet the distinctions between these classes in reality seem to have been somewhat fluid. No doubt Druids could divine and bards conduct rituals, after their own fashion.

As for bloody rites of sacrifice, classical accounts of Druidry must be treated with fair caution, for authors such as Caesar, Siculus, Suetonius, and Lucan had a vested interest in calling into disrepute the one force in Celtica that could potentially mobilize the Celts against their Roman persecutors: the Druids.

You will also often read statements like 'the only records of the Druids are preserved in classical writings'. This is actually non-sense, for the myths committed to the manuscripts of the Dark and early Middle Ages contain a mine of information. In fact, these insular sources are by far the more enlightening, but have come down to us in a confused form via the monasteries, with all their monkish biases. Blame for this situation cannot entirely be laid at the feet of the Romans or Christians, however. One thing is known of Druidical practice beyond doubt: its wisdom was not to be committed to writing. Caesar even tells us that it was unlawful amongst Druids. Oral recitation was the method of lore-keeping, and given the long, arduous training within the Druidical orders it is obvious a vast body of material was meticulously systematized and committed to memory. We must also distinguish here between the tradition of oral memorization in ancient times, which involved quite technical and exacting mnemonic procedures, and the popular oral tradition of later times where arcane elements half slumber in the folk memory of the people. Druidical lore was something you learnt by heart; there was room for embroidery of basic storylines, but little place, the sources suggest, for error or distortion.

Philip Carr-Gomm well expresses the paradox of practising Druidry today when he says that:

> Studying and practising Druidry can be a puzzling affair. Look at it one day and it seems as if there's nothing there: a few third hand accounts from biased Greek or Roman observers, a few inferences to be drawn from linguistic and archaeological research, and a mass of later material, mainly from the seventeenth century onwards, that is replete with speculation, fantasy, or downright trickery. Look at it another day and a treasure chest is opened: the sacred geometry of the megalithic sites built by the proto-Druids reveals awesome

cosmological understanding, early Irish and Welsh literature inspires us with tales filled with references to Druidry and paganism, the classical references reveal tantalising glimpses of a highly developed spiritual tradition, and folklore studies show how even today many of our customs and traditions derive from our Druidic and Celtic heritage.[xiv]

Much of the cynicism regarding contemporary Druidry comes from guilt by association with the worst excesses of the seventeenth- and eighteenth-century Druid Revival, whose state of knowledge was even slimmer than ours. Yet that revival also did us a service, in that it thrust the Druids back into popular consciousness and helped lay the foundation for a movement which continues to this day. Those interested in learning more about this area are recommended John Matthews' *The Druid Source Book* (1997) as a useful compilation of sources.

While the lack of hard facts and the abundance of debatable theories which thrive in the lush field of Celtic revivalism may make the continuation of Druidic practice appear absurd in some people's eyes, this judgement really comes from a misunderstanding of the intent of modern day Druids (and other contemporary Pagans). As Carr-Gomm, the Chief Druid of the Order of Bards, Ovates and Druids, further comments:

> The biggest mistake that we can make when we approach literary source material about Druidry is to imagine that this material is the primary source of the Druid tradition, when in fact it is the secondary. The primary source can never be presented in literature, because it can only be found in places where we must set books aside – in places where both this world and the Otherworld are strongly present – by sacred springs and holy wells, by seashore or in stone circles, beside great trees or strong mountains.[xv]

In other words, we will never come to understand a Nature-venerating religion by burying ourselves in the dead wood of chronicles and archives. Contemporary Druidry, like Paganism in general, is not a dogmatic, doctrinal religion based in obscure, musty texts. Rather, it is concerned with a living, evolving relationship with creation. It is about experiencing a deep rapport with the roots of the self and with others in one's community. The body of the goddess herself – the land, sea, sky and all they hold – is the true book over whose pages we should ever pore.

Yet the sources are still of great importance, for they give some indication of how the Celts of the pre-Christian era may have actually understood and interfaced with the natural world. The Celtic heritage undoubtedly provides profound bridges between society and Nature, connections such as we are seeking to re-establish today. These were people who saw the sacred in every part of the natural world and whose priesthood worshipped outside towns and temples, in the wilderness, in sacred groves. And these considerations take us to the heart of the enigmas of Ogam, where natural objects – in this case the great trees of the forest – take on significations of a very particular nature. They are totems and connectors to planes of deep, otherworldly knowing and insight.

The Sacred Grove

While both the hazel and apple, touched upon earlier, seem to be of greater importance to classical Druidry than the much vaunted oak and mistletoe, all trees in fact have a sacredness and great body of lore associated with them in the Druidical tradition. For the *nemeton* (sacred grove) is the true site of Druidic worship. This woodland focus seems to be an ancient survival relating to the immemorial body of treelore that once stretched across Eurasia, to the archaic theme of the World Tree, and to the shaman's rite of initiation on that tree. And if the Cosmic Tree is the pillar of creation, then the sacred grove is its matrix. The trees in the Druidical grove are the outward symbols of all sorts of magical and religious principles; they are living manifestations of certain divine forces and mighty guardians of creation. The Ogam Tree Alphabet, representing the woodland trees, thus becomes a grove of meanings, an index of such qualities and forces, a domain of magical initiation.

Indeed, we find enshrined in Ogam a kind of blueprint or guidebook to the Mysteries, a symbolic model of the sacred grove wherein the religious observances and rituals of the Druids were conducted in antiquity. The set of divinatory associations of the tree-letters thus become much more than mere fortune-telling tokens; they embody in microcosmic form the map which the Druids saw in Nature, leading the soul forward in its progress through the labyrinth of experience. In practising Ogam divination, we are reopening a sacred circle within which we may commune and receive the ancestral wisdom, in a form relevant to us in the here and now. Thus our partial knowledge is supplemented by the springs of wisdom which run eternal and which are not subject to the decay of outer tradition and its vestments.

Today, the art of Ogam interpretation is being awakened and its Grove of Meaning reactivated, just as neo-Pagan groups everywhere are replanting sacred groves in the Greenworld. The rebirth of this ancestral wisdom comes after great ages of darkness, for a double-edged axe was to fall upon the groves of the ancient Celtic world. The Romans deliberately targeted *nemetonia* as part of their offensive against Druidic religion and in their wake the Church carried on the destruction. All over Gaul the sacred groves were axed, as too they ultimately were in the place traditionally regarded as the seat of the Druids: Iona (the island of Anglesey) in the Irish Sea. There, while 'the Druids, lifting up their hands to heaven and pouring forth dreadful imprecations, scared our soldiers', Tacitus tells us, 'between the ranks dashed women in black attire like the Furies, with hair dishevelled, waving brands.'[xvi]

It is no surprise that priestesses such as these should have appeared, armed with such vehemence, for the myths of the Celts clearly reveal that the *temenos* or sacred enclosure represented by the otherworldly island is a largely feminine domain; a symbolic womb of the goddess, a realm to which the souls of the dead are ferried and from which the new born emanate.

Druidesses and the Goddess

When Irish lore tells us that Dana is mother of all the gods, there is no dissembling as to the status of the goddess in ancient Ireland. The equality between men and women in Celtic culture, too, exceeded that of many parts of the 'civilized' world of the time. But what can be gleaned regarding the goddess-centred aspects of ancient Celtic society? This is a subject which is bedevilled by the lack of a consensus in the interpretation of what 'hard' (that is, archaeological) data survives. Irish literature has also spawned branching schools of interpretation, and undoubtedly modern fiction, like Marion Zimmer Bradley's *Mists of Avalon*, while beautiful and compelling, has given rise to romanticized visions.

In the *Lebor Gabála* (*The Book of Invasions*), which will be revisited in greater depth below, each of the successive five waves of invaders is led by Druids who participate in the project of colonization, seeking sovereignty in the form of the goddess of the land. This has lent credibility to the notion in some minds that Druidry has roots in, or contains traces of, the forgotten practices of the preceding megalith-building peoples, an obscure folk who are mythicized in the early literature as the Hyperborean Túatha dé Danaan, Fomóri and Fir Bolg. Little is known of them, but their shadowy presence may be the source of certain elements peculiar to early Irish myth. Certainly, the superhuman feats attributed to the Druids in their epic magical contests – employing spells in legions, invoking dark mists, raising storms, and bringing showers of fire and blood down from the skies – are ancient shamanistic powers that reveal the Druids' essential unity with the elements, whose Queen in the vernacular literature is Dana herself.

The early sources (both native and classical) also speak of Druidesses. Indeed, in the story of *The Coming of Lugh*, the great Cian, Lugh's father, when in a moment of direst need 'went then to the woman-Druid, Birog of the Mountain, for her help'.[xvii] Of the Túatha dé Danaan two great Druidesses, Beonill and Danaan, are mentioned in the Mythological Cycle – really the ancient Mother Goddesses Bóann (mother of Óengus and namesake of the River Boyne) and Dana, Danu or Anu, the mother of the gods herself. Also named as druidesses are the famous figures of Badb, Macha and Mórrígan,[xviii] the Celtic triple goddesses of battle and death. Although the existence in historical times of actual Druidesses (as opposed to other kinds of priestesses) is hotly debated, these mythical 'Druidesses' provide a model for female avatars in contemporary Druidry to follow. Some writers have even taken them to be remainders of possible pre-Celtic origins of Druidism in matrifocal or female-centred, megalithic cults, suggesting that modern day Druidesses may spring from an even older lineage than Druidry itself!

Finally, many of the heroes of later Celtic legend are trained by woman warriors (or warrior goddesses) such as Cú Chulainn at the hands of Scáthach and Lancelot in the keeping of the Lady of the Lake. Celtic women fought alongside men as equals and, as in Norse culture, seem to have been especially respected for their powers of magic and clairvoyance. Vopiscus (third century CE) records a tale to the effect that the Emperor Diocletian consulted 'a certain Druidess' while staying in a tavern in Gaul. The woman adroitly foretold his future success.[xix] While perhaps apocryphal, this and similar accounts confirm that there were seeresses amongst the Celts highly respected for their pronouncements. Perhaps there was an organized cult of Druidesses, possibly they were priestesses in their own right, separate or interrelating with the Druids, and it may even be that the Druidesses' rites and practices were indeed of a more ancient extraction.

The Cave of Learning

Many accounts of Druidic training stress the fact that learning was undertaken in the dark, to aid memory, and it is clear where the roots of this custom are to be found. Pomponius Mela (18 – c. 75 CE) writes of 'a course of instruction lasting as long as twenty years, meeting in secret either in a cave or in secluded dales.'[xx] The cave, like the *nemeton* (which Roman sources often stress as being dark, antediluvian places), is a feminine, womb-like symbol, relating the mysteries of the goddess. In the *Kadair Kerridwen* (Chair of Ceridwen), a beautiful poem dating to at least the Welsh Gogynfeirdd movement of the late eleventh to mid-fourteenth centuries, the poet describes his initiation as taking place in the hall of the goddess Ceridwen. He sings of it:

> While I was held prisoner, sweet inspiration educated me
> And laws were imparted me in a speech which had no words.[xxi]

He also speaks of inspiration 'coming from the cauldron', how he comes to occupy the Chair of Ceridwen, and as its protector asks rhetorically

> The chair and cauldron of Ceridwen, have they no defence?
> My tongue is it not free in the Goddess's sanctuary (enclosure)?[xxii]

All this occurs after Taliesin has been swallowed by Ceridwen and reborn, suggesting that his 'imprisonment' took place in her womb (that is, in the cave or 'cell of learning') and refers in fact to some order of bardic initiation. It is a tantalizing thought that this poem may echo a far older rite performed in a real cave, recalling perhaps customs that have roots in the Palaeolithic era, for what else are the illuminated cave complexes of early Europe if not initiatory temples?

The spartan Druidic colleges, where novice bards spent long, arduous years in *clochan* (small cave-like huts), were in existence at least as early as classical times, and remnants of this system survived until surprisingly recently in some areas; as late as the eighteenth century in Scotland. With the rise of Christianity, the categories of Druid, bard and ovate had collapsed into the single class of the *filid* (poets), but in the early medieval period Druidic schools still stood alongside Christian monasteries and, at Bangor for instance, some monasteries had formerly been Druidic colleges. Caesar reports in *De Bello Gallico* (*The Gallic Wars*) 'that in the schools . . . the Druids . . . learn by heart a great number of verses, and therefore some persons remain twenty years under training.'[xxiii] As far as Ireland was concerned, the duration seems to have been twelve years. Eugene O'Curry records the following account of their curriculum in his *Manners and Customs of the Ancient Irish*:

Year 1: 50 Ogams or alphabets. Elementary Grammar. Twenty tales.
Year 2: 50 Ogams. Six easy lessons in Philosophy. Some Specified poems. Thirty tales.
Year 3: 50 Ogams. Six minor lessons in Philosophy. Certain Specified Poems. Grammar. Forty poems.
Year 4: The *Bretha Nemed* or Law of Privileges. Twenty Poems of the Species called *Eman* (Births). Fifty Tales.
Year 5: Grammar. Sixty Tales.
Year 6: The Secret Language of the Poets. Forty Poems of the Species called *Nuath* (Twins). Seventy or Eighty Tales.
Year 7: *Brosnacha* (Miscellanies). The Law of Bardism.
Year 8: Prosody. Glosses (the meaning of obscure words), *Tein Laegheda* (Illumination of Song), *Imbas Forosnai* (Light of Foresight), *Dicheltel do Chennibh* (Extempore Incantation), *Dendsenchas* (Land Lore).
Year 9: A specified number of compositions of the kind called *Sennet* (?), *Luasca* (three oscillating springs over a Druid's head?), *Nena* (?), *Eochraid* (keys), *Sruith* (streams) and *Duili Feda*

(Wisdom Tales). To master 175 tales to this and the next two years.

Year 10: A further number of the compositions listed above (part of the 175 tales).

Year 11: 100 of the compositions known as *Anamuin*.

Year 12: 120 *Cetals* (Orations). The Four Arts of Poetry. During this and the two years previous to master the 175 tales, along with 175 of the tales learned by Annruth – 350 tales in all.[xxiv]

We shall probably never know what much of this syllabus involved. Yet there are several points of great interest. Firstly, of course, comes the memorization in the first three years of 150 varieties of Ogam. This clearly shows that Ogam was a fundamental part of bardic lore and its presence at the beginning of the course suggests that it is the foundation of much that followed. Alongside such areas as 'grammar', 'privileges' and 'births' (i.e. genealogies), there are a number of more mysterious elements that present themselves for our contemplation. The Secret Language of the Poets taught in the sixth year is a title elsewhere used to describe Ogam itself in its more esoteric aspects, while the *Imbas Forosnai* (Light of Foresight) of the eighth year is well known to have been a complex divinatory practice.[xxv] A highly fictionalized account of this rite is presented, for those interested, in Caiseal Mór's novel *Song of the Earth* (1992).

Much of this learning programme is clearly esoteric in nature. Take, for instance, the ninth year, nine being the most sacred of numbers in Celtic thought. Whatever the exact procedures of the *Sennet*, *Luasca*, *Sruith* and *Duili Feda*, they obviously involve mystical knowledge rather than anything purely factual or academic. Such topics as 'three oscillating springs over a Druid's head', 'keys', 'streams' and 'wisdom tales' all suggest an entry into a higher degree of initiated knowledge. We can notice, also, the overall emphasis on the poems and tales of the oral tradition which a bard had to memorize – along with the set oration – which R. S. A. Macalister estimated at some sixty thousand lines![xxvi] It is clear that the traditional storylines encoded all sorts of information, not to mention wisdom.

Once again, this course of this learning always returns, as a salmon does to its spawning ground, to the wisdom of the goddess. In the Irish legal tracts known as the *Senchas Már* this link is reinforced again and again; in a late Irish piece, *Immacallam in dá Thuarad* (*The Colloquy of the Bards*), in which St Patrick discusses heathen lore with the Druid Caoilte, the *filé* Néde talks of memory as ultimately springing from the fount of the Great Goddess Dana:

> I am the son of Poetry,
> Poetry, son of Reflection,
> Reflection, son of Meditation,
> Meditation, son of Lore,
> Lore, son of Research,
> Research, son of Great Knowledge,
> Great Knowledge, son of Intelligence,
> Intelligence, son of Comprehension,
> Comprehension, son of Wisdom,
> Wisdom, son of the three gods of Dana.[xxvii]

Dana, the Mother Goddess, doubles here for Brigid, daughter of the supreme god known as the Dagda, for 'It is Brigid who is poetess or the wise-woman whom the poets worship, because of her great and wondrous protection. It is for this reason that she is called the Goddess of Poets.'[xxviii] In this respect, the Irish Brigid corresponds to the Welsh witch Ceridwen, patroness of the Gogynfeirdd bards.

Such a deep-rooted and widespread wisdom tradition as the ancient sources suggest does not simply disappear without trace. Some elements, of course, are lost, while others transmogrify and take on new forms. The Druids had to overcome their dislike of the written word to allow what tales and accounts have come down to us respecting Celtic religious ideas. In fact, the monastic life of the fifth to the eighth centuries (a crucial twilight period for paganism) continued to be overshadowed in certain respects by indigenous belief. Many of the scribes were drawn from the *filid* class; they were poets who preserved in essence the bardic learning, and this heritage was still current at the time that the great sagas were being set to parchment.

There is evidence of a caste of Druids still in existence in the late tenth-century in Ireland, despite persecution at the hands of Patrick.[xxix] Indeed, Ireland's learning in this period made it the lighthouse of Europe and we can reasonably expect to find remnants of the Druidical religion of ancient Ireland scattered, if anywhere, in the great manuscripts into which the oral traditions were somewhat haphazardly codified in the Middle Ages.

Illuminated Leaves

Clearly, the earliest available insular (i.e. 'native') literature is the most promising source for the treelore and lore of the trees surrounding Ogam. This raises its own problems, leading as it does through a maze of manuscripts or 'branches' of poetic tradition, but below we look at some of the major relevant 'Cycles'. You will find here an overview of the great books from which this lore is derived, remembering that these are in many cases miscellanies of stories and other material from wildly different sources and even epochs. (What is more, the manuscripts seldom correspond to how later scholars have chosen to define the 'branches' of tales concerned, for often the one tale is found in different, garbled or incomplete forms across several surviving manuscripts.) Some readers may, however, prefer to skip to the pages which follow.

Of chief interest is certainly the Irish tradition, which is by far the best preserved of Celtic vernacular literatures. First and perhaps foremost is the *Lebor na Huidre* (*Book of the Dun Cow*), a dilapidated fragment of one hundred and thirty-eight pages which nonetheless contains some of the most ancient and important tales of the old gods and heroes, including the famous *Taín Bó Cuilnge* (*Cattle Raid of Cooley*). It is signed by the hand of Maelmuiri, a scribe who died in 1106. Next comes the *Lebor Laigen* (*Book of Leinster*), of similar antiquity, attributed to Finn Mac Gorman, Bishop of Kildare, which also furnishes many tales relating to the hero Cú Chulainn. Of the fourteenth-century *Book of Ballymote* and *Yellow Book of Lecan*, the former provides crucial information about Ogam, as we have seen. The *Book of Lecan* and *Book of Lismore*, of the fifteenth century, form the last two of the 'six great collections', although there are a number of other lesser works that still contain valuable material.

More limited in scope but still valuable in themselves and for comparative purposes are the Welsh, Scottish and Breton traditions. Wales has its own revered manuscripts, known as the

'Four Ancient Books of Wales', the oldest of which is the evoca-
tively named *Black Book of Caermarthen*, from the late twelfth
century. Following this are the *Book of Aneurin* (late thirteenth
century), *Book of Taliesin* (fourteenth century) and *Red Book of
Hergest* (fourteenth and fifteenth centuries). The last of these
contains, among other things, the celebrated materials known as
known as the *Branwen Ferch Lyr* (the Four Branches of the
Mabinogion), collected into that form in the nineteenth century
by Lady Charlotte Guest, but widely regarded as dating in
content to no earlier than the ninth century. (In fact, *The White
Book of Rhydderch*, its earliest manuscript form, was written
around 1300.) The previous three collate poems and prophecies
attributed to the three great bards supposed to have lived in the
sixth century, Myrddin (Merlin), Taliesin, and Aneurin.
However, due to the habit of later poets adopting these presti-
gious names as personal titles, these wonderful poems cannot
be dated with certainty to before the ninth century. Indeed,
some derive from the Gogynfeirdd revival of the eleventh to
fourteenth centuries, while certain eighteenth- and nineteenth-
century translators added their own 'emendations', much to the
chagrin of later scholars. Also of note are Scottish materials from
the fourteenth, fifteenth and sixteenth centuries: they deal with
some of the characters of the Irish Túatha dé Danaan, as well as
Finn, Ossian, the Fenians and Cú Chulainn, and were perhaps
borrowed from Ireland as popular tales. Brittany, too, has
contributed a scattering of poems and tales, some in manuscript
form but most surviving in the popular oral tradition, although
the lines of transmission are often hopelessly blurred.

Finally, there are the later bodies of medieval romance
which relate in piecemeal fashion to the old Celtic world. The
Arthurian cycle of Britain and France is the celebrated example,
but more distant materials such as the Frankish *Chanson du
Gestes* also figure as tangentially Celtic in inspiration.

In this book we are mostly concerned with the Irish materials,
though the Welsh poems and myths connected with Merlin and
Taliesin are also indispensable. Many of the stories and themes
that figure in the manuscripts discussed above have been current
in the oral tradition in Ireland until quite recent times. Tall
stories are still told in the far flung coastlines of the West about

mythical heroes and heroines who inhabit the ancient tales, as they passed such and such a hill or camped in a local woodland. In Ogamfews, you will find that each tree-letter is linked to a tale (or cluster of tales) from this body of traditional Celtic literature, so that when you pull a tree-letter in a reading you are addressed by a storyline relevant to your own circumstance. This can be far richer than straightforward advice, for it places within your own hands the opportunity to crack the shell of the tale and taste the kernel of the message that lies within it for you and you alone. And by taking up the interpretation of these tales we are ourselves acquiring and reinvesting with new significance the magnificent hoard of stories from the Celtic world, just as our ancestors turned to them for wisdom and guidance, and as will, we trust, our children's children.

Irish Literature

Irish literature has four great 'cycles' of related tales. These are the Mythological Cycle, which deals largely with the gods and goddesses of Ancient Ireland; the Ulster Cycle, a heroic set of stories which Ireland's most illustrious champion, Cú Chulainn, dominates; the Fenian or Ossianic Cycle, where Finn mac Cumhail, the mystical hero who tastes of the salmon of inspiration, figures along with his son, Ossian; and finally the Historical Cycle, a miscellaneous collection of stories relating to the kings and High Kings of Irish legend and history. These cycles, it should be remembered, are essentially a modern system of classification. In the tradition to which they are native, the sagas are ordered by story-telling type: Destructions, Cattle-raids, Courtships, Battles, Cave Stories, Voyages, Tragedies, Adventures, Banquets, Sieges, Plunderings, Elopements, Eruptions, Visions, Love Stories, Hostings, and Invasions.[xxx] There was little distinction between 'myth' and 'history'.

In addition to the Cycles, there are folkloric materials of various extraction, which comprise a sort of thicket of traditional beliefs and 'superstitions', many of them doubtless derived from the old stock of the Celtic Faery Faith. In what follows we look to the first three of the great cycles, leaving, for the time being, the Historical Cycle to one side.

I: The Mythological Cycle

Foremost in ancient Irish Literature is the Mythological Cycle, which essentially recounts a series of semi-mythical colonizations of the Emerald Isle. The main source is the *Lebor Gabála* (*Book of Invasions* or *Book of the Conquest of Ireland*), whose contents were recorded in the eighth to the ninth centuries – though parts of it likely predate this by at least several hundred years. The Five Waves of Invasion chronicle the coming of Partholon's crew, followed by the Nemedians, with the Fir Bolg and associates at their heels, after which the Túatha dé Danaan (People of the goddess Danu) arrive, to be overcome by the last wave, the Gaels. Since the Celts have left no record of a creation account, these tales survive as a kind of epic dramatization of the origins of the Irish.

Much of the material exists on the boundary between half-remembered history and the domain of mythology, and suffers from a degree of Christianization. However, while scribes in the early medieval monasteries edited and censored the pagan material at their disposal, they also appear to have exercised some care in its preservation. Though many elements have surely been lost, much survives that is certainly pre-Christian in character. The main techniques used by the scribes to obscure (or perhaps disguise) the pagan content of these 'myths' was to link Ireland's ancient past to biblical history and cast its gods and goddesses as heroic mortals possessed of extraordinary skills. No doubt they also choose to omit certain 'objectionable' elements, where these exceeded churchly scruples, but as we have seen the distinction between monk and *filé* seems to have been somewhat fluid in the early days of the monasteries. Taking these facts into account, we can salvage a considerable amount of genuine material, whatever riddles it may still pose for us.

Of the Mythological Cycle, the Fourth Wave of Invasion is the most important in terms of the religious conceptions of the early Irish, as known to us today. The Túatha dé Danaan, children of the chthonic Earth Mother Dana, are the old gods of Ireland, the closest we have to a pantheon of Celtic divinities. They replace the 'evil' Fomóri, dark spirits of the land who were probably the divinities of an even earlier set of beliefs. Here are introduced some of the most enduring characters of later legend, for the Túatha dé Danaan are the Ancient Ones who ultimately retreated with the coming of the Gael to live in the *sidhe* and became the Faery Folk of the Otherworld. Though overcome by the tides of history, they continue to live in the annals of folklore as the Little People who haunt sacred sites and the crossroads of country lanes, still able to catch the unwary off guard and conduct them into the world of Fey.

Here we meet Dana, the Great Mother of all the gods and goddesses, whose veritable host of 'children' include Núada Airgetám (of the Silver Hand), the Warrior King who is superseded by the inimitable Lugh Lamfada (of the Long Arm), a Celtic sun god who gave his name to Lyons; the Dagda – the 'Good God' – that great buffoon of a supreme being, often pictured as a ill-kempt fellow in ill-fitting robes who possesses an insatiable appetite and a magical cauldron that never empties; his wife, Bóann, after whom the River Boyne is named; Óengus Mac Óg, the fair faced 'god of love' and beauty; the Mórrígu, a fierce war-goddess who went on to inspire the later Arthurian legends of Morgan Le Fay, the Morgain of Marion Zimmer Bradley's *Mists of Avalon*; Díancecht, the god of medicine and healing; Manannán mac Lir, son of the Irish sea-god and later a ruler of the ocean and Otherworld himself; and Ogma the Sun Face, god of wisdom, learning and eloquence, inventor of the Ogam script, to name but a few.

We should always bear in mind, however, that the boundaries between the old gods are fluid, with the functions of one god often overlapping another. The Mórrígu, for instance, shares her battle-hag perch with her 'sisters' Neman and Macha, and all three collectively form the triple-goddess figure known as the Badb (said 'Bav'). In Celtic myth, it is *themes* which are often more important than individual characters, for many ancient ritual formulae – such as the drops of inspiration which certain magician-heroes taste – occur in different tales involving separate mythological players. Such themes are the shining threads which guide us through the labyrinth of materials we have inherited from the world of the Celts. They also form the clusters of storylines that we apply to ourselves through the art of Ogam divination, as we sit in the sacred grove of the ages, drinking from

the magical well that is found there, contemplating our circumstances and refreshing our hearts and minds.

II: The Fenian Cycle

The tales of Finn mac Cumhail and his roving warrior bands, the
Fianna, are one of the strangest and most wondrous collections of
Celtic lore. Finn is an enigmatic figure: poet, lover, warrior, hero,
wizard. The twelfth-century *Macgnimartha Finn* (*The Boyhood
Feats of Finn*) tells of how as a young man he received enlighten-
ment on the banks of the River Boinn (Boyne):

> And . . . he . . . went on to learn poetry from Finegas, a poet that was
> living at the Boinn, for the poets thought it was always on the brink
> of water poetry was revealed to them. And he did not give him his
> own name, but he took the name Deimne. Seven years, now, Finegas
> had stopped at the Boinn, watching the salmon, for it was in the
> prophecy that he would eat the salmon of knowledge that would
> come there, and that he would have all knowledge after. And when
> at the last the salmon of knowledge came, he brought it to where
> Finn was, and bade him to roast it, but he bade him not to eat any
> of it. And when Finn brought him the salmon after a while he said:
> 'Did you eat any of it at all boy?' 'I did not,' said Finn; 'but I burned
> my thumb putting down a blister that rose on the skin, and after
> doing that I put my thumb in my mouth.' 'What is your name, boy?'
> said Finegas. 'Deimne,' said he. 'It is not, but it is Finn your name is,
> and it is to you and not myself the salmon was given in prophecy.'
> With that he gave Finn the whole of the salmon, and from that time
> Finn had the knowledge that came from the nuts of the nine hazels
> of wisdom that grow beside the well that is below the sea.[xxxi]

From this point on Finn has only to place his thumb in his mouth
to come by any desired knowledge. What is more, a little later he
gets 'a second wisdom' from the 'well of the moon', which grants
the gift of 'foretelling' (clairvoyance) upon the recipient.

The connections between the salmon of wisdom, nine hazels,
wisdom and prophetic ability clearly point to the value of the
Fenian cycle to Ogam interpretation; more so, because much of
Finn's life and that of his 'forester band' is played out within the
wild, woodland environments of ancient Éire, with frequent and
illuminating references to its trees, bushes and shrubs. Indeed, we
will encounter Finn and his friends in Ogamfews on more than
one occasion.

III: The Ulster Cycle

Irish literature's most celebrated epic, the *Taín Bó Cuilnge*, concerns the exploits of the great hero Cú Chulainn. Though it and other sources concerning his life, such as the eleventh–twelfth century *Serglige Con Culainn Inso Sís & Óenét Emir* (*The Wasting Sickness of Cú Chulainn & The Only Jealousy of Emer*), clearly feel more legendary, Cú Chulainn is more than a mere action man: he has the 'hero-light' and is identifiable as a sun god figure. In his youth he is taught arms by Scáthach, a war goddess related in character to the Mórrígu and her sisters. Indeed, this cycle contains a considerable amount of material relevant to our study of the ogamfews and their significations.

As we have seen, Cú Chulainn is himself the reputed author of a Word Ogam, and as such is a type of guide in ogamlore. As the most illustrious hero of Irish tradition, Cú Chulainn teaches the path of duty, honour and valour, just as Finn teaches inspiration, Morainn fair judgement, Óengus higher love, Merlin the deepest lore of wizardry, and Taliesin the sacred songs in which such spells are couched. Yet, if this cast should appear too heavily masculine, it pays to recall once again that the ultimate source of all this lore in Celtic tradition lies in the spring that feeds the Druidic grove: the wisdom of the goddess.

It is, after all, the Ever Living Lady from the Land of Promise (in one or other of her aspects) who tends the cauldron from which questing heroes and heroines alike seek to drink as they wander the paths of the Greenworld. This is very clearly borne out by the stories of Merlin and Taliesin.

Merlin and Taliesin

Apart from the celebrated tales of the Mabinogion and other ancient remnants, the Welsh manuscripts are most notable for having preserved for us legends concerning – and poems supposed to have been written by – two of the most extraordinary figures of Celtic lore. The first, Merlin, needs little introduction, being widely known, at least in stereotypic form, from the Arthurian romances. The arch-wizard and counsellor to the King, who confounded the court wizards of Vortigern while still a precocious child, continues to cast his spell from his castle of glass into our own times. Taliesin, a figure of paramount significance to contemporary Druidry, is of equal stature and he provides valuable insights into the psyche of Celtic paganism. It might be said that Merlin seems to be an archetypal Druid and Taliesin the exemplary bard, but it should be noted that the sources cast both characters in the role of shaman-poets. It is indeed noteworthy that there is a strand of Celtic lore surrounding these figures which seems to be partially separate from the more judicious Druids; that of warrior shamans whose anarchic, even mad behaviour may lead us into the deepest substratum of Celtic 'Nature' religion.

Certainly, there is much food for thought here in any study of ogamlore, as such figures have an intimate association with the great trees of the Ogam grove.

Myrddin Wylt

Merlin has many faces and more than one manifestation in history. Lovers of Arthurian romance will be familiar with the Myrddin Ambrosius – crystallized in Geoffrey of Monmouth's *Historia Regum Britanniae* (*History of the Kings of Britain*) of about 1135 – who lived 'long ago in the reign of King Vortigern', that is, from the mid-fifth century. But there is another figure haunting the fringes of the medieval romances who is more mysterious still. That is the Myrddin Wylt (Merlin the Wild) who, although historically of a slightly later period, evokes far more archaic resonances.

Geoffrey of Monmouth's original *Vita Merlini* (*Life of Merlin*) tells of this other Merlin, who is primarily a wildman of the woods, ecstatic shaman and poet. Out of Strathclyde in the lowlands of Scotland of the sixth to the seventh centuries comes record of one Merlin the Briton, who is allied as counsellor to his lord Gwendeleu against the cruel Rydderch. Gwendeleu is ruler of an essentially pagan kingdom and court defending itself against the Christianized Rydderch. When his lord is defeated and the court shattered, Merlin goes mad and flees to the forest of Kellydon where he lives the life of a outcast. To add insult to injury Geoffrey has Ganieda, Merlin's own sister, become Rydderch's wife! Finally captured, Merlin is brought to court and, seeing a leaf in his sister's hair, laughs sardonically. When Rydderch demands to know the cause of his mirth, Merlin informs him that she got that leaf lying under a tree with her lover. The King then sets up certain proofs by which the sooth-sayer is to prove himself, to his ultimate chagrin!

What is most fascinating in all this is Merlin's sojourn in the woods. It is in this phase of his strange, mythicized life that he utters the famous pieces known collectively as the *Prophecies of Merlin*. That Merlin, replete as he is with Druidical characteristics, retreats into the forest is instructive in itself, for the forest grove is the site of Druidic worship. As Lucan wrote, 'they worship the gods in the woods without recourse to temples.'[xxxii] That he turns mad – in the definition of the later period through which these materials have come down to us – is also greatly significant. For the 'madness' of Merlin has clear parallels with the shamanistic ecstasy of initiates to the mysteries of Nature religions across Europe and beyond. It is a profoundly embedded theme in Irish literature too, as we shall see.

The Apple Tree

You may wish to read the most famous prophecy attributed to Merlin in an orchard, for it is known as *The Apple Tree*. Although various portions of the poem are later grafts, the nucleus of the material is undoubtedly ancient and parts may even be attributed to the shadowy figure of Myrddin Wylt himself. In *The Apple Tree*, Merlin laments his fate: exclusion from the court, poverty and want of human kindness. And it is at the same time a lyrical celebration of the natural world, full of praise and wonder for forest, lake and mountain. Through all of this, Merlin's only friend is the apple tree, under whose spreading branches he shelters, remembering his former life, and prophesying for the future. These fragments give an idea of the overall strain of the work.

> Sweet apple tree, you of the lovely branches
> Putting forth vigorous buds on all sides . . .
> Sweet apple tree with yellow reflections,
> You who grow on a hill above the moor . . .
> Sweet apple tree of lush foliage,
> I have fought beneath you to please a maiden . . .
> Sweet apple tree that grows in the clearing . . . [xxxiii]

Now, the apple has more than just naturalistic associations, as we have seen, and as the commentary on the *quert-few* (ꕡ) in Ogamfews elaborates. It is a grand gateway tree linked to the Otherworld. Its branch is the badge of the initiated *filé*, and its fruit are the apples of healing and immortality found in Avallach or Avalon, the island of apples to which Arthur is ultimately taken on his funeral barge.

Merlin here presents, in fact, the archetype of the shaman–poet prophesying with the wisdom of the Otherworld. Like other sacrificial figures, such as Odin, Christ, or the Buddha, he undergoes his great transformation beneath the branches of a gateway tree. And in other Celtic sources, we find parallels to Merlin in the equally strange figures of Lailoken and Suibhné, demonstrating that Merlin himself is merely one manifestation of deeply embedded cultural theme. The Lailoken referred to in the twelfth-century *Life of Saint Kentigern* provides valuable corroboration of the widespread nature of the wildman storyline: he is banished to a wood, goes mad and from his rock prophesies bitterly. But it is in the legends associated with Suibhné, particularly as found in the twelfth-century *Buile Shuibni* (*The Frenzy of Suibhné*), that we find the most illuminating parallels with the ecstasies and sufferings of Merlin.

The Madness of Suibhné

Suibhné of Argyll throws St Rónán's psalter into a lake, exhibiting a similar impatience with the new religion to that of the reprobate pagan, Merlin. After some ongoing skirmishing, the saint curses Suibhné, who is gripped by madness and flees by air in the likeness of a bird. Spending seven years in woods in Glenn Bolcáin in Ireland, Suibhné prophesies and composes poetry. At the end of the seven years he lives an entire year in a yew tree in Ros Ercáin. His son-in-law's ministrations cure him briefly, but madness still grips him and he returns to the woods, climbs a tree and recalls his life in the forest, its trees, and the wild places of Ireland. He remains in the forest for some time and – as conveniently foretold in Rónán's prediction – does not live long after leaving it.

A number of elements in this tale are noteworthy. First is Suibhné's symbolic bird-flight (an ancient shamanistic theme), his ecstasy and his versifying. The year within a tree trunk is clearly ritualistic; as the *idho-few* (卌) associated with the yew shows, this is a tree of death and transformation, literal or symbolic. The recitation from a treetop is a classic shamanistic theme, derived from the ancient motif widespread across Europe and Asia of the shaman's ascent of the World Tree into the upper-worlds of the gods. What is more, as the verses reproduced below reveal, Suibhné's poetry comes out in a type of magical formula, entwined with treelore. In the following passages he elaborates the virtue of the trees of the woods, of the sacred grove:

> Thou oak, bushy, leafy,
> Thou art high beyond trees;
> O hazlet, little branching one,
> O fragrance of hazel-nuts.
>
> O alder, thou art not hostile,
> Delightful is thy hue,
> Thou art not rending and prickling
> In the gap wherein thou art.
>
> O little blackthorn, little thorny one;
> O little black sloe tree;
> O water cress, little green-topped one,
> From the brink of the *ousel* [?] spring.
>
> O *minen* of the pathways,
> Thou art sweet beyond herbs,
> O little green one, very green one,
> O herb on which grows the strawberry.
>
> O apple-tree, little apple-tree,
> Much art thou shaken;
> O quicken, little berried one,
> Delightful is thy bloom.
>
> O briar, little arched one,
> Thou grantest no fair terms,
> Thou ceasest not to tear me,
> Till thou hast thy fill of blood.
>
> O yew-tree, little yew-tree,
> In churchyards thou art conspicuous;
> O ivy, little ivy,
> Thou art familiar in the dusky wood.

O holly, little sheltering one,
Thou door against the wind;
O ash-tree, thou baleful one,
Hand weapon of the warrior.

O birch, smooth and blessed,
Thou melodious, proud one,
Delightful each entwining branch
In the top of thy crown.

The aspen a-trembling;
By turns I hear
Its leaves a-racing –
Meseems 'tis the foray!

My aversion in woods –
I conceal it not from anyone –
Is the leafy stirk of the oak
Swaying evermore.[xxxiv]

The trees in this poem correspond closely to the Ogam letters. Most importantly, they reveal to us yet again the essential story of the Druidic or shamanistic initiate reciting lore of the woodland, singing the praises of the denizens of the forest.

What we can conclude from all this? Essentially, that the Merlin/Lailoken/Suibhné figure stems from the older and wider archetype of the wild man of the woods who learns the forest's lore in a state of ecstasy. Shaman of the treetops and also master of the beasts whose many transformations include the horned figure of the stag, Merlin is an initiate to the mysteries of the goddess. This is the true meaning of his laughter at the leaf in his sister's hair, for it is he who has lain with her under a tree, as Jean Markale has demonstrated, based on the widespread underlying theme of sacred incest in these stories.[xxxv] Whatever the Freudian interpretation of this, in Celtic culture it relates to initiation into the mysteries of the goddess, just as Finn mac Cumhail tastes of the salmon of the water of the River Boyne (and thus the Mother Goddess Bóann after which it is named) and the Welsh bard Taliesin becomes the grain of corn that impregnates Keridwen, making him his own father. Incest here is being employed not literally but as a metaphor for ultimate union with the divine (the Mother Goddess), a transcendence of duality, and realization of absolute oneness. It is, in other words, masking a profound religious theme.

Breton legends regarding Merlin associate him intimately with a spring or 'fountain' at the centre of a wood. The tree and the well are once again connected in Celtic thought, for the well lies at the centre of the sacred grove. As the twelfth-century Romance writer Chrétien de Troyes describes it in his *Yves*, in the language of that later period:

> [Go] to a spring not far from here . . . You'll see the spring boiling, although it's colder than marble. It's in the shade of the loveliest tree that Nature ever managed to create. It keeps its leaves the whole year round and doesn't shed them, however hard the winter . . . [xxxvi]

We know that the spring is the prototype of the sacred well and is linked to the chthonic aspects of the goddess. Merlin is the priest of the spring under a tree in whose branches the birds of the Otherworld sing: he is guardian of the well in the *nemeton*. This function makes him a powerful counsellor in the art of Ogam interpretation, as is his spiritual consort: the mysterious otherwordly woman who tends the well.

Taliesin

Taliesin, like Merlin, is a child of mysterious circumstances. His story – which was elaborated in the texts of the Gogynfeirdd bards, although many of the themes, incidents and poetic motifs may predate the eleventh century – begins with the trials of a lad named Gwion Bach. Its importance to our exploration cannot be overstated, and it is a story used today in rites of initiation in several contemporary Druidic orders.

> Gwion is conducted into the service of the witch Ceridwen as a lad, along with his apparent foster-father, the old blind man Modra. Keridwen has sent for some of the rarest herbs in the world to fill her cauldron. She is mixing a concoction designed to gift her ugly, misshapen son Avagddu with the inspiration of the poets, so he will at least be loved for his wisdom. She asks Taliesin and Modra to watch the cauldron while she sleeps, with the direst of warnings lest they dare to taste or spill a drop of its contents. However, late at night Gwion puts too much wood on the fire; the cauldron bubbles high, and three drops fall on the back of his hand. Unthinkingly he applies his tongue to the burn and thus imbibes the elixir meant for Avagddu.

At this point Taliesin receives the great draught of wisdom, but he also realises the danger he faces at Keridwen's hands, for she has awoken. He flees the house and, finding himself in a field, shapeshifts into a hare. Keridwen follows in the form of a greyhound bitch, snapping at his heels. She closes on him as he reaches a riverbank, where Gwion shapeshifts into a salmon and tries to lose himself deep in the waters of the stream. But Keridwen becomes a sharp-toothed otter and pursues him. Just as he is almost caught, Gwion breaks the surface of the water and transforms himself into a graceful bird, swift of flight. But Keridwen takes the form of a hawk and makes ready to swoop. Gwion dives towards a barn in the countryside far below, becoming, as he falls, a single grain and taking his place in a huge pile of corn, fit for threshing. But Keridwen spies out his hiding place, and in the shape of a black hen takes him up into her beak in a single gulp.

Soon Keridwen finds herself with child, but cannot bear to destroy the infant. Instead she casts him upon the waters of the Boinn, from which he is eventually taken up by the hapless Elphin. Elphin names the child Taliesin (Radiant Brow) and becomes his foster-father. Taliesin, while still an infant, goes on to confound the bards at the court of Maelgwn, the king, winning much honour for his master and ultimately himself. His compositions, or those attributed to him, become some of the most celebrated in Welsh tradition.[xxxvii]

This tale can be interpreted with reasonable ease. Gwion represents the non-initiated soul, like the young Finn preceding his tasting of the miraculous salmon. He enters into the service of Keridwen, the Goddess of the Cauldron of Life, Death and Rebirth, who swallows him into her womb or cell of learning. He will emerge as an Initiate to the Mysteries.

The chase scene represents the Initiate's transition through the Four Elements of Earth (the hare), Water (the stream), Air (as a bird), and Fire (in the form of the sun symbol of the grain of ripened corn). This is also a set of animal totems which constitute the seasons of the year. Thus Taliesin passes through the wheel of the turning year, dancing the sacred, shapeshifting dance of the seasons. Finally caught by Keridwen, he becomes the seed (grain of corn) that impregnates her and thus is his own father. The womb of the goddess is the tomb and the womb of rebirth. His new manifestation as Taliesin reveals him as an initiated *filé* or bard, a divine child replete with knowledge. Like Merlin he sings of his knowledge in a number of ecstatic verses, including the famous 'I have beens' where he recalls all the many shapes or incarnations he has taken.

There is a final parallel with Merlin/Lailoken/Suibhné in Taliesin's supposed authorship of the *Cad Goddeu*, a Welsh poem known as *The Battle of the Trees*. On the surface of it, the *Cad Goddeu* chronicles a battle where the soldiers are instructed (by the Lord, no less!) to take the form of trees of the woods. The most simplistic explanation would be that this is a camouflage technique utilized to gain advantage in battle, as in *Macbeth*'s Burnham Wood scene. But it seems likely that the *Cad Goddeu* is a much more symbolic work. Its background is probably mythological and the 'battle' doubtless involved the secret Druidic identities of the great trees.

> *The Cad Goddeu*
>
> The alder-trees, at the head of the army,
> Formed the advance guard,
> The willows and the service trees
> Lined up behind them,
> The plums, which are rare,
> Astounded the men.
>
> The new medlars
> Were a pivot to the battle,
> The bushes of thorny roses
> Struggled against a great mass,
> The raspberries, ranged in thickets,
> Showed as no others
> How fragile is life.
>
> The privet and the honeysuckle
> With ivy on the front line
> Set off into battle with the gorse.
> The cherry-tree handled the aggressors,
> The birch, despite his noble mind,
> Was placed at the rear,
> Not because of his cowardice,
> But because of his height.
> The golden clover proved
> To the stranger how wild was his nature.

The pines stood at the front
In the centre of the fray
Which I exalted greatly
In the presence of the kings.
The elm and his followers
Did not move a foot.
They fought against the centre
Against the flanks and the rear.

Of the hazel-trees, one could see
That their warlike rage was most great.
Lucky the privet's role,
He was the bull of battle, the master of the world.
Morawg and Morydd
Did great deeds in the shape of pines.
The holly was spattered with green,
He was of all the most valiant.[xxxviii]

This difficult poem remains enigmatic, but it clearly echoes the tradition of recital of treelore that we followed through *The Madness of Suibhné*. Once again, the Celtic shaman-poet sings of the otherworldly trees in the sacred grove of meaning.

The Green Man and May Queen

In recent times there has been a tremendous revival of the archetype of the Green Man, a figure of folklore represented in medieval cathedral sculpture of the Dark and Middle Ages, and more recently on signs outside many an English country inn. This rustic-looking figure with his crop of green leaves or vines spilling from his grinning mouth is actually a complex character. Although some scholars have recently questioned his pagan origins, to contemporary Pagans he signifies humanity's oneness with Nature, on the one hand, and the living, intelligent spirit of the Greenworld, on the other. He has been connected with many figures of folklore, including Hern the Hunter, Cernunnos, Robin Hood and, much later, Jack of the Green.

His female counterpart is the May Queen, Flower Maiden, or

Maid Marian of mythology and folklore. She represents both the female facet of the divinity in Nature and the archetype of the 'natural woman'.

Although of a different provenance than the Irish and Welsh divinities, heroes and shaman figures we have been exploring, the Green Man and May Queen provide us with a symbolic bridge between our current age and the ancestral lore of the Celts. We have seen that the great shamanic lore of the trees is an essential ingredient of what has come down to us of Celtic spirituality, and that the sacred groves of the Druids may yet live on in symbolic form in the Ogam script. But if the old stories the Ogams invoke are to be more than mere tales, we need mediators who can help us to interpret them in new and useful ways. To my mind, the figures of the Green Man and May Queen fulfil this role. They remind us of the protectors and guardians of the Greenworld who emanate from many an Irish saga or even Arthurian romance. It is as if all the wisdom of the ancient Greenworld were concentrated in this mystical pair in a form that speaks directly and urgently to our epoch. The god and goddess of Nature need to reawaken in our hearts so that they can manifest their wisdom afresh in this perilous age. Their return to the stage of contemporary affairs through the revival of Paganism, ecological awareness, the Green movement, and techniques such as Ogam divination are all part of this process. They not only point us towards re-establishing our equilibrium with Nature, they are vivid reflections of our own higher natures. By partaking in the cycle of cultural regeneration they offer, we potentially bring healing and restoration not only to ourselves but to the world around us.

We have encountered many branches of Celtic tradition in the course of Ogamlore, but the Green Man and May Queen figures integrate them all into the one, dual archetype for the modern age: that of our holistic link to Nature and her role in instructing our minds and hearts. Ogamlore is a form of sacred knowledge gifted by the sun-faced divinity, Ogma, who aids us in our growth just as the sun nourishes the Greenworld. The twenty tree-letters of the ancient Ogam script compose an alphabet steeped in the Druidic treelore of the old Celtic dominions. Although the old trees figure as totems and connectors to the energies of the Greenworld, they also function on a symbolic level. They are signposts or gateways, each representing a traditional tale or set of tales and understandings from the oral tradition. When we draw an ogamfew, these elements are activated and made relevant to us in the here and now. We penetrate to the roots of the matter at hand, where the springs of inspiration nourish the good Earth.

Ogam is a versatile and inspiring system of divination, but its virtues are not limited to mere fortune-telling. While they can be very accurate as a predictive system, there is a far deeper significance to the ogamfews. In fact, the tree-letters represent the transformations of the divinity through a cycle of birth and death and, as the wheel of Ogam turns, rebirth too. Those transformations relate to the mysterious journey of the seed through its stages of gestation, growth, flowering, decay and renewal, for the seed is the divinity in Nature. The real mystery is that *we too are that seed* as we journey through the cycle of life's seasons. This was the great teaching of the mystery religions of the ancient world. *Ogam* brings the Celtic variant of that mystery alive for us today.

II
Ogamfews

Yet trees are not 'trees', until so named and seen –
and never were so named, till those had been
who speech's involuted breath unfurled,
faint echo and dim picture of the world . . .

J. R. R. Tolkien, from *Mythopoeia*[xxxix]

Guide to the Ogams

In Ogamfews, you will find the twenty tree-letters of the Tree Alphabet presented in the BethLuisFearn sequence, followed by four additional divinatory tokens, the Four Treasures (see below). Each has been given a title of contemporary relevance such as 'Guidance' or 'Obstacles', but the traditional name and variant names of the tree-letters are also presented.

The Word Ogams

You will find that the Word Ogams are given prominence on the page, as these kennings provide us with echoes from the sacred oral tradition. They fulfil the function of the divinatory poem, such as we find in the Rune poems, connected to the Runes, and the oracular verses of the *I Ching*. However, as they are obscure and sometimes contradictory, you may wish to proceed directly to the following sections. Their divinatory significations are generally explained in the following interpretative texts, and you can get to know them over time. On a magical level, they are useful in the longer term as a gateway into the oldest strata of ogamlore. Do not, however, expect to crack their riddling codes all at once.

Visualization

Next comes the Visualization. This is a short description designed to provide you with a mental image of the inner essence of the tree-letter in question. You may prefer your own visualization if, for example, you find that a burly male figure seems more appealing to you as an image of Protection (l, *luis*, rowan) than, say, a mighty goddess. The images chosen stem from traditional sources – you will usually find them in the tales which follow – but remember that the beauty and power of Celtic tradition is its flexibility and the fact that a multiplicity of tales and images are employed to illustrate the one, grander theme. What is more, here we are using mythology in a creative and empowering way, and these Visualizations may be used as aids to creative Visualization and vision-questing. At this point, fixed images become fluid and animated.

Meaning

We now come to the heart of the matter, the Meaning section. This is where the message of the ogam concerned becomes an omen of personal significance. This is the advice addressed by the Celtic Oracle to you, or to the one for whom you are reading. Through the synchronous processes of divination it can carry messages to you from the realms of the gods.

You will notice that each ogam is multifaceted and has more than one possible interpretation. Mull over the range of meanings until the right one clicks into place in your mind and heart. Although they have many different aspects, each ogam is at the same time quite definite and can accurately correspond to quite specific situations. Sit with this section for a while; its implications may be more far reaching than at first you realize.

Natural Characteristics

Next there is a description of the Natural Characteristics of the tree in question. Here we gain insight as to why the Celts chose to use this tree to illustrate a certain principle. It is also valuable for focusing our attention upon the living, green entity that underlies the identity of the tree-letter in question.

Of course, not all who divine with Ogam live in lands where these trees are native to their surrounding environment. If so, perhaps you could think of trees indigenous to your area that illustrate a similar principle in Nature. Most places have rich archives of lore concerned with the natural world, if only we open to them.

Storylines

Now we come to the Storylines associated with each ogam you have drawn. As noted, most ogams have more than one tale connected to them, so here you may find several interwoven threads. If certain storylines speak to you most deeply, you may like to seek these out further in many of the fine collections available today (see the Bibliography at the end of this book). In these stories you will uncover a vast wealth of wisdom and enlightenment.

The art of applying mythological models and understanding to daily life is one that is enjoying a great resurgence in popularity. With the influence of C. G. Jung, Joseph Campbell and others, we are relearning the deep value of such tales, for they hold the accumulated folk wisdom, the psychology and the spirituality of many ages and are a timeless fount of inspiration.

Folklore and Magic

Finally, you will find the Folklore section. This provides a brief commentary on the recorded customs and beliefs surrounding the tree in question. Folklore in some cases contains echoes and traces of much that was once lore in the greater sense, and the beauty of it is that some of these elements persist in certain areas until this very day. Yet contemporary folklore also involves the revival and reinterpretation of ancient customs: we need to reclaim it as a living and vital field, with as much to teach as the more respectable arts and sciences.

Attached to the folkloric material are the magical practices, past and present, which relate to the tree-letters. What is magic and why should it be connected to Ogam divination? This is too vast a question to address here, but if we note that the word *magic* shares a root with *image* and *imagination*, we realize that magic is really the art of using metal images to change physical reality.

Through visualizing a force or energy, or working with it through a symbolic object such as a wand or cup, we send strong signals into the invisible world as to our needs and wishes. This gives the universe the opportunity to respond to our requests, and actually participate in shaping the character of events, to some degree. In other words, if divination is the diagnosis, magic is one potential treatment for certain problems. However, those wishing to utilize the information on magic and rite here should thoroughly verse themselves in the wider field before experimenting. It pays to remember that purity of heart and motive are crucial to such work, if the results are to be beneficial.

*

The art of divination is, like any other, one which develops with time and practice. Yet people are often stunned to see how the light of Ogma penetrates into the corners of their lives and illuminates much that had been obscure. Apart from anything else, it opens a sacred space within which we may commune with ourselves and gain insight into our circumstances, aided by higher powers of peace and benevolence. While hallowed, divination is also a form of sacred play, a game of self-knowledge where we can observe our own progress in the stakes of life. You will learn more about this in Ogamcasting, the final part of this book, where the techniques and procedures of divining with Ogam are explained in some detail.

Aicme Beth

Birth

T

Beth (Birch)

Names: *beth, beith, beithe* (said BEH). Botanical name: *Betula alba* (*Betula pendula*); silver birch. Status: peasant tree. Sound: b.

Elaborations on the Ogam Names
Of withered trunk, fair-haired the birch.
Word Ogam of Morainn mac Moín
Birch is faded trunk and fair hair.
Word Ogam of Cú Chulainn
Birch equals browed beauty,
worthy of pursuit.
Word Ogam of Óengus
Birch is most silver of skin.

Visualization

The Birch Goddess of Birth is enshrined in the trunk of the birch tree, her upward-branching arms outstretched.

Meaning

Beth, standing as it does at the entrance to the Ogam grove, is a tree-letter of beginnings. It is a herald of change, of things to come. Expect the unexpected, for a previous phase is concluding and novel things are ready to manifest. Magically, birch has long been used to assist in clearing out the old, in purification, and in birthing the new.

Several ogams betoken the death of the old, but birch espe-cially represents the emergence of a bright new element from the fabric of what has gone before. This is a tree-letter of inception. Whatever is dawning in your life at this time, it is likely to be a joyful occurrence. Yet, though a gentle ogam, *beth* is nonetheless firm, for birth seldom comes without some measure of pain.

Though *beth* does not necessarily relate to childbirth itself – more generally auguring the birthing of a new phase, project or relationship – similar principles operate. Now is the time to devote your energy to preparing the ground for that which is ready to issue forth. Imagine that you are tending a seed which will need considerable care to come to fruition. Yet letting things take their own course is also vital. Think of yourself as a midwife of the new.

Like the birch, this tree-letter embodies the principle of self-propagation. It teaches us about the cycle of continuous manifes-tation of the new from the soil of the old. The lesson here is how to handle, as harmoniously as possible, the constant transforma-tion such processes bring. Cyclical change is the basic order of Nature. The sooner we can accept and embrace the changes that come our way, the quicker happiness follows.

Reversed, this ogam suggests you may be stuck in the soil of the old. If you cling to the dead wood of the past, you will end up withering and becoming stale to life. Let what is in the past pass, for holding on to outmoded thoughts, ideas or relationships is standing in the way of your growth. Do not fear the new, it her-alds renewal and regeneration.

Keywords
Old phase concluded, purification, renewal. Beginnings, heralds change, the appearance of the new. Constant change, cyclical law, process. Childbirth.

Reversed
Being stuck, stale, withering. Need to let go of the past.

Natural Characteristics
The identification of the birch with the birth of the new stems from several of the tree's features. In its natural habitat, birch grows most readily on the forest's edge, and so it is often the tree

first encountered as one enters northern European woodland.
One of the earliest trees to leaf in spring, birch marks the seasonal return of the life-force in the Greenworld. Moreover, this is
a self-propagating tree that has both male and female catkins,
illustrating the principle of life arising out of life.

As it ages birch may well of described as being 'of withered
trunk', but it is a tree of prolific growth which provides a fruitful
environment for fungi, including the hallucinogenic fly agaric
mushroom, and it also paves the way for a host of other woodland
dwellers. Ecologically, it embodies self-sacrifice.

The silver birch when in full vigour, its white trunk 'most silver
of skin', also marks the tree as a type of entrance to the Otherworld,
for in Celtic myth animals and objects connected to the
Otherworld are often albino. Birch is a feminine, Faery tree known
in folklore as the Lady of the Woods, and like the fair-haired, otherwordly women of Celtic myth, it carries the call to adventure for
the questing hero. Where the birch points, there one must follow,
for its branches hold the keys to the unfolding of destiny.

Storylines

The birch's most important appearance in Irish literature is in a
Fenian Cycle romance preserved in a seventeenth-century manuscript, the contents of which may nonetheless date to as early as
the tenth century. In the *Tóruigheacht Dhiarmada Agus Ghrianne*
(*The Pursuit of Diarmaid and Gráinne*), the themes of withering,
fair-hair, and the 'beauty spot' all fall together in a meaningful
whole. Gráinne is one of those fair heroines of Celtic myth;
described time and again as inhabiting a 'sunny house', she has
clear solar associations. As the daughter of the High King and
fairest woman in the land, she parallels the many otherwordly
women who lead heroes onto the path of adventure in Celtic
myth. But the maiden is to be married to the ageing hero, Finn.
When she first meets him she recoils at his grey-haired and hoary
appearance. Gráinne thinks resentfully to herself how it is not
fitting that she should be wedded to 'a man that is older than my
father'.[xl]

Instead, she becomes enamoured of Finn's nephew, Diarmaid,
literally a 'browed beauty', for the hero has a love-spot on his
forehead that causes maidens to fall helplessly in love with him.

Our heroine pursues this Celtic Adonis relentlessly, forcing him to flee with her by invoking a *geiss* (ritual bond) that states he may not refuse the request of a lady. Honour-bound to offer her loyalty and protection, he reluctantly agrees. On the run, the couple come to a place called Doire-dá-Bhoth (the Wood of the Two Huts) and there Diarmaid performs a strange and magical ritual involving birch:

> And Diarmuid cut down the wood round about them, and he made a fence having seven doors of woven twigs, and he set out a bed of soft rushes and of the tops of the birch-tree for Grania in the very middle of the wood.[xli]

The 'tops of the birch tree' that Diarmaid uses to house Gráinne form 'burdles' of twigs known in folklore as witches' knots, thus creating a kind of protected circle within which the couple sleep. The whole episode is highly symbolic, with its theme of the withering of the old king, representing the old order, in favour of the new, symbolically within the compass of the birch burdle. This is replicated across a number of Celtic tales: it is a *fabula*, or archetypal story-line. The drama of the young lover taking the place of his ageing liege – the King is dead, long live the King! – is found most notably in the romances of such celebrated lovers as Mider and Étaín and Tristan and Yseut and, of course, in the lovers' triangle of Arthur, Guinevere and Lancelot.

The birch has also been linked to the great sorcerer of Welsh tradition, Gwyddyon, nephew of Math (although ash is his *primary* tree). He appears in the Welsh poem the *Cad Goddeu* as 'Gwyddyon the birch', according to the Celtic scholar and poet, Jean Markale. The birch here is apparently the ruler of a troop of otherwordly trees who act as soldiers in the strange battle that the poem describes. The birch's role over the others trees is, as Markale puts it, that of 'transforming their withered aspect and bringing them back to life'.[xlii] This accords perfectly with the theme of life emerging from the soil of the old that we have been following

Folklore and Magic

Birch garlands were often given as tokens of love in folk custom, and birch wands were used in love magic. Birch, or the *beth* ogam, may still be used in love magic today, although you must be careful about what you end up bringing into reality! The maypole itself was often made of birch, connecting the tree with fertility and regeneration themes. Dancing around the maypole is a wonderful affirmation of the great powers of procreation and a joyous celebration and is undergoing revival in contemporary Pagan circles.

Until comparatively recently, there was a custom of 'birching' prisoners that reveals the link between the birch and purgation. The offender was soundly whipped with branches of birch. This form of corporal punishment has roots in festive practices of ritual flagellation in which birch wands were used to drive out the old and prepare for the coming of the new. The use of birch for this purpose further underlines the tree's purifying and revivifying qualities.

Protection

ᚂ

Luis (Rowan)

Names: *luis* (said LWEE). Botanical name: *Sorbus aucuparia* or *Fraxinus* or *Pyrus* (also known as quicken-tree and mountain ash). Status: shrub. Sound: l.

Elaborations on the Ogam Names
Delight of eye is Mountain Ash owing to the beauty of its berries.
Word Ogam of Morainn mac Moín
Rowan is delight of eye, quicken-tree; to wit, the flame.
Word Ogam of Cú Chulainn
Rowan is strength of cattle, the elm.
Word Ogam of Óengus
Rowan is friend of cattle.

Visualization

A wreath of rowan forms a magic pentangle above a doorway.

Meaning

Luis is a tree-letter of protection, defence and sanctuary. A traditional ward against the evil eye, witchcraft and other dangers, its primary significance is protection from harm. Whatever may be menacing you, rowan signals that you are safe, provided that you behave wisely and take appropriate measures.

The theme of magical protection was a common one in the ancient world. While today we may not be so ready to attribute misfortune to dark witchcraft and sorcery, there are many dangers in life to guard against. Rowan's appearance in a reading reassures you that you are being taken care of and should fear no harm.

This does not mean, however, that you should allow yourself to become complacent. The very presence of *luis* in a reading suggests a lurking danger of one kind or another, against which you may need to take precautions. The threat could be to your happiness, health or prosperity. Perhaps there are people working mischief or malice against you or wider environmental factors that are conspiring to threaten your security.

Yet the fact that you have drawn rowan is an assurance that you have the means to outwit any danger. Rowan is a tree-letter of supernatural protection, a good-luck charm confirming the presence of friendly powers at work on your behalf. Acknowledging your guardian spirits, whether as ancestors or animal totems, will help allow them to carry out their role of furthering your interests and shielding you from ill.

Signs and amulets of protection are used in many cultures across the world. A sprig of rowan above a doorway to protect a home is a traditional application of this ogam. The protective rune Υ (*algiz*) is popular in contemporary Pagan circles today, but the best known and most widely used is surely the pentagram, symbolically enclosed within its magical circle. Such 'wards' can be worn as talismans to grant the wearer increased powers of protection.

Reversed, this tree-letter warns that your defences may be down. Either you are too open and vulnerable to attack or perhaps negative influences are circling in your vicinity, looking for a point of entry. This warning is not meant to make you paranoid but to prepare you. Eliminate weak areas in your defences and avoid patterns of behaviour that lead you into the path of danger. Call upon your powers of protection. Access the magic within; it will not fail you.

Keywords
Protection, defence, sanctuary. Precautions against dangers, safety, shielding from harm. Amulets, wards and spells of protection.

Reversed
Defences down, vulnerability, danger.

Natural Characteristics

The most significant natural features of rowan are its white flowers, which sprout in summer, and its red berries. The Ogam Elaborations make clear that its title 'delight of eye' is based on the scarlet appearance rowan takes on by virtue of these berries, and in the great Irish epic *Tochmarc Étaín* (*The Wooing of Étaín*), the beautiful Étaín's lips are praised for being 'red as the berries of the rowan tree'.[xliii] When the *Word Ogam of Morainn mac Moín* alludes to rowan as 'the flame', it is probably describing how the tree can set the hillside ablaze with the hue of its berries.

In order to understand the significance of these facts, we have first to realize that in Celtic cultures the pairing of red and white was thought to be especially significant. In a number of Irish and Welsh tales, animals with white bodies and red ears, such as pigs and hounds, appear in the path of a hero or king. These are beasts of the Otherworld, for red and white are the colour of the *sidhe* (those who dwell in the burial mounds). This association makes the rowan extremely potent in Celtic thought, a tree of magic and witchcraft. Indeed, Graves tells us that one of its names is 'the witch' and that witch-wands of rowan were commonly used for dowsing.

Storylines

Like birch and heather, the rowan tree plays an important role in the Irish legend of *Tóruigheacht Dhiarmada Agus Ghrianne* (*The Pursuit of Diarmaid and Gráinne*). Diarmaid and Gráinne are on the run from Finn, whose jealousy over the young lovers' elopement knows no bounds. It is a life and death situation, for Finn is determined to avenge himself upon his faithless wife and nephew. After a number of trials, the lovers come to the Wood of Dubhros, the site of 'a wonderful quicken tree'. This tree had grown from a berry dropped unwittingly by a member of the Túatha dé Danaan (the old gods of Ireland) when they were passing through the district. This is how its discovery by their messengers is described:

> And it happened one time after the tree was grown, there were messengers of the Tuatha de Danaan going through the woods of Dubhros. And they heard a great noise of birds and bees, and they went where the noise was, and they saw the beautiful Druid tree. They went back then and told what they had seen, and all the chief men of the Tuatha de Danaan when they heard it knew the tree must have been grown from a berry of the Land of the Ever-Living Ones.[xliv]

A guardian volunteers his services in protection of the tree. His name is Searbhán Lochlannach (the Surly Viking of Lochlann). Yet his appearance – 'very black and ugly he was, having crooked teeth, and only one eye in the middle of his forehead' – identifies him as an archetypal character recognizable in a number of myths. Searbhán is the Wild Man of the woods, the protector of the Greenworld who later finds an echo in Arthurian Romance as the Green Knight, whose challenge to the Arthurian court is accepted by the hero Gawain.

Here in these woods Diarmaid and Gráinne shelter, after making an agreement of peace and surety with Searbhán. For a time they are safe, because no one will enter the woods. However, through a series of misadventures Diarmaid is forced to kill the Wild Man and Finn is then able to enter the forest with his soldiers. The lovers hide in the uppermost branches of the rowan, where formerly the 'bed of the Surly One was'. They are safe here for a time and Óengus, the god of love, arranges to transport the fair Gráinne in safety to his residence, Bruigh na Boyne. In this story from the Fenian Cycle the quicken tree is clearly steeped in associations with protection, defence, and sanctuary.

Folklore and Magic

In the latter two Word Ogams *luis* is described as the 'strength' or 'friend' of cattle, an allusion to the role of the rowan in magic to drive evil spirits away from cattle, to prevent them from souring the milk. Of course, cattle were of great importance to the Celts as a source of wealth, as the many cattle-raid tales make clear. Anything that could interfere with them was naturally associated with the powers of darkness and much later, in the European witch-craze, we find accusations of witchcraft levelled at people because their neighbours wanted to blame somebody for barrenness or disease afflicting their animals. This may be based on a much older cultural theme, for in the Irish Mythological Cycle we are told that that the Queen of Witches and great battle goddess, the Mórrígu, 'was much given to meddling with cattle'.[xlv]

In terms of traditional tree magic, it is rowan that acts as a ward against such misfortune. Thus in times of trouble and danger, you may wish to invoke the protective energies of *luis*.

Rowan was planted at sacred sites, especially stone circles and oracular shrines, doubtless to protect them from malevolent energies. There are great protective thickets of rowan in the Baltic 'amber islands' which share in the Celtic legends associated with Avalon, the most sacred of all isles. Rowan itself is said to be protected by dragons or serpents, who are well known as guardian spirits of their environs.

Guidance

ᚓ

Fearn (Alder)

Names: *fearn*, *fern* (said FAIR-n). Botanical name: *Alnus glutinosa*. Status: chieftain-tree. Sound: f.

Elaborations on the Ogam Names
Alder, the van of the warrior bands,
for thereof are the shields.

Word Ogam of Morainn mac Moín
Alder is shield of the warrior bands,
owing to their redness.

Word Ogam of Cú Chulainn
Alder is protection of the heart,
a shield.

Word Ogam of Óengus
Alder is guarding of milk
or milk bucket.

Visualization

The oracular head of the god Bran sits on a shield, ringed by singing birds.

Meaning

Fearn is the alder, a tree-letter of counsel and guidance. You will benefit at this time by being receptive to good advice, both from outer sources and from within. If you are in challenging circumstances, this ogam suggests that good counsel is close to hand. In general, it directs you to the sources of guidance and inspiration you have to draw upon.

On a practical level, if you are experiencing difficulties it is important to listen to the right advice. Whether in personal, social or legal matters, you will want to be in full possession of the facts. At this time, an older person or figure of authority may be in a position to help or advise you, to your benefit. Listen carefully for the substance of what is being conveyed.

The best guidance comes from within, but accessing the wisdom of the heart is often a challenge. We need to learn how and when to mute the conscious mind and become receptive to the prompts of the sage within. As the tree-letter of oracular knowledge, *fearn* counsels you to seek answers from the deep waters of the self. Don't blindly follow outside advice; be your own oracle.

Various magical practices are designed to assist the accessing of our guides. Ancestral advisors, animal or bird totems and spirit guides have in traditional cultures long been recognized as vital in the quest for discovering our own wisdom. Usually the simple desire to meet and learn from such otherworldly helpers opens a dialogue with them.

Fearn is also a tree-letter of the Faery gifts of prophetic ability, music, poetry and the arts, sources of inspiration which the Celts saw as springing from the Otherworld. It teaches the value of creativity, insight and intuitive synthesis, and encourages you to let your creative self come to the fore and lead the way forward.

Reversed, alder may signify a blockage in your receptivity to good counsel. Either you are not listening to those around you or you are ignoring the subtle promptings from within. Strive to make an accurate assessment of the situation. Meditate on your own feelings and intuitions. What is your heart trying to say? Alternatively, *fearn* could refer to a creative blockage, like writer's block. It may be best to try a different tangent and turn to other things until your issue resolves itself. Relaxation and entertainment may be what is needed to lighten your state of mind.

Keywords
Counsel, guidance, oracular knowledge. Sacred word, whisperings. Correct advice from a person in authority. The sage within, spirit guides, inspiration, creativity.

Reversed
Blockages to good counsel, ignoring promptings, creative blockage. Need to lighten and relax.

Natural Characteristics

Alder is a water-loving tree, often found on the banks of streams and rivers, providing shade for plants and fish. Its nitrogen-salt-forming root system also benefits the surrounding soil. In winter – after it has shed its leaves – black cones from the previous season and unopened catkins adorn the tree. These 'heads', which remain after the alder's branches are bare, may have suggested its connection to the 'talking head' of tribal god Bran the Blessed to the ancient Britons.

Alder is a hardwood that was especially employed in the making of shields, as the Word Ogams show. Its role as the 'shield of the warrior bands' is also alluded to in the Welsh poem the *Cad Goddeu*, an emblematic 'Battle of the Trees' where

> The alder-trees, at the head of the army,
> Formed the advanced guard.[xlvi]

This leads to the divinatory correspondence of being shielded from harm, especially through receiving the right advice. The tree was also used in the construction of fords, bridge supports and house foundations lending, as we shall see, the *fearn* ogam its associations of strong foundation, lasting support, and the bridging of reason and intuition.

Storylines

We know that the god Bran is the alder, as he is named as such by Gwyddyon himself: 'The high branches of the alder-tree are on your shield. Your name is Bran of the dazzling branches . . . The high branches of the alder-tree are in your hand; Bran you are by the branches you bear . . . 'xlvii To clinch the case, Bran's sister Branwen has a son named Gwern, meaning alder-tree.xlviii

In the second branch of the *Mabinogion* we find the story of one Bendigied Vran, a title of Bran's. The romance of *Branwen: The Daughter of Lyr* tells of how Bran (here humanized as King of Wales) has given his sister Branwen in marriage to the Irish king Matholwch. But she is mistreated by him and sends a bird as messenger to Bran, who then leads an expedition against Ireland. Afterwards, he gives a rather strange command to his followers:

> And Bendigied Vran commanded them that they should cut off his head. 'And take you my head,' said he, 'and bear it even unto the White Mount, in London, and bury it there, with the face towards France. And a long time will you be upon the road. In Harlech you will be feasting seven years, the birds of Rhiannon singing unto you the while. And all that time the head will be to you as pleasant company as ever it was upon my body.'xlix

From this ensues four-score years in which Bran's head continues to guide and encourage his retinue in the episode known as 'the Entertaining of the Noble Head'! What is significant here is the theme of the oracular head, a widespread motif in the Celtic and Norse world that suggests the role of a god, king or mighty personage in instructing his followers from beyond the grave.

The Celts believed that the vital power of a person resided in the head, but the theme of the oracular head may further suggest a form of ancestor worship in which the spirits of the departed return to advise the living from their perspective of higher knowledge in the Otherworld. Interestingly, the word *bran* is an old Celtic root and is the Irish, Welsh and Breton word for crow. Crows, along with other birds, are emblems of protection and sources of other-worldly guidance in Celtic mythology. They proffer warning or advice, to those who listen, and Druids and bards were said to be able to understand the language of these and other birds.

Bran is, therefore, a type of oracular god who, like the crow after whom he may be named, sings to his people with the secrets of the Land of the Ever Living Ones. The benefits of this function are revealed in the fact that Bran's followers are joyous, full of mirth and never tire. Like the alder in the *Word Ogam of Cú Chulainn*, Bran's relationship to them is as a 'protection of the heart, a shield'.

Folklore and Magic

The Welsh Bran has been widely linked to the Irish Bron, son of Lir (the god of the ocean), and the character Bran mac Faibal, hero of a famous *immrama* (sea-going) voyage. Later he turns up in Arthurian Romance as Bron, the Fisher King who guards the Grail. This association with the element of water highlights another link between Bran and the alder. In *Branwen: The Daughter of Lyr* Bran arrives in Ireland to rescue his sister but his army finds the way blocked by the Linon River. 'I will be the bridge,' Bran declares, lying down for his followers to cross. Similarly, alder-wood is what the Celts used as the foundations of bridges, jetties and their 'floating towns', built on lakes.

Finally, the *Word Ogam of Óengus* tells us that alder is for the 'guarding of milk (or milk bucket)'. This refers to the use of alder-wood in making milking-buckets, for which role its water-resistant quality made it well suited. The vessel holding milk resonates with the sacred cauldrons of Celtic myth and cup of inspiration, including the later Holy Grail. Bran-the-Alder is one of its magical guardians. In modern magic, *fearn* may be invoked to attract good counsel and open up our communication with the Otherworld.

Intuition

ᚔ

Saille (Willow)

Names: *saille*, *sail* (said SAHL-yuh). Botanical name: *Salix* spp., esp. *Salix alba* (also known as the sally-tree). Status: peasant tree. Sound: s.

Elaborations on the Ogam Names
Willow, the colour of a lifeless one,
owing to the resemblance of its colour to a dead person.
Word Ogam of Morainn mac Moín
Willow is hue of the lifeless,
hue of one dead.
Word Ogam of Cú Chulainn
Willow equals beginning of loss,
willow.
Word Ogam of Óengus
Willow equals strength of bees.

Visualization

The moon caught in the branches of a willow-tree that grows beside a silver stream.

Meaning

Saille is a tree-letter of feeling and intuition. This is a time of particular sensitivity, both to outside influences and to the internal realm of sensations and impressions. Like a seasoned seafarer, you are able to sense the changing tides of events by instinct and experience. While it is important to be receptive to the flow, take care not to become swamped by the flux of impressions.

Saille's description as having the 'hue of the lifeless' (i.e. white or pale) identifies it with the moon, which, like the willow itself, has obvious associations with water. This ogam consequently corresponds in divination to the 'feminine' qualities of intuitive perception, emotion and cyclical progress.

The 'lifeless hue' of the Word Ogams also links *saille* to the spirit world and psychic realms, for willow was traditionally associated with witchcraft, divination and clairvoyant states. Coming into your own in these areas takes you into a domain of knowing that lies beyond rational explanation. This leads to insight and empowerment.

Celtic cultures acknowledged the powers of seership as a natural part of the fabric of life. Individuals with 'the Sight' were well respected and frequently consulted. Such highly developed powers of perception were actively cultivated through training and exercise, as their value to the individual and community was – and still is – great indeed.

Being open to these currents is healthy and natural. It also leads to you feeling your way into situations, and thus to emotional sensitivity. Yet at this time you may be so aware of other people's states of mind that these begin to impinge on you. Take care to avoid being bogged down in the watery realms; without some firm ground, the waves can overwhelm us.

Saille is also sometimes identified as an ogam of love, but it tends to relate more to the bewitching dreams and watery illusions of love than to literal relationships. In romance there may be a tendency to fantasize and project imagined qualities on the other person, though when well placed this ogam may also signal the development of a deep rapport between partners.

Reversed, *saille* may signal that you are out of your depth. Perhaps you are venturing too deep without sufficient support or internal stability. The inner tides rise to claim us as easily as real waves. Be warned that a person can drown in the watery element or float perilously adrift in the caves of the unconscious. Now may be the time to fight your way up to the surface!

Keywords

Intuition, feeling, lunar influences. The spirit world, witchcraft, divination, psychic states. Feeling, emotional sensitivity, perceptions. In love, dreams and fantasy, bewitchment.

Reversed

Being out of your depth, overwhelmed, lost. Need to surface for light and air.

Natural Characteristics

There are numerous varieties of willow, though the Word Ogam references to the 'colour of a dead person' specifically suggest the white willow or *Salix alba*. Probably the most notable feature of willows is their love of water, the tree's favourite habitats being stream and river banks, marshy areas and fords. In this they have an affinity with the preceding tree-letter, the alder. As the couplet goes:

> Of watery race Alders and Willows spread
> O'er silver brooks their melancholy shade.[1]

This connection with watery, liminal zones was probably the most impressive of the tree's natural characteristics to the Celtic imagination. The phrase *Lí n-aimbi* in the *Word Ogam of Morainn mac Moín* literally means 'hue of the not living',[ii] and links the tree not only with the moon but with the mysterious 'white' or 'shining' denizens of the Celtic Otherworld.

Willow was also a wood much favoured for use in wickerwork, which is symbolic of the interweaving of conscious and unconscious knowledge. It was used to make baskets, wicker walls in mud huts, and coracles. The coracle – a boat constructed out of a branch framework upon which skin or canvas is stretched – invokes many associations. It leads the traveller into liminal, watery zones, yet also bears him or her safely over the deep.

Storylines

Saille is widely identified in modern Ogam divination with the moon goddess, reflecting classical mythology, in which the willow is her tree. Circe, for instance, was once a funereal goddess of the willow grove; her grove is dedicated to Hecate, a goddess of moon-magic and witchcraft also associated with this tree. Hecate's role as a sorceress who haunted crossroads and graveyards by night helps to explain the lingering association of the willow with witchcraft and the night into European folk-lore. Similarly, the Sumerian Goddess Belili, who ruled over the moon, love and the Underworld, is associated with the willow. Graves linked this figure with the Celtic river goddess Belisama, whom he took to be the lunar counterpart of the sun god Beli.

While the Moon was originally regarded as male by the Celts, a number of figures in Celtic myth are reminiscent of the Mediterranean lunar goddess. In the eighth-century *immrama* saga entitled *Immram Curaig Maíle Dúin* (*The Voyage of Maeldúin's Boat*), the crew arrive at a mysterious location named the Island of the Crystal Keep, where we find another female figure cloaked in the following terms:

> They saw approaching a white-necked woman attired in a robe of swan's brilliance, a woman of wisdom and fair deeds.
>
> About her white mantle an edging of red gold, delightfully lustrous; upon her feet sandals of silver – a singular casting!
>
> Her mantle was fastened by a brooch of fair silver, with twisted gold work, fine craftsmanship.
>
> Yellow locks of golden hue hung from her head, her going was gracious, royal was her stately mien.
>
> Beneath the fair bridge, like a holy place, was hidden a well of pure water, a stout well-cover over it.
>
> The beautiful and greatly favoured woman was busy pouring out draughts of the invigorating liquid . . . [lii]

But she is most evident in the figure of Ceridwen. Ceridwen is the Welsh Queen of Witches. In the sixteenth century *Hanes*

Taliesin (*Story of Taliesin*), elements of which could date to the ninth century or even earlier, she is depicted as a powerful woman of magic who gathers herbs to work potent spells. It is even possible that Ceridwen was partly inspired by Mediterranean sources, suggesting an early mixture of Celtic and classical lore. Her connection to water and the night (and by implication the moon) is revealed in the fact that she presides over a cauldron of death and rebirth in the Otherworld and, in the form of a black hen, swallows the lad Gwion into the darkness of her womb. He emerges nine months later reborn as Taliesin, 'Radiant brow', skilled in prophecy, divination and poetry.

Folklore and Magic

Folklore associates willow with divining or 'witching' rods, specifically those used in the art of dowsing for water. This role is connected to the tree's water-loving function and underlines *saille*'s connection to divination, psychic powers and clairvoyance.

Willow's link with divination may be alluded to in a strange scene from the Mythological Cycle. Here a group of clowns perform tricks in the house of Manannán mac Lir, god of the ocean.

> And one of these tricks was, a man of them to take nine straight willow rods, and to throw them up to the rafters of the house, and to catch them again as they came down, and he standing on one leg, and having but one leg free.[liii]

Such clowning gestures may be an allusion to ancient ritual practice, as nine is a sacred number and the action of standing on one foot a Druidical procedure linked to clairvoyance. *The Song of the Forest Trees* warns us 'Burn not the willow, a tree sacred to poets'[liv] (you will recall that poets were originally a class of Druid); and in the classical world Orpheus is depicted receiving the gift of 'mystic eloquence' by touching willow trees in a sacred grove. Thus, in modern magic, *saille* may be invoked to strengthen one's powers of intuition and witchcraft.

Transformation Nion (Ash)

ᚇ

Names: *nion, nuin* (said NEE-uhn). Botanical name: *Fraxinus excelsior*. Status: peasant-tree.
Sound: n.
Elaborations on the Ogam Names
Ash, a check on peace is Ash
for from it are made the spear shafts
by which peace is broken.
Word Ogam of Morainn mac Moín
Ash is checking of peace,
maw of a weaver's beam applied to wood.
Word Ogam of Cú Chulainn
Ash equals flight or boast of beauty,
a weaver's beam.
Word Ogam of Óengus
Ash equals the flight or boast
of women.

Visualization

The arch-magician god Gwyddyon stands tall with a mighty ash-tree as his wand.

Meaning

Nion is the ash, a great and sacred tree in Celtic mythology connected to the magician god Gwyddyon, a shapeshifter and sorcerer who presides over the processes of transformation and manifestation. These are complementary poles: transformation implies being shaped by outer circumstances, manifestation means melding reality to your own ends.

Life is a cycle of constant change, from one state, stage or condition to another. This is fraught with challenge and, at times, great difficulty. Friction and conflict are often necessary to force us into the next stage of personal evolution; transformation is often precipitated by a crisis, which pushes us out of our comfort zones and confirms the need for change. Yet accepting this challenge ultimately leads to a wider, more expansive reality.

This ogam is also linked to fate. This does not mean that destiny is iron-cast, but points to the unique fate-path that you have to pursue in this world – one which, although it contains many possible options, is singular to you and to no one else. *Nion* counsels you to regard the continuous unfolding of events as signposts, prompting and guiding you on your journey.

It also challenges you to take up the wand of manifestation and make reality anew for yourself. Positivity, creative visualization, ritual and spell-craft are all instruments of manifestation you may wish to draw upon. Wands are not the only magical tool connected to this tree-letter. Ash was also a wood favoured for the construction of arrows, symbolizing the art of taking aim and striking the centre of the target.

Reversed, you are more likely to be on the receiving end of circumstances than acting as their master. Fate is pushing you along on its course, for good or ill. You may be progressing, but without control or guidance. Take care not to be swept up too much in the tide or become a pawn to external events. You may also find yourself a victim of cyclical patterns, which need to be addressed at the root. Remember, you can manifest misfortune for yourself as much as good fortune.

Keywords
Shape-shifting, transformation, changes, growth, fate and destiny. Pathways, possibilities, options, potential. Cycles of change, evolution, crisis, expanded reality.

Reversed
Lack of control, victim of circumstances, pawn to events. The need to take control.

Natural Characteristics

One of the ash's greatest features is the massive height to which the tree grows; up to one hundred and fifty feet. It has quite a sheer trunk with widely spaced branches, and this pole-like appearance contributed to its association in Celtic and Norse thought as the *axis mundi*: the central column and axis that supports the sky. As such it also appears as a type of bridge between the earth and heavens. The ash also has a deep and widespread root-system that tends to deplete the surrounding soil, ensuring that the tree inhabits its own space, thereby underlining its special character in the Celtic imagination. Other notable features of the ash are its phallic-shaped buds at the tips of branch stems and the fact that it is one of the last trees to leaf and so its bare, grey trunk remains prominent late into season.

Ogam wands were originally made of ash, and the root-word *nin* means 'letters'. The Celts also favoured ash as a wood for crafting spears and arrows. Its role in weaponry is reflected in the kennings 'checking of peace', and probably 'maw of a weaver's beam', for weavers were sometimes identified with the fateful battle-hags or washerwomen of Celtic myth who choose those to be slain in battle. This links it on a more general level with fate and destiny.

Storylines

The ash has a particularly strong correspondence with Gwyddyon, the master magician of Welsh legend famous for his magic wand, a Celtic equivalent of Odin. Odin it is in Norse mythology who is associated with the ash-tree, Yggdrasil, which forms the central axis of the nine worlds. (In fact, the name of the World Ash actually means 'Odin's horse'.) As the Celtic Odin, the ash is one of Gwyddyon's trees, along with the birch.

In the Mabinogion tale *Math, the Son of Mathonwy*, we find that the goddess Arianrhod has imprisoned the young Lleu Llaw Gyffes, a Welsh equivalent of the Celtic sun god known in Ireland as Lugh. Arianrhod has placed a *geiss* (a curse, in this case) on the boy that will keep him from bearing arms and thus from his greater destiny. The powers of darkness are, symbolically speaking, holding the light at bay, and Gwyddyon is forced to resort to trickery to rescue Lleu.

> In the early twilight Gwydion arose, and he called unto him his magic and his power. And by the time the day dawned, there resounded through the land an uproar, and trumpets and shouts. When it was now day, they heard a knocking at the door of the chamber, and therewith Arianrhod asking that it might be opened . . . [lv]

What Gwyddyon has done is employ his enchantments to create the sound of a battle outside Arianrhod's castle, a 'checking of peace' in the words of the *Word Ogam of Morainn mac Moín*. This ploy compels Arianrhod to unwittingly give a sword and shield to the youthful hero, for finding that she 'cannot see the colour of the ocean by reason of all the ships', Arianrhod panics. By this deception, Lleu reclaims his true destiny and is finally armed as a warrior.

. This tale is paralleled in Greek mythology, where the solar hero Achilles is so beautiful in his youth that he must be hidden amongst women, a possible source for the Word Ogam references to 'flight or boast of beauty' and 'flight or boast of women'. He cannot be released until his coming of age, which is marked when he receives an ashen spear – an important ancestral weapon handed to him ritualistically by his father Peleus – as a wedding gift in his marriage to the immortal goddess Thetis.

In both cases we see a symbolic transformation or rite of passage from childhood to adulthood and from being controlled by fate to having it in one's own hands. The underlying theme is the release of the sun (representing the new, growth-promoting, emergent order) from the dark stronghold in which it has been imprisoned. From this flow *nion*'s associations in contemporary divination as a tree-letter of empowerment in matters of transformation and destiny. In drawing *nion*, it is as if you have been handed a magical wand of ash with which to work your will in the world.

Folklore and Magic

The *Dindsenchus* (*Lore of Places*) tells of five sacred trees of ancient Éire, three of which were ashes: Eo Munga, Daithi and Tortiu. The ashes are praised for their height, the shelter they provide, and their nobility. Eo Munga is celebrated in these terms:

> Eo Munga, great was the fair tree,
> High its top above the rest;
> Thirty cubits – it was no trifle –
> That was the measure of its girth.

> Three hundred cubits was the height of the blameless tree,
> Its shadow sheltered a thousand:
> In secrecy it remained in the north and the east
> Till the time of Conn of the Hundred Fights.[lvi]

The holy tree, along with its companions, suffered the same fate as many of the sacred groves under Roman rule: it was felled by pious Christians, the 'bright trunk laid low' as the Church pursued its vendetta against pagan 'idolatry'.

Pagan associations there are indeed with the ash. It was much famed as a Druidical wand – Gwyddyon's wand was probably ash, just as his Norse counterpart Odin possessed a spear made of ash and used its twigs as runestaves in divination. The Druidical rod in Celtic magic was a highly charged instrument that could raise storms, bring down curses, confer invisibility and, especially, shapeshift human beings into animals. Modern-day Druids and contemporary Pagans also make wands to use as channels for divine forces in magic and ritual, sometimes of ash. Such wands are often carved with spirals and are always treated with great reverence.

Aicme Húath

Obstacles

⊥

Húath (Hawthorn)

Names: *húath, uath, huathe* (said HOO-ah).
Botanical name: *Crataegus* spp. (also known as whitethorn). Status: peasant-tree. Sound: h.
Elaborations on the Ogam Names
Whitethorn, a meet of hounds is whitethorn, formidable owing to its thorns.
Word Ogam of Morainn mac Moín
Hawthorn is pack of wolves,
terror to anyone.
Word Ogam of Cú Chulainn
Hawthorn is difficult night,
hawthorn.
Word Ogam of Óengus
Hawthorn is whitening of face.

Visualization

A hawthorn bristling with spikes and adorned with dark red berries stands blocking the middle of a wayfarer's path.

Meaning

Húath is a tree-letter of obstacles and obstructions. While this does not necessarily mean that what you wish for is impossible, it does suggest that you may have to go the long way round. There are conditions which will have to be met and hostile forces to counter. This situation will call for patience and restraint, though the end result could well be more pleasing than first appearances suggest.

The hawthorn is a Faery tree in Irish folklore that stands as a magical barrier, testing those who would pass it on their way. Whatever obstacle this may represent in your life, it cannot be simply ignored – or uprooted, however much you may like to apply force to the situation. Indeed, such action would only result in misfortune; keep your sword at bay.

Look carefully at the situation and the type of response it requires. Preconditions may well be set that you must fulfil if the outcome is to be as you wish. There is no short cut or easy way around. You must bow to necessity and accept the nature of the territory in which you find yourself. However, keep your goal in mind and do not be dissuaded or disheartened.

Like the prickly thorn bush, *húath* promises only pain and entanglement if you push aggressively forward into its domain. Even with right action, you may be hounded with doubts and fears, the 'pack of wolves' of the *Word Ogam of Morainn mac Moín*.

The desire to press ahead could lead to emotional upset and sleepless nights. Try not to get too entangled with whatever the issue is, romantic, financial, practical or psychological. Detachment is necessary at times to preserve your sanity and allow you time to rest, recuperate and prepare for what is ahead. Perhaps this delay or setback is here for your growth. Draw on your well of patience and skill; it will not fail you.

There are also strong traditions which link hawthorn to sexual love and erotic matters – including marriage – though in this book that role is fulfilled by *onn* (gorse) or *úr* (heather). If this reading centres around romantic issues, there could well be complications in your love life. This does not mean things are hopeless. Remember the old adage: 'The course to true love never did smoothly run.'

Reversed, *húath* represents an absolute barrier to your ambitions or desires. If you persist with this course of action you will gore yourself on life's thorns and wind up in hopeless bondage, or deeply shamed. You are bound as if by threads of the Faery realm. Whatever you think you want or need, you must bow gracefully to necessity. Retreat is the only sane course; any other path will only lead to anguish and humiliation.

Keywords
Obstructions, obstacles, pre-conditions, hostile forces. Desire, entanglements. Fear, shame, embarrassment. Complications in love.

Reversed
An absolute barrier, necessity. Anguish, humiliation.

Natural Characteristics

The name *húath* is likely descended from the root *sceathe* (meaning 'to be scathed' or harmed) and the physical qualities of the hawthorn go part way to explain its aura of foreboding. A small tree related to the rose, hawthorn often grows alone in the wild. However, it has long been used in hedgerows throughout the British Isles, on account of its impenetrable form. Its most striking features are its flowers and berries. The flowers are snow-white, with five-fold petals, while its small green berries ripen into a rich, dark red in autumn.

Red and white are the primary colours of the Celtic Other-world and mark hawthorn as a Faery tree, in close company with the rowan and holly: indeed, these were trees often believed to have been planted by the Fey. Especially when hedged, hawthorn is densely branched from its central trunk and these branches are armed with short, sharp thorns. This makes it an effective barrier, and coupled with the superstitions surrounding the tree lends it a formidable role as a tree of magical deterrence against those who trespass in its territory.

Storylines

Húath's obstructive quality is well illustrated in the Welsh tale of *Kilhwch and Olwen*. Kilhwch has fallen madly in love with the fair Olwen, daughter of Yspadden Penkawr. One of Olwen's titles is 'She of the White Track', which links her to the hawthorn, with its trail of white blossoms, and her father's name literally means 'giant hawthorn'. Yspadden's irascible nature sums up the testing, obstructive character of the hawthorn, for he poses every type of imaginable obstacle to Kilhwch, acting as a barrier between his daughter and the amorous hero.

Kilhwch persuades Arthur's warriors to help him in his quest, but Yspadden deals with them foully, throwing poisoned darts into the company. Here we can see a metaphor for the thorns of the hawthorn, connected to dark magic, for the 'poison' corresponds to a traditional type of curse called the *Glám diachenn* (see below). Yspadden finally sets for Kilhwch thirty-nine virtually impossible tasks, revolving around the capture of thirteen magical treasures, which require the full assistance of Arthur's knights.

Among them, Kilhwch must slay a mighty she-wolf and her cubs, recover the Cauldron of the Master of the Abyss, and rescue Mabon (the god of light) from a dungeon! The wolves mentioned may correspond the 'pack of wolves' which the *Word Ogam of Morainn mac Moín* associates with hawthorn. Furthermore, the *Word Ogam of Cú Chulainn* names hawthorn as 'difficult night', echoing Yspadden's own words to Kilhwch after he has set his terrible tasks: 'Difficulties shalt thou meet with, and nights without sleep, in seeking this . . . '[lvii] Before Kilhwch can attain his desire he must confront obstacle upon obstacle, and the scenario is similar for the person who draws the *húath* ogam.

This tree-letter is also sometimes connected to another figure from the *Mabinogion*, the beautiful Blodeuwedd. She is a maiden made of flowers by the arch-enchanter Gwyddyon, created for Llew (the Irish sun god Lugh). Llew delights in Blodeuwedd, but his joy is short lived. Gronw, a rider from the underworld, out with his hounds on a hunt, appears and seduces her. They spend three nights together and then plot to murder Llew, who subsequently undergoes a three-fold death followed by gruesome trials before he is rejuvenated. Here, again, the testing qualities of *húath* are all too evident.

Folklore and Magic

Hawthorn was employed by the *filid* (poets) in Ireland in the *Glám diachenn* (a satire, a ritual curse) that could be levelled against one's enemies. We read in the *Book of Ballymote* that:

[T]he poet had to go with six companions . . . They turned their backs to a hawthorn bush . . . With the wind blowing from the north each of them held a sling shot and a hawthorn wand in his hand and chanted a verse against the king over these two objects . . . Each of them then put down his stone and his branch on the root of the hawthorn bush.[lviii]

Here the forces of the mound are invoked and then one projects the curse, symbolically speaking, using the medium of the sling. 'And with that satire . . . I will put shame on them and enchantment, the way they will not be able to stand . . .'[lix] Any *aer* (curse, satire) was no laughing matter to the Celts. It could not only destroy a reputation, but hex and even physically blight the victim. It is not recommended that you employ *húath* magically for such purposes.

There is another aspect of hawthorn that marks it as quite a favourable and propitious tree. Flowering in May (in the northern hemisphere), it signals that the time has come to celebrate the rising sap of sexuality that blossoms in the Greenworld. Hawthorn has a longstanding association with fertility ceremonies, including maypole dancing. A garland of its leaves was often placed at the tip of the phallic maypole. Its dense, thorny branches and the fact that the tree's flowers are traditionally likened to a woman's musk may well have suggested female sexual organs to the Celts.

With the coming of Christianity, this erotic symbolism was perverted so that hawthorn came to stand for restraint and chastity. It now represented an allegorical barrier against sinful behaviour, a warning against excess. Its thorns came to symbolize a moral menace; they embodied the dangers of pleasures of the flesh.

Hawthorn has long been used to guard and protect burial mounds, the dwelling of the *sidhe*. The hawthorn on Wearyall Hill at Glastonbury is a famous example. In Ireland the belief persists that felling a hawthorn will bring great misfortune, and when in recent years the DeLorean car factory planned to develop a mound on which a hawthorn stood, the Irish workmen refused to remove it. John DeLorean oversaw its eventual clearing, to his detriment, for ruin financial and personal soon followed.

Duration

ll

Duir (Oak)

Names: *duir* (said DOO-r). Botanical name: *Quercus robur.*
Status: chieftain-tree. Sound: d.

Elaborations on the Ogam Names
Oak, higher than bushes is an Oak.
Word Ogam of Morainn mac Moín
Oak is highest of bushes,
with respect to its wood in the forest.
Word Ogam of Cú Chulainn
Oak equals kneeling work,
bright and shining work.
Word Ogam of Óengus
Oak equals craft or carpenters' work.

Visualization

The Oak King stands within a dolmen's arch, limbs of strong wood, hair of leaf, crowned with mistletoe.

Meaning

Duir, oak, has long been seen as the King of the Woodland in the British Isles. It is a stout tree in height and girth, long lived too, its wood excellent for working. The Gaelic name *duir* reflects both the practical and magical qualities of oak: its word roots link to the words 'en*dur*ance', '*dur*ation' and '*dur*rway'. This is a tree-letter of established strength, maturity, and nobility. You stand at the peak of your powers, mighty like the oak.

The oak is a tree that takes time to mature but once established it is great in strength. Its roots dig deep into the nourishing earth, its trunk stands hardy to all weathers and its branches spread magnificently over its surroundings. Be like the oak, firmly rooted, secure in your own nature, branching out in fruitful directions. Here you have come into your power, having survived weathering at the hands of the elements – storms, losses, defeats, darkness, terrors. This ogam teaches the wisdom of endurance, both physical and spiritual: it also takes you beyond mere survival into an established mode of life.

Perhaps you have found your feet in your vocation or ascended a knotty rung in the ladder of life. Your position is favourable and likely to strengthen. Emotionally you are becoming more grounded and able to endure the assaults of experience. You could also be involved in parenting, or some other responsible role, and doing well. In mental and creative matters, your talents are finding expression. You are deepening and mellowing, like good mead encased in oak.

As mentioned, the word 'doorway' is related to *duir*. This was not simply because of the suitability of the oak in the carpenter's work. Oak is a sign of progress, as if a door stands ahead of you, signalling your transition into a higher state. As such you also become a doorway for others, a sheltering and protective force. This situation is not one which will pass quickly but a lasting state or condition. Allow yourself to relax into this role, full of goodwill and wit, for there is a noble aspect to this ogam. Oak is one of the great chieftain-trees.

Reversed, *duir* warns that you may be behaving in a manner unbefitting your strengths and resources. Are you undermining your own position by not acting as sensibly or honourably as you might? Are you letting yourself down or overplaying your hand? Moments of weakness and confusion are only human, but do not let them become a habit!

Keywords
Endurance, duration, established strength, maturity, nobility. An established mode of life, responsible vocation, strong foundation. Progress, protective force, goodwill.

Reversed
Unbefitting behaviour, weakness, confusion. Abusing strength, position.

Natural Characteristics

Oak is a mighty tree which can grow up to a hundred and fifteen feet with girths of between thirty and forty feet. The *Word Ogam of Morainn mac Moín* describes oak as the 'highest of bushes', which is, however, not literally true; it is more a reflection of the tree's venerable status in Celtic culture. Oak is one of the eight chieftain trees listed in the *Book of Ballymote* and was valued not only for its wood but for its sheltering role in woodland and field. Apart from the English oak (*Quercus robur*) and sessile oak

(*Quercus petraea*) native to the British Isles, there are about six hundred species worldwide.

With a lifespan of up to and over seven hundred years, it is one of the longest-living forest dwellers in the northern hemisphere, though it is far outstripped by the yew. Oak grows quickly at first but is slow to mature, with seventy or eighty years elapsing before it produces acorns. From early times, acorns were used as feed for pigs, adding to the tree's reputation as a great provider. The incredible resilience and beauty of its wood have made it a much loved tree, yet have also seen its decline due to over-felling at various points in its history.

Oak has a tendency to attract lightning in storms and the tree is often struck. Yet it endures this hardship well, and many twisted, blasted oaks testify great skill in surviving the elemental powers. It role as a 'lightning rod' has linked oak mythologically with various thunder god figures across pagan Europe, and it has sometimes been seen as actually embodying the lightning's flame.

Storylines

The oak has two major levels of correspondence: to storm, thunder and lightning gods on the one hand, and on the other to the sacred king figures who are the thunder god's earthly representatives. The god most clearly corresponding to the oak in the Celtic sphere is Taranis, the Gaelic version of the Norse gods Thor and Tyr, the Greek Zeus, Roman Jupiter and Judaic Jehovah. Taranis literally means 'thunderer', and he was worshipped not only in Gaul but from the north of Britain to the Adriatic coast. A sturdy warrior-king, Taranis was a god who used his power and position to protect and further the human cause. The Dagda, the supreme god of early Celtic mythology, is also connected to the oak: he owns a harp named Dur-dá-Bla (the Oak of Two Blossoms) and his abode at Bruig na Bóinde (Newgrange, the mystical centre of Ireland) was anciently reputed to have an oak grove at its heart. Many other gods, goddesses and heroes are associated with this holy tree.

In the *Immrama Brain maic Febhail* (*The Voyage of Bran*), the hero is told by Manannán mac Lir (God of the Ocean) of his 'flowery plain' beneath the sea, in the Land of the Ever Living Ones: 'There is a wood of beautiful acorns under the head of your little boat.'[lx] Oaks certainly grew in the Celtic Otherworld, for in the *Echtra Cormaic i Tir Tairngiri* (*The Adventures of Cormac in the Land of Promise*) we read that the legendary King Cormac arrives at that enchanted land and amid many wonders sees this strange spectacle.

> Then he saw a man kindling a fire, and he used to throw a thick oak upon it. And he would come back with a second tree, the first one would be burned out. 'I will be looking at you no longer,' Cormac said then, 'for there is no one here to tell me your story, and I think I could find good sense in your meanings if I understood them,' he said.[lxi]

Immediately after, Cormac comes to a *dun* (house), 'very large and royal', where he meets the Lord and Lady of the Land of the Ever Living Ones. Cormac is of royal lineage and will one day become king, so it is a fair guess that the enigmatic woodchopper's action of throwing oak after oak on the fire relates to the succession of kingship. Cormac is being initiated into his own future role as the Oak King.

There is evidence to suggest that the oak is also connected to the most famous of legendary Celtic rulers, Arthur. This is no surprise, for the oak was widely used as an image for kingship: when the last Welsh king, Llywelyn ab Gruffyd (1246–82), was slain in battle against the Anglo-Normans he was lamented by a bard in these terms: 'My heart freezes with terrible grief/ Because of the king, oaken door of Aberffraw . . . '[lxii]

Folklore and Magic

The oak is popularly associated with the Druids and a previous generation of scholars tended to regard Druidism as a kind of 'cult of the oak'. This in part stems from the claim that the roots of the word Druid lie in *duir-id*, literally 'wise one of the oak'. First suggested by Pliny(25–79 CE), this etymology is not currently fashionable. There is no doubt, however, that oak was an extremely holy tree to the pagan Celts: Pliny writes:

> The Druids – so their magicians are called – held nothing more sacred than the mistletoe and the tree that bears it, always supposing that tree to be an oak. But they choose groves formed of oaks for the sake of the tree alone, and they never perform any of their rites except in the presence of a branch of it; so that it seems probable that the priests themselves may derive their name from the Greek word for that tree.[lxiii]

There is plenty of evidence for Druidical oak groves. In the island of Skye, an oak grove near Loch Siant was held so sacred one could not remove a single twig from its trees, and this veneration was not limited to the Celtic domain.

Greece's oaks were inhabited by powerful deities known as dryads. The Chaonian forest at Dodona was consecrated to Zeus as the god of thunder and there bronze gongs hung on the oak trees – probably they were beaten and their utterances regarded as divine speech. Aeschylus calls oak the Tree of Life, and its rustling leaves whispered the speech of Zeus. A similar theme appears in Judeo-Christian mythology, for Genesis XVIII tells us that Abraham entertained God himself in an oak grove at Mamre.

The 'kneeling work, bright and shining work' mentioned in the *Word Ogam of Óengus* could refer to worship of (or a worshipful attention to) the oak. Oaks are indeed marvellous trees to contact as powerful guardians of the Greenworld; there is a much-loved oak in my own back garden which I find radiates great calm and surety. You can approach oak as a guardian tree which will instil in you a deep sense of solidity and strength in times of trouble.

Challenge

ℐℐℐ

Tinne (Holly)

Name: *tinne* (said CHIN-yuh). Botanical name: *Ilex aquifolium* Status: shrub. Sound: t.

Elaborations on the Ogam Names
Holly, a third of a wheel is Holly,
because holly is one of the three timbers
of the chariot wheel.

Word Ogam of Morainn mac Moín
Birch is faded trunk and fair hair.

Word Ogam of Cú Chulainn
Holly equals a third of weapons,
an iron bar.

Word Ogam of Óengus
Holly equals fires of coal.

Visualization

A holly tree rises from the flames of a fiery forge, adorned with blood-red berries.

Meaning

Tinne is a tree-letter of challenge and defence. Its appearance suggests that you will be tested, perhaps to the limits of your strength and courage. You must face the matter squarely, taking measures to defend and protect yourself. Though this is a sore trial to go through, you will emerge stronger and wiser from it.

In all our lives there are times when circumstances seem to conspire against us. Whether it is at work, in love or some other arena of your personal life, challenge lies everywhere. Your position is being either openly attacked or insidiously undermined and it is time to take action. You have strengths to draw upon: enter into your power and meet the adversity. There is nothing else for it.

It may also be that some inner turmoil is buffeting you or barring your progress. Perhaps your state of mind is the challenge to be overcome. Emotionally, you could get burnt or be afflicted by the fires of passion. Spiritually, you may be amidst the flames of the forge of transformation. Yet, fuelled by a fighting spirit, you will arise anew from the ashes.

This trial is par for the course of life's winding pathways: no one can expect to escape without fateful brushes with hostile forces, and as such you are not alone. The illustrious company of your ancestors and all others who have stood against and weathered such assaults goes with you. Arm yourself with the magical weapons of courage and endurance which they gift you.

Reversed, *tinne* suggests that fate is raining blow after blow upon you and your strength is not standing up to the onslaught. Emotionally, this is a slash and burn scenario. Try to get yourself out of the situation as quickly as possible. If your position cannot be defended, flee it; there is no shame in this. You need to escape the fray of battle and pick yourself up again. Time will rebuild your strength.

Keywords

Challenge, testing, trials. Your position is under attack. Emotional, spiritual testing. Issues of defence, need to take action, arm yourself for the fight. Transformation, strengthening, tempering.

Reversed
Assault, damage, onslaught. Take flight, flee, rebuild your strength.

Natural Characteristics

It has been suggested that the original identity of this ogam was actually 'an iron bar or weapon' rather than a tree. However, if the identification of *tinne* with holly was a later one, it is still profoundly meaningful, on account of holly's link to weapons and wounding. Holly, left to itself in the wild, may attain a height of up to seventy feet, though this is seldom allowed to happen. The tree is generally treated as a type of shrub these days and cultivated to diminutive proportions in gardens and hedges. This was not always so, for holly once formed part of the vast primordial forests that covered much of central and southern Europe.

The most striking feature of holly is undoubtedly its profusion of spiny leaves. These have many lobes (that is, folds ending in sharp points), especially on the lower branches. Thus holly often forms a type of natural thicket. Also notable are its berries – the 'fires of coal' perhaps of the *Word Ogam of Óengus* – which turn red in autumn. This links holly to the Celtic Otherworld and to the forge of the god of smiths, Goibniu. Its wood was once used as the spokes of chariot wheels and spear shafts, contributing to its associations of challenge and defence.

Storylines

Holly's most famous legendary appearance is found in the fourteenth-century tale of *Sir Gawain and the Green Knight*. Here a surly giant approaches Arthur's court in the following fashion:

> In one of his hands he had a spray [club] of holly, which is at its greenest when the woods are bare, and in his other hand an axe, a huge and monstrous one, a cruel battle-axe to describe in words, if anyone could . . . The man came forward and entered the hall, making for the high table, regardless of danger; and he greeted no one, but looked high over their heads. When at last he spoke, 'Where,' he said, 'is the ruler of this company? I would very much like to set eyes on that man and have speech with him.'[lxiv]

The Green Knight then challenges the warriors that are present to a grim trial of strength: they may take up the sword to cut off his head, but he must afterwards have the right of returning the blow. Only Gawain will rise to the challenge, and there begins a great series of adventures, for Gawain must ultimately accompany the Knight to his castle and there undergo fearsome trials in a rite of passage that will mark him out as the bravest and staunchest of Arthur's companions.

When Gawain goes to meet him he must enter a wood 'wonderfully wild', for the Green Knight is the Lord of the Underworld and his wife is its Lady. This bristling figure armed with a club of holly is reminiscent of various Wild Man figures of Irish myth, including Gruagach, and his cousin in early British mythology, the hairy, leaf-clad Wild Man Gogmagog: the antagonist who must be overthrown before the hero can unite with the goddess.

This guardian figure plays his part differently masked in a story from the Mythological Cycle: as a clown performing tricks, though his testing and challenging function is the same.

> Old striped clothes he had, and puddle water splashing in his shoes, and his sword sticking out naked behind him, and his ears through the old cloak that was over his head, and in his hand he had three spears of hollywood scorched and blackened.[lxv]

The deceiving clown turns out to be none other than Manannán mac Lir (Lord of the Realm of the Ever Living), his spears scorched and blackened with the fires of transformation.

Finally, the Ogam Elaboration which names holly as 'a third of a wheel' may refer to more than just chariots. After all, the wheel is sacred to the three Weaving Sisters of ancient European mythology, reflected in the Greek Fates and Norse Norns. Their powerful influence is plainly revealed in this scene from the Fenian Cycle, which may be influenced by Greek myth, where they are cast as hateful hags, daughters to Conaran of the Túatha dé Danaan.

> The three women went then to the opening of a cave that was in the hills, and there they sat down together, and they put three strong enchanted hanks of yarn on crooked holly sticks, and began to reel them off outside the cave.

They were not long there till Finn and Conan came towards them, and saw the three ugly old hags at their work, their coarse hair tossed, their eyes red and bleary, their teeth sharp and crooked, their arms very long, their nails like the tips of cows' horns, and the three spindles in their hands.[lxvi]

The Fenian heroes are held in thrall by a trembling and weakness, symbolic of the bonds of fate woven by these women (note their use of holly sticks as spindles). The description of the Fate goddesses as vile crones reflects the patriarchal quality of the Fenian stories, with their warrior ethos, but the fact that the heroes overcome these hags and escape the bonds of enchantment is still a powerful lesson in confronting and freeing oneself from hostile forces.

Folklore and Magic

Traditionally, *tinne* has been closely linked to the preceding ogam, *duir*. Oak and holly fall alongside each other in the Ogam sequence but equally significant is the fact that /d/ and /t/ are voiced and unvoiced forms of the same consonant. In folklore the connection is expressed in the ancient drama of the Oak King and Holly King battling each other for supremacy over the turning wheel of the year.

Oak represents the power in the waxing half of the year that comes to fruition with the Summer Solstice, while Holly, with its aura of challenge and darkness, marks the beginning of the waning half, culminating in the Winter Solstice. This is why, to this day, holly is associated with Christmas, whose date corresponds to midwinter (December 22–25) in the northern hemisphere. Long after the pagan significance of this ancient rite became obscured, mummers and maskers continued to dramatize the ritual battle of holly and oak in village pantomimes and fetes. Although it may be used as a household decoration – upon an altar for instance at the Winter Solstice – holly is not generally invoked in contemporary ogam magic, for obvious reasons.

Enlightenment   Coll (Hazel)

IIII

Name: *coll* (said CULL). Botanical name:
Corylus avellana.
Status: chieftain-tree. Sound: c.
Elaborations on the Ogam Names
Hazel, fair wood that is Hazel,
everyone is eating of its nuts.
Word Ogam of Morainn mac Moín
Hazel is fairest of trees,
that is hazel, owing to its beauty in woods.
Word Ogam of Cú Chulainn
Hazel equals sweetest of woods,
a nut.
Word Ogam of Óengus
Hazel equals friend of cracking.

Visualization

A branching hazel spreads over a bend in a stream. A salmon
leaps from the water to catch one of the hazel nuts in midair.

Meaning

Coll is one of the most significant tree-letters of the Ogam
sequence, for from the branches of the hazel tree fall the Nuts
of Wisdom. Finn mac Cumhail was a young apprentice in Irish
myth who gained wisdom after eating a salmon that fed on the
sacred hazelnuts, and this tale points to *coll's* role as an ogam of
profound insight, even enlightenment.

In some cases *coll* may represent a period of apprenticeship in
which knowledge is being passed on to you from an outside source.
You are acquiring learning vital to your material or spiritual well-
being, and your own powers of understanding are blossoming.

As with knowledge, gaining wisdom implies effort, with many
hours spent in what may have seemed like a fruitless pursuit, as
you stare at the world of reflections without penetrating its
depths. Suddenly you realize that the light and the shadow and
you are all one and you enter into the heart of a great mystery, as
when the shell of a nut falls away and its kernel is revealed.

Of course, this perception may come unbidden and simply

occur in an instant according to Nature's own impulse, without thought or reflection. Being pure of heart and mentally unattached to the world of illusion, you see things as they are and penetrate to their inner substance. You crack the Nuts of Wisdom almost effortlessly.

This is a felicitous ogam to draw. You have reached a point in life's quest where you sit, as if on the bank of a great river, drawing on the waters of wisdom. The river represents the immortal Goddess of Wisdom, and the waters well up from the deepest springs of knowledge. Here you are nourished and refreshed on your journey.

Reversed, *coll* suggests a blockage in your search for wisdom and inspiration. You may be disillusioned and only able to perceive the faults and flaws in the world, others and yourself. Perhaps you despair of discovering any higher source of illumination and are therefore acting in darkness and ignorance. Or maybe you have simply tired on your quest and stopped in some desert land of soul, far from the waters of inspiration. Do not remain in such a state. There are well springs to be found; your quest is not fruitless.

Keywords
Wisdom, knowledge, enlightenment, inspiration. The springs of knowledge, deep knowing, practical and grounding knowledge.

Reversed
Blockages to wisdom and inspiration, disillusionment, despair, darkness, ignorance. The need to enlighten yourself.

Natural Characteristics

The hazel is a squat shrub that rarely attains to heights above thirty feet (though it has been recorded to reach as great a stature as sixty). Its fawn branches and lime-green leaves are full of grace and charm but do not quite explain the lines in the Ogam elaborations and *Word Ogam of Morainn mac Moín* which praise it as the 'fairest of trees'. For explanation of this we must look deeper into ogamlore.

Clearly, it is its nuts which distinguish hazel as a tree of special merit. Ripening in September (in the northern hemisphere), they may be eaten straight from the branches of the tree, from whose forks they spring. The value of hazelnuts as a food source is embodied in the *Word Ogam of Cú Chulainn*'s phrase for hazel 'sweetest of woods, a nut'. They were a prized form of protein and flavour in the diet of the Celts and are of course regarded as a delicacy to this day.

Storylines

It is no accident that the hazel is the ninth tree-letter of the Ogam alphabet, nine being the most sacred of all numbers in Celtic tradition. In the wisdom poetry the flesh of the hazel is a metaphor for spiritual nourishment and illumination. This universal theme has a specifically Celtic twist: the cracking of the shell relates to the penetration of the poetic kennings (puns, riddles) used by Druids and bards, and the kernel becomes its inner truth or meaning. This tradition reminds us of the Zen koan (e.g. 'What is the sound of one hand clapping?') which is designed to induce enlightenment in the mind of the one who contemplates its mysteries. Thus we have the kenning for hazel 'friend of cracking' in the *Word Ogam of Óengus*.

Mythologically, this theme is beautifully illustrated in the *Macgnimartha Finn* (*The Boyhood Deeds of Finn*). One of the Celtic world's most celebrated heroes, Finn was nursed from infancy in secrecy by his mother and a Druidess named Bodhmall in the woods of Slieve Bladhma. Finn's associations with woods and the Greenworld, moreover, endured all his days, as does the hero's link to women and though them to the Wisdom of the Great Goddess.

As a young warrior Finn slays a burly champion and inherits his magical crane-skin bag. This bag once resided in the house of Manannán mac Lir (god of the ocean and the Land of the Ever Living Ones) and held all sorts of treasures. After handing the bag to Crimall, his uncle, Finn goes on one of his greatest adventures. Here is how he attains the Salmon of Wisdom:

And then he said farewell to Crimnall and he went on to learn poetry from Finegas, a poet that was living at the Boinn, for the poets thought it was always on the brink of water poetry was revealed to them. And he did not give him his own name, but he took the name Deimne. Seven years, now, Finegas had stopped at the Boinn, watching for the salmon, for it was in the prophecy that he would eat the salmon of knowledge that would come there, and that he would have all knowledge after. And when at the last the salmon of knowledge came, he brought it to where Finn was, and bade him to roast it, but he bade him not to eat any of it.

And when Finn brought him the salmon after a while he said: 'Did you eat any of it at all boy?' 'I did not,' said Finn; 'but I burned my thumb putting down a blister that rose on the skin, and after doing that I put my thumb in my mouth.' 'What is your name, boy?' said Finegas. 'Deimne,' said he. 'It is not, but it is Finn your name is, and it is to you and not myself the salmon was given in prophecy.' With that he gave Finn the whole of the salmon, and from that time Finn had the knowledge that came from the nuts of the nine hazels of wisdom that grow beside the well that is below the sea.[lxvii]

After this feast, Finn is granted knowledge and the abilities of clairvoyance and prescience. The fact that poets thought 'it was always on the brink of water poetry was revealed to them' relates to the fact that water (especially rivers) were sacred to the goddess in Celtic Europe, and the Boyne relates to the Irish river goddess Bóann. Indeed, the Nuts of Wisdom which Finn eats in the totemic form of the Salmon of Knowledge are elsewhere pictured as one of the supreme springs of wisdom of the Túatha dé Danaan, the ancient gods of Ireland. Here is the description of Connla's celebrated well as found in the *Dindsenchas* (*Lore of Places*):

And they had a well below the sea where the nine hazels of wisdom were growing; that is, the hazels of inspiration and of the knowledge of poetry. And their leaves and their blossoms would break out in the same hour, and would fall on the well in a shower that raised a purple wave. And then the five salmon that were waiting there would eat the nuts, and their colour would come out in the red spots of their skin, and any person that would eat one of those salmon would know all wisdom and all poetry. And there were seven streams of wisdom that sprang from that well and turned back to it again; and the people of many arts have all drank from that well.[lxviii]

Finn and other bardic and Druidical figures, therefore, symbolicaly partake in otherworldly knowledge and inspiration by eating the nuts of the hazel. The Well below the Sea is clearly in Manannán's country (the Land of the Ever Living Ones), the ultimate abode of the old gods. Tasting of its fruit (or nuts, as the case may be) suggests an ancient shamanistic theme in which the shaman spirit-journeys into an under-the-sea realm and there is granted gifts of clairvoyance and precognition by chthonic powers. This is the path of the Celtic Druid, bard or ovate – 'the people of many arts' – who legend tells us 'have all drunk from that well'.

Folklore and Magic

The hazel was regarded as so holy that, along with the apple, wantonly felling it warranted the death penalty under Brehon law. It was known in Ireland as the 'food of the gods' and was closely associated with the Druids. Twigs of the tree were sometimes used in water dowsing and as wands in magical rites. It was also, in particular, a wishing stave considered the best of all woods when used in magic to manifest wishes and desires, and as such a wand of hazel was actually known as a 'Wishing Rod'.

You may wish to construct such a ritual wand of hazel or carve the *coll* ogam on a wishing wand, or treat the story of Finn mac Cumhail's enlightenment as a meditation.

Many town names are derived from cognates of *coll*. A common one is Carlton or Calton, from the Gaelic *Calltunn*, meaning 'town of the hazel'. A Calton near Edinburgh carries its name by virtue of a sacred grove which once existed there.[lxix] The hazel grove is one of the ultimate sacred enclosures in Celtic thought, a realm symbolically linked to the domain of the Great Goddess.

Wholeness

ⅢⅢ

Quert (Apple)

Names: *quert, queirt* (said KWAIRT). Botanical name: *Malus sylvestris*. Status: peasant-tree. Sound: q.

Elaborations on the Ogam Names
Apple, shelter of a wild hind is an Apple Tree.
Word Ogam of Morainn mac Moín
Apple is shelter of a hind,
lunatics or hinds.
Word Ogam of Cú Chulainn
Apple equals excellent emblem,
protection.
Word Ogam of Óengus
Apple equals force of a man.

Visualization

An apple tree with branches of silver and fruit of gold in a grove on an island in the sea, illuminated by the rays of the sun.

Meaning

Quert, apple, is one of the most wildly mystical trees of the Ogam sequence and with its appearance you have reached the heart of the Ogam grove. This tree-letter is an embodiment of health and vitality, the 'force of a man' or woman, as the *Word Ogam of Óengus* has it. It also often signifies healing, regeneration and wholeness after suffering of some kind or other.

Quert brings not just well-being but a spontaneous feeling of wholeness and a deep connection to the Universe. It often signals a period of rest and respite, allowing you take time out to simply *be* rather than always *doing*. If no such break is on the horizon, perhaps this ogam is gently warning you to make every effort to give yourself time to relax and recuperate, before your body or mind force you to do so.

The apple tree in Celtic myth is associated with Avalon, the Island of Apples. A transcendental location in the Otherworld, Avalon is connected with the Land of Youth or Land of the Ever Living. Drawing this ogam means that your vital energy is strong at this time but should still be tended. If you have been sick in body, or consumed by some mental or emotional condition, the heavy going is coming to an end. As an ogam of recovery, *quert* encourages new growth, a phase when your vigour and vitality are refreshed and strengthened. As your well-being returns, you are able to recognize this whole cycle of events as part of a 'redemptive catastrophe' that has actually brought growth and regeneration into your life.

Reversed, *quert* suggests an affliction which you are finding it hard to throw off. Sickness and ill-health may be gaining the upper hand, or perhaps you are struggling with heavy-heartedness or depression. Harsh experiences may have left you shattered with little energy to draw on to aid yourself. It is essential, however, that you marshal your remaining forces. Seek the best help or advice available and direct all your efforts towards self-healing and recovery.

Keywords
Health, vitality. Healing, regeneration, recovery. Psychological integration, wholeness. Rest, respite, relaxation, recuperation.

Reversed
Sickness, ill-health, depression. The need to marshal one's forces and energy.

Natural Characteristics

The apple tree is too well known to need much detail here, but it pays to note that the original apple tree of the British Isles was actually the crab apple. Crab apple trees are found in the wild even today; small, wizened bushes, some varieties still carry thorns on their trunk as their arboreal ancestors did. Crab apples are undersized, sour fruit seldom eaten today but nonetheless suit-able for jams and preserves.

There were a number of varieties of apple in existence in the ancient world (Pliny cites twenty-two), but it was not until the eighteenth century that hybridization produced the incredible diversity of plants known today under the term *Malus domestica*. Needless to say, the apple is one of the most popular fruits consumed by humans, prized for its crispness and sweetness, especially organic varieties. An enduring belief in the efficacy of apple in health and healing is preserved in the folk saying 'an apple a day . . . ' This notion has deep roots, as we shall see.

Storylines

The 'golden apples of the sun' in Celtic mythology are a magical fruit that confer well-being, longevity and even immortality upon the recipient. In a famous episode from the Irish epic *Oidheadh Clainne Tuireann* (*The Fate of the Children of Tuireann*), Lugh describes the apples.

> No other apples will do but these, for they are the most beautiful and have the most virtue in them of the apples of the whole world. And it is what they are like, they are of the colour of burned gold, and they are the size of the head of a child a month old, and there is the taste of honey on them, and they do not leave the pains of wounds or the vexation of sickness on any one that eats them, and they do not lessen by being eaten forever.[lxx]

The East is of course the realm of the rising sun, and the apple may figure here as a type of microcosmic solar disc, embodying the light, life-giving and regenerative rays of the sun.

It is, however, the farthermost West with which apples are most commonly associated in Irish mythology. The name Avalon is familiar to us from Arthurian Romance; it literally means 'island of apples'. The otherwordly isle to which Arthur is ferried by the three maidens (or 'a ship entirely occupied by women' in the words of *La Mort le Roi Artu*) was known in Irish myth as Avallach or Emain Ablach. It was celebrated as a paradisal destination, a place of healing and restoration, qualities also evoked by Arthurian legend, where the wounded King Arthur – after being tended by the ministrations of his sister Morgan le Fey – is interred there. 'For I must', as Arthur says with his final breath in *The Morte D'arthur*, 'go into the vale of Avilion to heal me of my grievous wound.'[lxxi]

This strikes close to the heart of the more ancient Celtic themes associated with Emain Ablach, which is one of the host of 'many-coloured islands of the West' which provide a series of stepping stones between this world and the next in Irish cosmology, and is often ruled by mythical women, who may recall clans of pagan priestesses. Readers of Marion Zimmer Bradley's *Mists of Avalon* will be familiar with this theme, but such women also appear in the ancient sea-going saga entitled *Immram Curaig Maíle Dúin* (*The Voyage of Maeldúin's Boat*), when the hero and his crew wash up there:

> The green-backed wave brought them over the calm sea to an island,
> With a mound and fortress full of folk.
> Beautiful maidens dwelt therein, as they could see;
> The bath they tended was filled with the brightest water.[lxxii]

Healing sanctuaries hallowed to the goddess did actually exist, such as the famous baths at Bath, sacred to Sulis. Real clans of priestess also lived on various islands considered to be the physical manifestation of the metaphysical Avalon. Roman accounts of the sack of the Druidical island of Iona, for instance, paint a vivid picture of black-robed priestess spitting curses at stunned legionaries.

In the late Irish piece known as *Immacallam in dá Thuarad* (*The*

Colloquy of the Bards), it is related how Óengus offered the three miraculous apple trees from the magical oak wood at Bruig na Bóinde (Newgrange, County Meath) as part of a wedding gift for the Milesians. These are otherworldly trees, 'one in full bloom, one shedding its blossoms, and the third covered with ripe fruit'.

Emhain of the Apple Trees (Emhain Ablach) is described as 'a house of peace', and from there hails an otherworldly woman who visits Bran mac Febal, with a branch of silver laden with white blossoms. She sings to the spell-struck host:

> I bring a branch of the apple-tree from Emhain, from the far island around which are the shining horses of the Son of Lir . . . There is an old tree there with blossoms, and birds calling from among them; every colour is shining there . . . [lxxiii]

The branch betokens the hero's acceptance into otherworldly society, as it were, and his possession of the gifts of the *sidhe* (Faery-folk). In the *Echtra Cormaic i Tír Tairngiri* (*The Adventures of Cormac in the Land of Promise*), Cormac is called to that mysterious country by a similar means: this time the 'shining branch' has 'nine apples of red gold' that cured all troubles 'when that branch was shaken for him'.[lxxiv] Its sweet music confers bliss and contentment upon the listener. Celtic poetry is indeed full of praise for the apple; its many virtues are sung, among other sources, by the poet Merlin in his 'madness'.

Folklore and Magic

The fruit of the apple-tree has solar associations, as shown by the English word apple (Breton and Welsh *aval*), which shares a root with the names of the Greek solar god Apollo and Celtic god Belenos, after whom the fire festival of Beltaine is named. As 'the Celtic Apollo', Belanos was a sun god also associated with thermal springs and their healing properties. His festival was one of the four great seasonal celebrations of the Celtic pagan year.

Beltaine in the Old World falls on 31 April (though it was originally celebrated on 1 May), midway between Spring equinox and Summer solstice, at the time when stags' antlers sprouted anew, and there are fragmentary records of rituals at this time of year, involving youths wearing antlered headdresses, undergoing the trials of a mock chase. The one who successfully evades the cavalcade has been labelled by some folklorists the Stag Lord.

It is interesting that Merlin, who is often identified with stags, shelters under an apple tree when in the grip of madness, for *The Word Ogam of Morann* describes *quert* as the 'shelter of a hind' and elaborates a little later 'lunatics or hinds'. It is as if the arch-wizard stops here in the midst of his gruelling ritual drama for rest and replenishment. *Quert* may, correspondingly, be invoked in matters of health and well-being, as a kind of tonic for those suffering from weariness of the soul.

Aicme Muin

| Harvest | Muin (Vine) |

Harvest

+

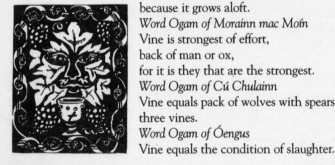

Muin (Vine)

Name: *Muin* (said MUHN). Botanical name: *Vitis vinifera* (sometimes also bramble or black berry). Status: chieftain-tree. Sound: m.
Elaborations on the Ogam Names
Muin is a vine tree highest of beauty is *Muin* because it grows aloft.
Word Ogam of Morainn mac Moín
Vine is strongest of effort,
back of man or ox,
for it is they that are the strongest.
Word Ogam of Cú Chulainn
Vine equals pack of wolves with spears,
three vines.
Word Ogam of Óengus
Vine equals the condition of slaughter.

Visualization

A Green Man crowns a vineyard scene. Vines sprouting from his smiling mouth, he drinks from a golden chalice.

Meaning

Muin, vine, is a tree-letter of work completed and consequent celebration. It suggests that you have reached a stage where your efforts stand finished and you can now take a pause to enjoy the fruits of your labour. This ushers in a season of festivity, itself reflecting the deeper mysteries of divine ecstasy.

Wine and mead are the product of a whole archetypal cycle of cultivation. To ferment a beverage takes much planning, effort and commitment – the strain on the 'back of man or ox' of Morainn's *Word Ogam*. The ground must be planted and weeded, the vines reared and protected, the pests driven off, and then comes the period of waiting. This is a good metaphor for any project that we see through from the conceptual stage to its ultimate flowering.

Muin corresponds to the traditional harvest time, which in the ancient calendar was a period of respite, intoxication, and bacchic ecstasy. This is when we let go of the restraints and inhibitions that characterize our everyday life and give ourselves over to pleasure, fun, and exhilaration. In due proportion, such revelry is healthy and proper to the natural order of things. Celebrate the bounty of the season!

Underlying the ancient rites of the harvest is an even deeper spiritual theme of self-cultivation, divine inspiration, and ecstasy. Across the ancient world the symbol of 'intoxicating liquor' was used as a metaphor for divinely inspired states of consciousness. The sacred festivals, with their songs and dance, were designed to lift the soul – and body – closer to the higher realms, which in the Celtic religion are pictured as places of continual feasting and plenty.

Reversed, *muin* warns of excess and its consequences. If you continually indulge yourself and dwell in excess, you will end up being destroyed. The harvest season and its fruits are part of a cycle; at other times we must clear the ground, plant and sow, work and toil. Do not be seduced into a rootless existence of pure pleasure-seeking: the tide that seems so intoxicating can claim you without warning and leave you broken and useless on its shores.

Keywords
Work completed, a project successfully concluded. Harvesting, festivity, celebration. Divine ecstasy, inspiration, fun and feasting. Festival life, seasonal celebration.

Reversed
Excess and its consequences, seduction of senses, a rootless existence.

Natural Characteristics

Muin is widely identified with the grape, a vine which was introduced to Britain in the Bronze Age, from which time leaves and clusters of grapes appear as decoration in art objects. However, it proved difficult to cultivate in such a cool climate and despite more sustained attempts in Roman times, importation from Gaul or Spain was often the easier option. This gives a further spin to the *Word Ogam of Morainn mac Moín* when it calls *muin* 'strongest of effort' (*tresim fedma*).

Vines, in general, are sinuous, tenacious plants whose spiralling patterns are reflected in the lacertine motifs of traditional Celtic knotwork. There were also liquor-producing vines other than the grape cultivated in the old Celtic world for their intoxicating qualities, though mead (based on honey) appears to have been the favoured beverage. Some commentators identify this tree-letter as 'bramble' (blackberry) or mulberry, from which mead is also distilled, and one *Book of Ballymote* Ogam list says of *muin* 'mead from it'.[lxxv] In either case we are dealing with a plant whose berries can be fermented to produce intoxicating liquor.

Storylines

Like the vine itself, the mythology of the grape was originally far more developed in the classical world than in the Western fringes of Celtica. Dionysus and Bacchus are well-known Greek and Roman gods of the grape and its intoxicating qualities. The early Greek Dionysus – also associated with ivy (the next ogam) – appears to have once functioned more as a god of religious ecstasy than a mere figurehead at drunken orgies. This later role was squarely inherited by the Roman Bacchus, who stood as a shameless and grinning embodiment of orgiastic revelry.

The Celtic and Norse worlds certainly had their own cult of divine intoxication in early times, but it was centred on mead rather than the grape. Either way, these cults revolved around the mysteries of fermentation, with the fermenting of the honey or fruit becoming a metaphor for the transformation of the initiate.

This exalted state of consciousness may be alluded to in the Ogam Elaboration phrase which names *muin* 'highest of beauty'.

The mead cult is particularly well attested to in Norse mythology, with the theme of the Cauldron of Divine Mead over which Odin ultimately comes to preside. Ceridwen's Cauldron, from which Taliesin drinks in Welsh mythology, provides a strong Celtic parallel, and this intoxicating brew is linked, among other things, to divine inspiration and poetry. In the medieval Welsh poem known as *The Fold of the Bards* Taliesin says

> It is high time to go to the drinking,
> And share with the skilful,
> And sing dense verse,
> According to the country's custom.[lxxvi]

Other divine draughts in Celtic myth flow from the Cauldron of the Dagda, which grants succour and renewal, and the Cauldron of the Abyss for which Arthur quests in early Welsh romance.

Alcohol was not merely employed for revelry or as a symbol of ecstatic consciousness. The Cú Chulainn epics, in particular, make no bones about the fact that strong drink was used to help induce the infamous Celtic 'battle fury' that was equivalent to the Viking berserker rage, though other herbs and drugs were also employed. It is used in this way in Irish epics such as the eighth century *Fled Bricrenu* (*Bricriu's Feast*) and *Taín Bó Cuilnge* (*The Cattle Raid of Cooley*), where strong drink is used to ply warriors into service by the bloodthirsty Queen Medb (Maeve)– her name itself meaning 'mead'! Is this 'the condition of slaughter' of the *Word Ogam of Óengus*?

Folklore and Magic

It was the Romans who truly established grape-venerating cults similar to those in their own homelands in British soil. The Celtic-Romano governing class that developed in the first centuries CE after the original occupation regarded wine as a great luxury and sought it ardently, most often through trade with Gaul. This no doubt helped to established a grape cult where previously mead had been favoured.

Some of the Green Man figures (also known to scholars as 'foliate heads') which adorned churches and cathedrals in the

Middle Ages depict a shining face grinning or leering out of a profusion of vine leaves. Often a vine is sprouting from his mouth, and grape leaves form a natural crown and wreath around his head. In contemporary Paganism this figure is often interpreted as the Celtic Bacchus, celebrating the eruption of the life force from the Greenworld in one of its most invigorating and intoxicating forms. A sculptor friend of mine carved a cheeky, leering example of this wonderful figure, which sits above the table in the dining room at my home, grinning his blessing over the place of feasting. Needless to say, *muin* may be invoked for ecstatic states of consciousness and as a complement to an important celebration.

Tenacity

\#

Gort (Ivy)

Name: *gort* (said GORT). Botanical name: *Hedera helix*. Status: chieftain-tree. Sound: g

Elaborations on the Ogam Names
Ivy, Greener than pastures is Ivy.
Word Ogam of Morainn mac Moín
Ivy is sweeter than grasses;
to wit, the cornfield.
Word Ogam of Cú Chulainn
Ivy equals pleasing oil,
corn.
Word Ogam of Óengus
Ivy equals size of a warrior.

Visualization

Ivy clings to a sheer wall of rock, a wolf's face forming in its leaves.

Meaning

Gort is ivy, a tenacious and ruthless plant that flourishes in all kinds of environments. This is, correspondingly, a tree-letter of tenacity, of the raw survival instinct which enables you to triumph over circumstances, establish roots, and put forth new green leaves out of the stoniest of soils. This suggests a fair measure of adaptability and toil, and when reversed may mean that you are the object of ruthless treatment from the outside world.

Ivy is a plant which insinuates itself into the least promising of places, prospering in a wide range of climates. It can be as readily seen flourishing in the wastes of our cities as in the Greenworld. When ivy attaches itself to objects it can exploit the most minimal advantages to support its own needs. Similarly, this tree-letter teaches you the virtues of making use of what you find about you, however seemingly unpromising, and applying sheer force of will to create conditions favourable to your requirements.

Another less pleasant aspect of ivy is that it is a parasite that preys on its host and uses other plants and bushes to support itself. Perhaps some such force is restricting, constricting, or exploiting you. At times, we too must show a similar ruthlessness in order to survive. While you should not treat others unjustly, you may need to apply a measure of the warrior spirit yourself in order to carve out your own niche.

The spiralling form of ivy as it winds and twists its way upwards and outwards embodies a powerful and primal impulse of the life force, greatly respected by the Celts. Here is a blueprint of unfolding and outward expansion. We can see a similar principle at work on many levels of the cosmos, from the interlocking pattern of DNA in our blood to the spiral forms of galaxies. It is a basic archetype of growth and endurance.

Reversed, though, *gort* augurs challenge and difficulty. When ivy takes the form of an outside factor which exploits or constricts you, you may begin to weaken and wither. The world is full of hostile energies that know no law but their own self-interest. If you are facing such a person or situation, do not stick around to be bound and swallowed. Take up your sword and make a clean break of the constricting knots while you still can. There are fertile fields opening elsewhere.

Keywords
Tenacity, survival instinct, ruthlessness. The growth spiral, the primal impulse of the life-force, flourishment. Ruthless treatment, restricting, constriction, exploitation. Breaking barriers, reformulation of reality, achievements.

Reversed
Challenge, difficulty, restriction.

Natural Characteristics

Gort is identified as ivy in the Ogam Elaboration and by almost all commentators in contemporary Ogam divination. It is possible, however, that the word *gort* originally meant 'green field', as reflected in the Word Ogam references to pastures, grasses, cornfields, and corn. It has also been suggested that ivy had a doublet in the form of honeysuckle.

Interestingly, ivy was regarded as a chieftain-tree in Celtic thought. The sinuous vine with its deep green shimmering leaves was respected as a prolific symbol of growth and tenacity in the natural world. Its very ruthlessness saw it respected by the often warlike Celts; this may be the source of the *Word Ogam of Óengus* epithet that calls ivy 'size of a warrior'. As a plant, it is a fighter, and no mean antagonist at that.

Undoubtedly, ivy carried a certain aura of menace. A crawler that flourishes by sucking the verdure from more substantial plants, ivy's snaking tendrils insinuate themselves into the most unyielding cracks and crevices. When its host is another tree, it will eventually smother and destroy the very thing that has helped it to flourish. Honeysuckle, also linked to this ogam, appears as a slightly less virulent parasite that is nonetheless similar to ivy in its habits.

Storylines

There are clear mythological correspondences for ivy in the classical world. Dionysus, who came to join the ranks of the immortal gods, was depicted in Greek culture as crowned with a wreath of laurel and ivy. Indeed, it has been stated that 'Dionysus is the ivy; in the first instance he is ivy, nothing more, nothing less.'[lxxvii] Dionysus was, in one aspect, a minor thunder god, imbued with sacred fire, and ivy wood was once used as fire stick in the crucial task of kindling fire. Mastery of fire is itself a vital tool in human survival and endurance.

Ivy's identity in Celtic mythology is a little more complicated. It appears in a number of poems and storylines, testament in part to the plant's ubiquity. Ivy figures several times in *Buile Shuibni*

(*The Frenzy of Suibhné*), a poem in which the Merlin-like shaman-poet Suibhné sings of his inspiration in the wood of Bolcáin. He praises several important elements: ivy's pervasive presence, its enduring quality, its pride and prolific growth, as seen in these fragments of verse:

> O ivy, little ivy,
> thou art familiar in the dusky wood.

> Going through the ivy trees –
> I conceal it not, O warrior –
> like a good cast of a spear
> I went with the wind.

> Good [the wood's] enduring ivy-trees . . .

> A proud ivy bush
> which grows through a twisted tree . . .

In this poem an animal totem appears that points to ivy's mythological identity. The plant is associated with a wolf 'among the ivy trees' that the wizard must outwit in order to survive. As Suibhné says:

> Beyond every wolf among the ivy trees
> swiftly would he get advantage of me,
> so nimbly would I leap
> till I was on the mountain peak.[lxxviii]

The swiftness and ruthlessness of the wolf seem to be connected to that of the ivy; perhaps on some level they are mythological doubles of each other.

Ivy's link with a threat to survival also leaves a trace in a story connected to the Fenian hero Finn mac Cumhail, found in *Macgnimartha Finn* (*The Boyhood Feats of Finn*). Here the infant hero shelters in a hollow of ivy as a dangerous polecat passes by, an animal totem who functions in a similar way to the wolf above. Yet Finn himself acquires the choking powers of the ivy to use it to his benefit, thus defeating the danger:

> In a hollow of a tall ivy-clad tree is nursed that noble Fiann leader [Finn]. One day he is left alone and a polecat passes near the hollow. It comes for the infant with no terror. He closes his grasp round the polecat and he keeps choking it from early morn until eve.[lxxix]

So we can see that ivy, mythologically speaking, embodies two interrelated aspects. On the one hand it embodies the raw force of survival that will assert itself and endure at any cost to its surroundings. On the other, this very power is itself useful and necessary to survival and we may need to adopt it as a model for action. Magically *gort* provides the potency to ward off and bind the powers that threaten and menace us.

Folklore and Magic

There is another aspect to ivy expressed in folklore and festival. In England, the last sheaves of harvested wheat were often bound with ivy in a bundle known as the Harvest May, the Harvest Bride, or the Harvest Girl. The last farmer to harvest his crops was given this figurine as a penalty, for it was regarded as an omen of ill-luck for the following year (reflecting ivy's pernicious nature as a parasite in the plant world).

This custom has its roots in a much older mythological theme, for in *The Madness of Suibhné* we read that the wildman of the woods encounters an equally mad wild-woman with whom he couples on May Day among the 'ivy branches'.

> A crazy woman fleeing from her man –
> however, it is a strange tale –
> a man without clothes, without shoes,
> fleeing before the woman.

> Our desire when wild ducks come
> at Samhuin, up to May-day,
> in each brown wood without scarcity
> to be in ivy branches.[lxxx]

In later times this 'crazy woman' became the Ivy Girl of folklore and ultimately a mere mythological slang for a 'shrewish wife' or meddlesome woman, constricting and constraining her husband. Yet as the old folk song 'Let No Man Steal Your Thyme' shows, this formula could easily be reversed.

> A woman is a branchy tree
> and man the clinging vine
> and from her branches most faithlessly
> he'll take what he can find,
> he'll take what he can find.[lxxxi]

Gort may be invoked in magic as an aid to one's strength and survival skills; it is not, understandably, appropriate for love magic!

Cleansing

nGétal (Broom)

Names: *nGétal, Ngetal* (said NYEH-tl). Botanical name: *Genista* spp. Status: shrub. Sound: ng
Elaborations on the Ogam Names
Broom, a physician's strength is Broom.
Word Ogam of Morainn mac Moín
Broom is a physician's strength;
there is an affinity between panacea and broom.
Word Ogam of Cú Chulainn
Broom equals beginning of heroic deeds, healing.
Word Ogam of Óengus
Broom equals robe of physicians.

Visualization

A witches' broom surrounded by herbs of healing within a circle of yellow broom-flowers.

Meaning

nGétal, or broom, is a tree-letter of well-being and healing. It counsels you to tend to the health of your mind, body and spirit, and reminds you of the need to foster your vitality through rites of cleansing and renewal. This does not always imply ill-health on your part, though reversed the chances are higher.

Broom was often used, as its name suggests, in the construction of traditional witches' style 'besom' brooms. Such brooms are actually magical tools, used in cleaning out the negative energy and accumulated detritus of our psychic as well as physical lives. As such, they become symbols of cleansing, and *nGétal* stresses the importance of clearing away negativity, whether it resides in your psychological complexes, or in the physical centres of the body or dwelling place. Whatever the sick element to be purged – emotional, romantic, financial, or health-related – a symbolic clearing is a major step towards ridding yourself of the unwanted energy.

Another principle of traditional medicine (also called alternative or complementary medicine) is that we should be taking advantage of health and vitality-giving elements as part of our general *well-being*. Organic food, herbs, minerals, vitamins, salted baths, flower essences and exercise are not only natural remedies to illness but crucial parts of a healthy life. Try to maintain all these in balance so that you are not forced to resort to the stop-gap measures of 'conventional' Western medicine.

As far as physical illness is concerned, we should note that the emphasis of this ogam is on healing and the physician's art: it focuses on how we feed our health, not on disease. Prominently placed in a reading on matters of destiny, *nGétal* could even suggest a vocation for you in the healing arts, of one kind or another.

Reversed, *nGétal* raises the spectre of sickness or disease. This does not necessarily warn of a serious ailment, though it does imply that your health and vitality is not what it could be, on a physical, emotional, or spiritual level. Look to Nature, who in her goodness provides many sources of healing and restoration, and practise some kind of clearing ritual as a first step to treatment. NB: In the case of a serious illness, a range of medical opinions should of course be sought.

Keywords
Medicine, herblore, healing, panacea. Cleansing, sweeping out negativity, keeping one's 'house in order', a purgative. Complementary medicine, strengthening health and vitality. The healer's art.

Reversed
Sickness, disease, ailments. Need for cleansing and healing.

Natural Characteristics

Some commentators have had trouble establishing exactly what tree *nGétal* is. The full Ogam Elaboration line actually reads 'broom or reed'. Robert Graves chooses reed or 'water elder', but the Word Ogams all name this letter as broom, which seems consistent with the allusions to physicians, panacea, and healing. Word roots link *nGétal* with *getal*, possibly meaning 'wounding',[lxxxii] which is, of course, the other side of the healing equation.

Broom is a squat bush that grows thickly and virulently. In summer it is notable for its yellow blossoms, a solar emblem that helped establish its connection in the Celtic mind to light, vitality, and therefore healing. The Word Ogams all stress broom's medicinal role, and it certainly has considerable properties in this respect. Steve Blamires writes:

> A decoction of the young branches or seeds will cause violent vomiting if taken in too strong a dose or too large a measure, but a controlled intake is good at relieving conditions such as gout, sciatica, and painful joints. It affords relief to those who suffer from recurring bouts of malaria or fever. It is also a diuretic and helps break down stones in the kidneys and bladder. Oil can be drawn from the stems by heating them over an open fire, and this tincture is good at relieving toothaches. The same oil, if boiled and allowed to cool, is good at cleansing the head and skin of parasites such as lice.[lxxxiii]

The association of broom with healing and herblore is strengthened by the clearing and cleansing uses of besom brooms in folk magic (see below under Folklore).

Storylines

Mythologically, the broom's yellow flowers link it to the sun, and particularly to the solar hero Balan. According to Jean Markale, Balan appears masked as broom in the famous and enigmatic Welsh poem the *Cad Goddeu* or *Battle of the Trees*.

> Among the bushes taking part in the battle is the broom or *genista*, known in Welsh as *banadl* and in Breton as *balan*. And if we look at the Chansons de geste [French Romances], where so many of the supposed Saracens are actually Celtic heroes, we find a character named Balan . . . Saracen though he is, Balan is depicted as having fair hair, light coloured eyes and a white horse. He is the archetypal solar hero and the broomflower being golden yellow, his name merely adds to his basic character.[lxxxiv]

Balan lives in a castle with a drawbridge and has a daughter called Floripar ('Born of a Flower'), which reminds us of Blodeuwedd, the flower maiden of Welsh romance. Markale concludes that the broom or *balan* is the same Beli–Belinus after whom the fire festival of Beltaine is named.

As for gorse's link to medicine, the power of healing or 'physician's strength' is an important element in many tales. Among the chief gods of the Túatha dé Danaan is Dianecht, 'that understood healing', a great god of medicine practised in herblore, who presides over a Well of Healing. His most famous deed, the miraculous construction of an arm of silver for Lugh (to replace the that lost in battle), is related along with a far less noble act in *Cath Tánaiste Maige Tuired* (*The Second Battle of Moytura*). For Dianecht's son Míach shows even greater skill than his father, and jealousy erupts between them. Dianecht sets about to kill his own son, succeeding only after Míach manages to heal himself a number of times from grievous wounds. Thereafter we read:

> And herbs grew from [Míach's] grave, to the number of his joints and sinews, three hundred and sixty-five. And Airmed, his sister, came and spread out her cloak and laid out the herbs in it, according to their virtue. But Dianecht saw her doing that, and he came and mixed the herbs, so that no one knows all their right powers to this day.[lxxxv]

The number three hundred and sixty-five suggests the days of the year and possibly therefore some sort of ancient herbal calendar (or codex of seasonal wisdom), now largely lost to us. Herblore, however, was and is widely practised, despite these difficulties.

In the battle of the Túatha dé Danaan versus the Fir Bolgs, from the Mythological Cycle, it is told how, despite many champions coming to their death, 'the physicians on each side used to make a bath of healing, with every sort of healing plant or herb in it, the way they would be strong and sound for the next day's fight.'[lxxxvi] Such baths are commonly associated with the arts of healing in Celtic mythology, and many Irish tales praise their mystical properties. Herbs, of course, also have magical qualities associated with them in witchcraft. In the late Fenian Cycle piece *Immacallam in dá Thuarad* (*The Colloquy of the Bards*), in which St Patrick figures, it is related how a Druid named Caoilte performs this magical operation involving herbs:

And he understood the use of herbs, and one time he met with two women that were very downhearted because their husbands had gone from them to take other wives. And Caoilte gave them Druid herbs, and they put them in the water of a bath, and they sent away the new wives they had taken.[lxxxvii]

Here we see herbal lore used magically to address the afflictions of fate, and to this day many magical traditions involve the use of certain herbs in potions and spells. In spellcraft, a herb is often employed because of its traditional association (e.g. with love or abundance) or because of an occult correspondence based on a plant's scent, colour, or shape.

Folklore and Magic

The broom in folklore is connected to the traditional besom-style 'witches' broom', in which broom shoots are used for the making of the shaft. In fact, broom handles and the bunched twig brushes can be made from many woods. Obviously, brooms are used to clean and clear a space, and could correspond to the physician's role regarding the human body. Such brooms can be used as part of magical as well as mundane housekeeping, for literally sweeping out some negativity or misfortune. Such folk magic goes part way towards explaining why the broom has so long been regarded as the witches' inseparable friend.

Another facet of lore connected to the besom may be relevant here. It has been suggested that the image of the witch riding her broom actually comes from an ancient shamanistic ritual. An ointment is made from a mixture of plants, including a hallucinogen – such as the fly agaric mushroom – and applied to the broomstick. This the naked witch rides, so that the ointment is taken in through her sexual organs, which introduces the hallucinogen directly into her bloodstream. From this action springs ecstatic and trance-related states, the 'flight' of the witch. Witchcraft involves the use of all sorts of other healing potions and concoctions, and there are many valuable books on the magical, holistic functions of herbs available today. nGétal can be used as the basis of positive visualizations for those seeking healing or recovery from an illness, along with the appropriate medicinal treatment.

Wounding

Straif (Blackthorn)

Names: *straif, straiff, staiph, straibh* (said
STRAHF). Botanical name: *Prunus spinosa*.
Status: chieftain- tree. Sound: ss
Elaborations on the Ogam Names
Blackthorn, the hedge of a stream is Blackthorn.
Word Ogam of Morainn mac Moín
Blackthorn is careful effort, strongest of red;
it equals sloe which gives strong red dye on metal.
Word Ogam of Cú Chulainn
Blackthorn equals an arrow's mist,
smoke drifting up from a fire.
Word Ogam of Óengus
Blackthorn equals increasing of secrets.

Visualization

A blackthorn tree from whose branches sprout thorns, shafts of
swords, spears and arrows.

Meaning

Straif is a tree-letter associated with pain, wounding and damage.
The dense, spiny 'sloe-bush' is an unpleasant plant to tangle with
and drawing this ogam suggests that you have been, or will be, on
the receiving end of a rather thorny experience. Yet it is not
all bad, for *straif* also offers initiation into the mysteries of self-
conquest and transcendence.

Straif resonates with the images of the sword, the spear, and the
arrow – all, of course, instruments of war. Traditionally linked to
warfare, the blackthorn tree corresponds to the battles we wage
in the course of our lives, including wounds received and inflict-
ed. Yet as readers of the Tarot will know, swords function as a
more general symbol for conflict that can be mental, emotional,
and spiritual as much as physical. The sharp edge of the sword
creates division and separation.

Look carefully to see whether the origin of the current strife lies
in the outside world or your own mind. The mind is, in many ways,
a weapon much like the sword. It is useful for analysis, for dissect-
ing and categorizing, but this strength is also its chief weakness.
If you find yourself in constant fruitless skirmishes or buried in

protracted battles, could you be engaging in thoughts or engrained emotional patterns which are generating the negativity?

Bizarre as it may be, we often become habituated to our wounds and consequently manifest situations where our worst expectations are confirmed. Thus disappointment breeds disappointment and we can come to live in a perpetual mode of damage control. If this could be the case, remember that you can never control external events but you can change your reaction to them! Seek to cultivate peace within and resolution of the cycle without will naturally follow. Your health may depend on it.

Reversed, *straif* has a sombre role. There is a warning here, for the blackthorn is a gateway tree of transition and even death – the ultimate 'increasing of secrets'. Ruled by the *cailleach* or 'death crone', it represents the force that swallows and breaks down those elements which have spent their substance and need to be renewed. This is not necessarily an omen of physical death, though it sometimes augurs surgery. It can also warn of the dismemberment of the composite parts of your life so that they can be reintegrated on a higher plane.

Keywords
Pain, wounding, damage (physical or emotional). A thorny experience. Division, separation, conflict. The need to address this at its roots. Disruption, difficulty and adversity.

Reversed
A threat to the order of your life. Transition, dismemberment. Surgery.

Natural Characteristics

Blackthorn is a blasted-looking shrub, with twisting and angular branches, seldom reaching over twelve feet in height. A woodland-edge dweller, it was traditionally used in hedgerows, in which it often grows to form a dense, impenetrable thicket. It puts forth white blossoms in early spring, and later sloes (small round berries clustered on the tree's stems), hence the epithet sloe-bush.

Yet the most potent feature of blackthorn is undoubtedly its thorns. These are long, slender, and extremely sharp, taking the place of twigs at the branch endings. They are ill-famed for their ability to inflict painful wounds, which often turn septic. This, and the traditional likening of thorns to swords and spears, undoubtedly gave blackthorn its associations with strife, warfare, and wounding.

Storylines

Thorns, as a genus, have an aura threat and menace in Celtic mythology, though they can sometimes also offer protection from harm. The blackthorn was often identified with the *shillelagh* (club, cudgel) wielded by uncouth giants in Irish tales, and blackthorn or briar, as the Word Ogams reveal, is steeped in associations of blood and warfare ('red dye on metal', 'arrow's mist', etc.). We can see this idea in operation in the Fenian Cycle in the person of Conan, who sports a briar on his banner.

> And as to Conan, it is a briar he had on his banner, because he was always for quarrels and trouble. And it used to be said of him that he never saw a man without striking him, or a door left open without going in through it . . . [lxxxviii]

As for the kenning 'hedge of a stream', hedge here refers to a wall of warriors, armed with weapons as the sloe is with its thorns, rolling forward like a river. This association of themes can be seen in the *Taín Bó Cuilnge* (*Cattle Raid of Cooley*) in relation to the boyhood deeds of the hero Cú Chulainn:

> Your red-plagued blood will drip
> From numerous splintered shields.
> The army which will swarm with fires
> Is a legion which they lead in many companies.
> A torrent of blood will be showered
> Over Cú Chulainn as well as flesh.
> You will suffer from a wound of vengeance,
> Afflicted from encounters with a hedge of spears.
> By an iron point will the red shield be splintered,
> Blazing against pierced skin.[lxxxix]

The 'hedge of spears' that splinters shields, pierces skin, and unleashes a torrent of blood is very close to the Word Ogam associations of metal and blood.

Thorns are also linked with warriorship itself. In the Fenian Cycle, Finn is entrusted to the care of the 'Woman Druid' Bodhmall, reflecting the custom of Celtic heroes being trained in arms and magic by powerful women, just as Cú Chulainn is trained by Scáthach and Lancelot receives has sword from the

Lady of the Lake. *Macgnimartha Finn* (*The Boyhood Feats of Finn*) describes how Bodhmall and her companion Liath Luachra carry out this strange rite with Finn: 'One of them would run round a tree, and she having a thorn switch, and Finn after her with another switch, and each one trying to hit at the other . . . '[xc] This is part of his martial (and magical) training, and through *straif* we too are initiated into the mysteries of conflict and strife.

Because of its link to wounding and, therefore, potentially death, blackthorn partakes in the dark symbolism of the *cailleach* or 'death crone', a Celtic equivalent of the minor Norns of Norse mythology. Here is a description, also from the Fenian Cycle, of one of these grim hags, who haunt the battlefield and sickbed.

> [Glasan] lay down and pulled some of the bodies over him, and he was not there long till he saw an old hag coming into the house, having one leg and one arm and one upper tooth, that was long enough to serve her in place of a crutch. And when she came inside the door she took up the first dead body she met with, and threw it aside, for it was lean. And as she went on, she took two bites out of every fat body she met with, and threw away every lean one.[xci]

The fearsome *cailleach* is a dark aspect of the mother goddess, who breaks down dead elements and digests them. She is the earthen grave, the 'increasing of secrets' that takes place in the underworld. And yet she is also the goddess of the Cauldron of Rebirth who, in Celtic religion, re-members the corpse and brings it back to life again in the bright Otherworld, the Land of the Ever Living Ones over which she rules.

Folklore and Magic

Blackthorn has had a bad press throughout the ages. Its negative side certainly came to predominate in the popular imagination as time went on, the plant being identified by Inquisitors during the witch-craze as a tool of malevolent witchcraft, and even as the wood from which the Crown of Thorns was made! It is quite possible, moreover, that sloe was used in malicious magic.

However, there is another aspect to the shrub which links it, like hawthorn, to sexual and regenerative energies, which it both guards and, perversely, embodies. This can be seen in later fairy-tales, such as Sleeping Beauty, where a maiden lies within a circle of thorns, spell-struck by a wicked witch (an echo of the *cailleach* or hag of blackthorn fame?). A true knight must take up his sword to release her, so that renewal can take place. A variation on this can be found in the Scottish tale of *The Son of the King of Éirinn*. Here the heroine, while eloping with her lover, works magic using a thorn to create a thicket to protect them from her pursuing father.[xcii] Sloe is used on this rare occasion as a protective device, but it is not a tree-letter to invoke lightly for any purpose in magical operations!

Rue

Ruis (Elder)

Name: *ruis* (said RWEESH). Botanical name: *Sambucus nigra*.
Status: shrub. Sound: r
Elaborations on the Ogam Names
Elder, the redness of shame.
Word Ogam of Morainn mac Moín
Elder is intensest of blushes,
from the reddening or shame.
Word Ogam of Cú Chulainn
Elder equals glow of anger,
punishment.
Word Ogam of Óengus
Elder equals redness of faces.

Visualization

A face marked with the juice of red berries ringed by a wreath of woven elder-branches.

Meaning

Ruis, elder, is on the one hand a tree-letter of regret, shame, humiliation, and even retribution. The old English word 'rue' corresponds well to these qualities. However, you should not be alarmed, for despite its challenges, *ruis* is on the other hand a great teacher linked with magical powers and the ability to change and creatively transform the legacies of past actions.

Ruis is an ogam of regret over our deeds. Perhaps you are suffering embarrassment, and wishing an event or set of circumstances had never happened. The term 'shame' implies that you or someone else may be suffering a 'reddening of face' over some incident or other. Shame has the role of alerting us to the fact that we have lost the right path and need to correct our actions. It prevents us from continually taking the wrong turns and pursuing inappropriate ends.

Elder also corresponds to what we understand by the term *karma*. If we recognize that actions accumulate and take on a life of their own in our fate-path, then we can become empowered by this knowledge. Learning from mistakes will free you to harmonize with the unfolding of your unique destiny. Take the initiative to work on the fundamental threads of your life and weave them into new and transformative patterns.

Ruis can also involve matters of revenge, the 'glow of anger'. Often when affairs of one kind or another have not been satisfactorily resolved, vengefulness comes into play. Though the Celts were very warlike, with grievances being nursed obsessively, the Druids often mediated disputes and generally smoothed the water. Take a leaf from their book.

Reversed, *ruis* suggests that accounts are yet to be settled on some issue along the path that you have been walking. You cannot escape guilt through denial; humiliation only arises where regrets have not been addressed. Take action to purge yourself of these emotions; they are unhealthy and attract retribution. Similarly, do not dwell in vengefulness — it is better to let the higher powers dispose as they will than assume the role of arbiter. Weed your own garden before glaring across at your neighbour's patch.

Keywords
Rue, regret, shame, embarrassment, humiliation. Grievances, retribution, revenge, vendetta. Karma, being called to account, the need to rework destiny.

Reversed
Accounts to be settled, addressing regrets, purging humiliation, tending one's own patch.

Natural Characteristics
The elder is a tree of modest scale that seldom reaches above thirty feet in height. Its trunk is unusual, for as a sapling it sprouts several

stems and each of these grows upward in its own right, finally
drooping over with the weight of its own foliage. Elder thus develops into a kind of thicket of shoots. Perhaps these characteristics
translate into its traditional identity as a tree of shame or rue; a
thick profusion of shoots which bend under their own burden.

Elder has the features that mark out other Faery trees: white
flowers and reddish berries. Its small white flowers open in
summer and are starlike, with five petals. Among other insects,
they especially attract flies. Its purple berries ripen in autumn and
provide nourishment for birds. They also explain, on a naturalistic level, the Word Ogam references to 'reddening' and 'redness
of face' (and thence shame). Elderberry wine was also once a
commonly fermented beverage, though the tree itself was never
wantonly felled, for reasons explained below.

Storylines

Elder was traditionally associated with witches, and some folklorists have alleged an ancient belief in the 'Elder Mother' as the
in-dwelling spirit of the tree. In Scandinavia and Denmark she
was known as Elle or Hyldemoer, who would avenge harm done
to her wards, the elder trees. In later times she became a mere
hideous hag, as is so often the fate of ancient goddesses under
patriarchal religion.

In a tale from the Fenian Cycle, the elder-tree appears
mentioned in the same breath as a very ghoulish assembly. Finn
and his men travel 'over the Plain of Health to the Old Yew of
the Old Valley' in a metaphoric death, since the yew is widely
associated with death and the land of the dead. There they find
a house with a fire shining from it. 'I never knew of a house in the
valley,' says Finn, alerting us to the strange nature of this otherworldly abode. Finn and his men are welcomed in by a 'big grey
man' and enter the house.

> They sat down then on the hard boards of a bed, and the grey man
> kindled a fire, and he threw logs of elder-wood on it, till they went
> near being smothered with the smoke. They saw a hag in the house
> having three heads on her lean neck; and there was on the other side
> a man without a head, having one eye, and it in his breast. 'Rise up,
> you that are in the house, and make music for the King of the
> Fianna,' said the grey man then.

With that nine bodies rose out of the corner nearest to the Fianna, and nine heads rose up on the other side of the bed, and they raised nine harsh screeches together, that no one would like to be listening to. And then the hag answered them, and the headless man answered; and if all that music was harsh, there was none of it that you would not wish to hear sooner than the music of the one-eyed man. And the music that was sung went near to breaking the bones of their heads, and indeed it is no sweet music that was.[xciii]

This obscure incident yields a recognizable theme. The fact that the elder appears here in the Valley of the Yew (that is, the land of the dead) points to its role as a signal of unsettled business with the past. For we learn about the grotesque dwellers of the house: 'And those three that fought against them were the three Shapes out of the Valley of the Yew Tree that came to avenge their sister, Cuillen of the Wide Mouth',[xciv] whose death the Fianna have caused.

This 'rite of the smoking elder-wood' may be a remnant of a much wider mythological theme. Its warns that misdeeds breed vengeance, for Finn's men are almost smothered with elder-wood smoke, pointing to a dark chthonic function of the tree in Druidical lore. This 'smothering' clearly relates to the 'redness of face', 'shame', or 'arduous anger, punishment' of the Word Ogams. Consequently, it may suggest a post-death rite of passage in which the soul is confronted by the shades of his or her actions or 'faces the music', as it were. As Finn's escape shows, however, these trials can be overcome by strength and virtue.

Folklore and Magic

As mentioned, elder is associated with the Elder Mother in folklore. For this reason, one did not fell the tree lightly. Jacqueline Memory Paterson writes 'no forester of old would touch elder, let alone cut it, before asking the Elder Mother's permission three times over and even then he was still in dread of her possible wrath.'[xcv] Witches were thought to be able to transform themselves into elder, a source of superstitious fear in later times. Perhaps this underlines the theme of the elder as an embodiment of retribution. After all, crossing a witch was sure to lead to vengeance, and witches (male and female) in former times did not necessarily have qualms about using their powers for revenge or personal gain.

Christianity turned elder's associations of shame and regret to its own dogmatic ends. Elder stood accused of being yet another tree from which the cross was constructed and the one upon which Judas hanged himself. Although obviously nonsense, such a legend does evidence a certain continuity of lore, with elder's significance in paganism as a tree of rue being transferred to a Christian setting. In the Middle Ages, elder wands were in fact used for healing and, ironically, as a sprig against malevolent witchcraft – for such magical uses could see you burned during the witch-craze. In magic, elder may still be invoked in situations where one has been wronged and has no other means of redress. One entrusts the matter to the care of the Elder Mother, for it is she who avenges on behalf of her children.

Aicme Ailm

Elation
+

Ailm (Pine or Fir)

Names: *ailm, ailim* (said AHL-m). Botanical names: *Pinus sylvestris* or *Abies alba*. Status: shrub. Sound: a.

Elaborations on the Ogam Names
Ailm, a Fir tree, a Pine Tree.

Word Ogam of Morainn mac Moín
Pine is loudest of groanings,
for it is *ailm* or 'a a' a man says
while groaning in disease,
or wondering, marvelling
at whatever circumstances.

Word Ogam of Cú Chulainn
Pine equals beginning of a weaver's beam
or of calling, ahh.

Word Ogam of Óengus
Pine equals beginning of answers.

Visualization

From the great height of a pine tree's upper branches a vast landscape unfolds.

Meaning

Ailm is the pine: a tree of ecstasy and elation. All the traditions surrounding this ogam letter reveal it as one of enthusiasm, wonder and awe. There may also be some fear and trembling, especially if this ogam appears reversed. Yet either way, *ailm* always augurs something great.

The state of elation which comes with peak experiences is both enjoyable and illuminating. It brings heightened awareness, an expansion of consciousness in which we dwell on the positive elements and unfolding possibilities of our lives. Imagine yourself high in the branches of a tall pine; from here you gain a sense of perspective and can see all the way to the horizon and its limitless reaches.

Let your enthusiasm lead you dancing across the landscape of life.

This ogam also marks the dawning of understanding, as when something is revealed of the overall design of which we are apart. Here you catch your breath with wonder and realize that there is a symmetry behind the apparently random flux of daily life. *Ailm* is traditionally linked to the song of otherworldly birds who sing from its spiny branches, and here it is as if you catch the notes of their composition and understand, with a measure of awe.

Realizations of great significance can also be mingled with pain. Indeed, at times elation contains the seeds of its own shadow side: awareness of the incredible fragility of life and consciousness, poignancy at what is passing, and fear in the face of that which is beyond our comprehension. Yet *ailm* encourages you to allow yourself to experience and express the full force of your feelings. Vent your emotion, whether it is joy, pain, or rage.

Reversed, *ailm* tends to signal something fearful or even terrifying. Anguish may well up from the depths, threatening to overwhelm you. Perhaps you are experiencing grief or some other agony, and no words can bring consolation at this time. Confusion may also reign, frightening and paralysing you. Do your best to distinguish between the pain and the confusion, so you can begin to process the hurt and unravel the knots that entangle your heart.

Keywords
Elation, enthusiasm, wonder, awe. Peak experiences, heightened consciousness, perspective, great realizations. Pain, poignancy, fear. Expression of emotion.

Reversed
Fear, terror, anguish. Confusion, fright, paralysis. Need to untie the emotional knots.

Natural Characteristics

As the Ogam Elaboration makes plain, *ailm* represents a coniferous tree, either pine or fir. Conifer trees, with their spiny needles, are from a far older epoch than broadleaves. They were prevalent in the boreal period that came after the last great glacial age, and pine is thought to have been especially common at this time, growing in a variety of climes. Conifers can survive in dry soil and tend to inhabit a rather bare surrounding space, due to the cover created by their needles. They are, crucially, evergreen, giving them a verdant appearance in winter, when deciduous trees have shed their leaves and stand bare and skeletal.

Scots pine, juniper, and yew are the varieties native to the British Isles, with silver fir being introduced as late as the seventeenth century. Scots pine is now mostly limited to scattered remnants of woodland in the Scottish highlands. The distinguishing feature of this tree is its tall, straight trunk and horizontal or upward inclining branches. It can reach heights of up to one hundred feet, with smooth, coppery-red bark and stiff needles sprouting profusely from its cone laden branches. The silver fir is of similar stature and is thought to have been the original Yule-tree.

Storylines

Across Eurasian treelore, pine and fir are trees of religious terror, wonder, transformation and inspiration. In the Welsh Mabinogion tale *Yves: The Lady of the Fountain*, a great and mysterious tree makes an appearance, 'a tall tree, whose branches are greener than the greenest pine trees'.[xcvi] This tree reappears in the medieval French Arthurian romance of *Yvain* (*The Knight with the Lion*), by Chrétien de Troyes, as a wonderful pine which rises beside the spring of Barenton in the forest Broceliande in Brittany. The hero Yvain, on the advice of a woodsman who is also 'master of the beasts', is directed to this miraculous pine.

> As regards the tree I'm sure, and that's the truth of the matter, that it was the finest pine that ever grew on the earth. And I don't believe that it would ever rain so hard that one drop of water would get through: instead it would all run over it. Hanging from the tree I saw the basin of purest gold that was ever as yet for sale in any fair. As for the spring, you may take my word that it was boiling like hot water. The slab was of emerald, bored out like a cask; and underneath were four rubies that shone more bright and crimson than the morning sun when it appears in the east. [xcvii]

Yvain then sprinkles some of the spring water on the slab, ignoring the woodsman's warning. Immediately a violent and terrifying tempest of thunder and lightning breaks out, with rain, snow and hail slaking the pine tree and shattering the surrounding woodland.

> As soon as the storm passed, I saw, if anyone is prepared to believe me, so many birds gathered on the pine that there was not a branch or leaf to be seen that was not completely covered by birds, which made the tree still more beautiful. And these birds sang together in harmony, though each sang a different song so that I never heard the song of one being sung by another. [xcviii]

The Master of the Beasts who directs Yvain to the pine tree is an extremely ancient figure, dating to the earliest known European religious beliefs. Surrounded by the creatures of his domain, he is the protector of the timeless wood. And the ageless pine with its overarching branches is itself clearly an arboreal tree, from the dawn of creation. The presence of the spring here suggests the goddess and thus a polarity with the phallic pine. Finally, the vision of an otherwordly tree covered with birds who sing in unison strikes a deep chord in the shamanistic lore of Celtic journeys to the Otherworld.

We can notice, too, the sequence of emotion connected to this incident: curiosity, wonder, fearlessness, terror, and transformation. Yvain here undergoes a rite of passage on a wheel of elating emotions. He arrives at a place of marvel also fraught with danger, where the balance of beauty is so fine it may easily be upset and turn to devastation. Interestingly enough, the pine tree here inspires a similar mix of wonder and terror to that alluded to in the Word Ogams, where *ailm* is linked to the vowel sound 'a a' or 'ah' and consequently to an exclamation of suffering or amazement. The *Word Ogam of Morainn mac Moín* relates *ailm* to a groan of disease, wonder, or marvel; in the *Word Ogam of Óengus* it is 'the beginning of answers'. Pine, being evergreen, is often regarded as a timeless tree which straddles the poles of birth and death, and this may be why it inspires terror and wonder and how it provides 'answers'.

Wider Eurasian treelore may provide us with some answers regarding *ailm*, for both fir and pine are associated with the sufferings, sacrifice, and transformations of the divinity in several traditions. In Egypt, pine was linked to the great god Osiris, who was dismembered by his evil brother Seth. A similar theme is present in the later adoption of the Yule-log of silver fir at Christmas time, venerating the birth of Christ, another sacrificial divinity. Classical Greece explained the evergreen nature of pine and fir in the following myth. Attis was loved by Cybele, but he broke his vow of fidelity to her. In anger, she changed him into a pine or fir. The cult of Cybele and Attis, related to that of Dionysus, was an ecstatic cult, involving music, dance, and orgiastic revelry, and Dionysus/Bacchus was often represented by a pine cone. Could ecstatic dismemberment and re-memberment rituals such as those associated with Osiris, Attis, and Dionysus be distantly echoed in the groaning 'a a' and 'ah' in ecstasy or agony spoken of in the Word Ogams?

Folklore and Magic

In pagan Europe, bonfires of heaped pine branches were lit at the Winter Solstice, in a type of sympathetic magic designed to attract the sun back from the wintry depths of the underworld. In such rituals, the Yule logs and trees were often adorned with various shiny objects, and this custom later translated into the ornaments of the Christmas tree. Some contemporary Pagans reclaim these Yule-log rites, investing them with their own symbolism.

The star on top of the Christmas tree, incidentally, has been linked to the cult of the Nail of the North or pole star. This cult is not properly understood, but it was very widespread in the North and probably connected to cycles of transformation of a celestial divinity. The pine, itself a hyperborean tree linked in the Western European imagination to the farthermost North, is clearly appropriate to such a Northern cultus. It is sad that today the pine is associated with the gross regimentation of mass forestry, but beautiful examples can still be encountered in the wild in many parts of the world.

Ailm may be meditated upon and invoked in magic as an aid to gaining ecstatic, peak experiences. Interestingly, psychological studies have shown that the more we note, acknowledge, and dwell on the positive, peak experiences of our lives, the more they happen! And in magic, after all, a governing principle is that like attracts like.

Sexuality

Onn (Gorse)

Names: *Onn* (said UHN). Botanical name: *Ulex europaeus*. Status: chieftain-tree. Sound: o.
Elaborations on the Ogam Names
Onn that is Furze (Gorse).
Word Ogam of Morainn mac Moín
Gorse is helper of horses,
the wheels of the chariot.
Word Ogam of Cú Chulainn
Gorse equals strength of warriors,
fierceness.
Word Ogam of Óengus
Gorse equals gentlest of work.

Visualization

A yellow-haired maiden of the Land of Youth stands in her stronghold of gorse, adorned with a girdle of its golden flowers.

Meaning

Onn is a tree-letter of sexuality. Gorse has yellow, sweetly scent-
ed flowers which perfume the air in spring and are traditionally
associated with the musk of sexual arousal, especially that of
women. Its appearance in a reading augurs issues of attraction,
eros, and sexuality, though reversed it signifies the painful thorns
which can beset the bed of bliss.

Sexuality is a very positive force in Paganism, which does not
suppress the life of the flesh. This ogam encourages you to have a
healthy rapport with your body, a sense of beauty, a grace and
erotic charge that springs from your very pores and the swagger of
your hips. Allow yourself to enjoy and express your sexuality in a
free and natural manner.

Onn relates to you being-in-your-sexuality, and is an ogam of
passion. Where lovemaking is concerned, it relates especially to
the heat of sexual pleasure and its health and vitality promoting
role. This tree-letter counsels us to be sexually empowered in love
relationships.

Sexuality is part of the abundance of earthly life, but a healthy
sex life must at times be fostered, particularly in long-term relationships. Be sensual and enjoy the fruits of the flesh. Romantic
garments, lace, scents, musk, candles, magical enticements, and
foreplay are like the flowers of the gorse: adornments which grace
the bedroom or soft hillside alike. Allow your erotic nature to
come to the fore.

Reversed, the negative, thorny aspect of *onn* becomes prevalent. You are straying from the paths of happiness and endanger-
ing your happiness and perhaps health. There are many flowers
along the path of life; you do not need to pick them all: be careful to avoid the sharp thorns that litter the way. Entanglements
present themselves that should at all cost be avoided. Have a care
to avoid putting yourself at risk, emotionally or physically.

Keywords
Sexuality, arousal, eros, passion. Attraction, masculine and femi-
nine elements, binding force, being in the body, erotic charge.
Health and vitality. Erotica, enticements, foreplay.

Reversed
Thorns, endangerment, entanglements, risk taking.

Natural Characteristics

Onn (gorse) is a plant with associations both solar, by virtue of its yellow flowers, and dark or underworldly, by dint of its thorns. Gorse is a spiky, thorny bush that was often used in the construction of hedges, particularly in Ireland. However, it has always proved difficult to contain, as witnessed in its often disastrous importation to parts of the New World. Its thorns link gorse symbolically with the hawthorn and blackthorn, both trees and tree-letters with an aura of danger to them.

The association of gorse with springtime, and thus dawn, comes from the sunny yellow hue of its flowers and the fact that they are said to be the first visited by bees in the vernal season. Although it flowers most profusely in spring, gorse's yellow blossoms are perennial, with a scattering visible even in winter. Its honey-scented flowers encircled by thorns may have suggested to the Celts female genitalia: eternally in bloom but sharply defended.

Storylines

Gorse is undoubtedly linked with the sun and soil. As in the Norse world, the sun and its rays could be female in Celtic mythology as readily as they could be symbolized by male mythological figures. And there is a veritable host of women in Celtic myth 'golden haired' as the yellow-flowering gorse, many of them hailing from Land of the Ever Living. You can catch the scent of such delightful figures in the perfumed gorse as it flowers in the springtime.

We get a good idea of the type of Otherworld maidens who correspond to the 'golden-haired gorse' from a description from the Fenian Cycle of Eibhir of the plaited yellow hair, first wife of Finn's much loved son, Oisín:

> It was beyond the sea she lived, in a very sunny place; and her father's name was Iunsa, and her sunny house was thatched with feathers of birds, and the doorposts were of gold, and the doors of ribbed grass. And Oisin went looking for her, and he fought against the High King and against an army of the Firbolgs he had helping him; and he got the better of them all, and brought away Eibhir of the yellow hair to Ireland.[xcix]

The women of Celtic myth, however, are not all passive prizes waiting to be won. Oisín's second wife, Níamh 'the yellow-haired', comes for him from the Land of the Young and bears him away to her abode. Níamh is the daughter of the queen of that country and attended by 'a hundred beautiful young girls having cloaks of silk worked with gold'.[c]

This ogam has also been seen as corresponding to Adraste, the golden-haired goddess of the dawn, who was invoked by Boudicca as she went into battle against the Romans. We should remember that women often fought alongside men in Celtic cultures, and Adraste is depicted as a strong willed, battle-ready woman whose totem animal is the hare, a creature connected to prolific reproduction. The hare is also linked to the Earth itself (in which, after all, it burrows) and so Adraste and similar figures can be seen as divine protectresses who embody the sovereignty of the land. Powerful and fertile, they are also aggressively sexual.

The Word Ogams of Cú Chulainn and Óengus provide rather contradictory kennings for gorse. On the one hand, *onn* is 'strength of warriors, fierceness' and on the other 'the gentlest of work'. This, however, perfectly fits the interpretation of *onn* as a tree-letter of sexuality. The associations of warriorship and fierceness match the spiky thorns of the gorse bush and the thorny aspect of erotic energies; in Celtic thought thorns also imply aggression, defence and the primal, potent energies of the giant realm (see *húath*, page 83). Yet the golden flowers of gorse also point to its sweeter side, the nectar that lies beyond the thorns. The 'gentlest of work' could refer to the harvest of this nectar, to the act of lovemaking itself.

Folklore and Magic

Gorse was also associated with fire, on both a literal and a symbolic level. In one tale from the Fenian Cycle, the warrior Duban Donn makes a round of the Battle of the White Strand nine times, rushing about 'like flames over a high hill that is thick with furze'.[ci] Such flames were a common enough sight: burning gorse off hillsides is still widely practised. However, there is also a hint of symbolism here, for the image of burning gorse extends the plant's solar associations and resonates with the Beltaine fires that burned on many a 'high hill' in honour of Beli–Belanos in pagan times. Over such fires couples would jump in rustic fertility rites. The gorse fires, therefore, invoke their own erotic associations.

In magic, gorse is a somewhat volatile quantity to deal with. *Onn* is a chieftain-tree and very potent. It is linked to the bioenergetic activities of bees as they distil the quintessence that is nectar. Gorse flowers may be used in potions, to adorn to altars, or carried on one's person, perhaps in a pouch with other tokens of sympathetic love magic. Needless to say, the thorns of the plant should be avoided in this connection; their presence in any spell-casting is likely to backfire, perhaps spectacularly.

Lovers

卌

Úr (Heather)

Names: *úr, ura* (said OOR, OO-rah). Botanical name: *Calluna vulgaris*. Status: chieftain-tree.
Sound: u
Elaborations on the Ogam Names
Úr that is Heather.
Word Ogam of Morainn mac Moín
Heather is terrible tribe, in cold dwellings; *úr*, fresh; from *uir*, the mound of the earth.
Word Ogam of Cú Chulainn
Heather equals completion of lifelessness, the grave.
Word Ogam of Óengus
Heather equals growing of plants.

Visualization

Lovers lie in a bed of sheltering heather, on a bright hillside, under the rising sun.

Meaning

Úr is heather, the soft bed upon which lovers lie. Upright, this is a very favourable omen for a love affair or partnership, for *úr* is a tree-letter of the joys of love and romance. It tends to represent love that is meaningful and lasting, as opposed to a mere passing fancy.

In Celtic stories and folktales of epic lovers, heather often signals the point where love is consummated. In this it differs from *onn* (gorse), which is a tree-letter of sexuality itself. *Úr* is a sign of love as well as lovemaking. It signals a deepening union between lovers, a shifting from the chase to the actual meeting of primal opposites.

While this is an ogam of lovers, therefore, it also relates to partnership. At what point do lovers become partners? An important stage in this process is the acceptance of the shadow side of the other person. You may draw *úr* when there are challenges to surmount in a relationship, for heather also relates to the overcoming the psychological barriers which separate people.

There are many tales from the Celtic world of the 'beauty and beast' type. Often an ugly female figure approaches a noble warrior, demanding that he lie with her. If he accepts, she becomes the most beautiful woman in the world. This relates to moving beyond the phase of infatuation, when appearances and illusions tends to predominate, to being able to face (and embrace) the ugly, shadow side of the one you love. As the shadow is integrated, a relationship becomes more deeply grounded and puts down roots. Thus strengthened and supported, you and your lover can branch out and flower in many directions.

The traditional 'bed of heather' can also signal issues of sharing a space, of living together. Perhaps you are contemplating taking the step of moving in with your lover. Heather represents a comfortable foundation for such a transition, though it also retains its associations of passion, freedom, and open spaces. You should seek to preserve these elements within your life, especially when you live together day in and day out.

Reversed, *úr* is not the best sign for lovers. Perhaps you want more than the situation can support. Don't delude yourself or try to move too fast. Allow things to progress naturally. Likewise, in an established partnership, *úr* can suggest problems and conflicts. The shadow side may be surfacing and driving you apart. Try to be accepting and embrace whatever is occurring. A light touch will be the best approach in trying to guide affairs in a positive direction.

Keywords

Lovers, courtship, consummation. Partnership, relationship, mutual love, acceptance. Conquest of the shadow (in love), putting down roots, flowering together. Sharing a space, living together.

Reversed

Delusion, desire, problems, conflicts. Lighten up.

Natural Characteristics

Úr may originally have signified the Earth or the soil itself, as implied by the Word Ogams. Heather is, of course, a plant that flourishes on hillsides, moorland, and heath. Like gorse and similar bushes, it grows across the land rather than reaching upwards as trees do. This earthy predisposition, and the softness of the 'bed' it naturally forms, have established its close association with the Earth and intimate connection to love and passion in folk culture. Furrowed earth is itself a symbol of a fertile womb waiting to be inseminated.

Heather has tough stalks and bears little flowers of red, purple, or bluish hue. These are especially favoured by bees which congregate to gather its pollen in large numbers in summer. A hillside covered with heather is fair to see. Its association with female figures (indeed, goddesses) in Celtic times is echoed in the fact that Heather remains a popular name for girls, especially in Scotland.

Storylines

As mentioned, it is often upon a bed of heather that love is consummated in Celtic story and legend, and whereas gorse appears to embody sexuality itself, *úr* seems to represent the point where the shadows separating lovers are dissolved and they are truly and fully united in love.

It is instructive to note the timing of heather's appearance in *Tóruigheacht Dhiarmada Agus Ghrianne* (*The Pursuit of Diarmaid and Gráinne*), a tale from the Fenian Cycle which is replete with treelore. The renegade lovers Diarmuid and Gráinne are on the run from Finn, who is Gráinne's betrothed and Diarmuid's lord. Gráinne has forced Diarmuid to flee with her, using a *geiss* (magical taboo), but he stubbornly keeps faith with Finn, leaving unbroken bread on the trail as a sign that he has not taken Gráinne as his own. Finally, however, Diarmuid succumbs to her

charms and 'it was broken bread he left after him' the morning
after. A little later, Finn performs a divination ritual and espies
the bed on which the lovers are lying:

> [O]ne time [Finn] made out they were on a mountain, for he saw them
> with heather under them; and it was beside the sea they were, asleep
> on heather that Diarmuid had brought down from the hills for their
> bed; and so [Finn] went searching the hills and did not find them.

The heather upon which the pair lie underlines their status as
amorous lovers and provides a soft bed from which Gráinne composes love songs to her sweetheart.

> And Grania would be watching over Diarmuid while he slept, and she
> would make a sleepy song for him, and it is what she would be saying:
> 'Sleep a little, a little, for there is nothing to fear, Diarmuid,
> grandson of Duibhne: sleep here soundly, soundly, Diarmuid, to
> whom I have given my love . . .
> 'O heart of valour of the lands west of Greece, my heart will go
> breaking if I do not see you every day. The parting of us two will be
> the parting of two children of the one house; it will be the parting of
> life from the body, Diarmuid, hero of the bright lake of Carman.'[cii]

Heather appears time and again in popular tales with Celtic roots
as the locus of the lovers' tryst, often illicit. As the errant wife in
the Scottish ballad 'Black Jack Davey' cries to her jealous husband, when he tries to tempt her back to the good life:

> What care I for your goose-feather bed
> with sheets turned down so bravely
> when I may lie on the cold, ploughed ground
> along with Black Jack Davey?
> Then I'll kick off my high-heeled shoes
> all made of Spanish leather
> and I'll put on my lowland brogues
> and trip it o'er the heather!

This is not to say that heather's associations lie solely with adul-
terous love, but heather is here allied with the 'ploughed ground'
of the field, and thus the receiving embrace of the female. If there
is a diabolical edge to amorous folkloric figures like Black Jack
Davey who haunt the heathland, it may come with the territory,
for the 'earth' of the original 'úr' is the domain of fertility spirits
and the procreative energies of the old gods.

Folklore and Magic

The heather is a crucial location in another popular ballad which recalls an ancient Celtic theme. In the folk song 'King Henry', while out hunting the King encounters a hideous hag with teeth like 'tethered stakes' and lank hair; altogether a 'thing that comes from hell'. She instructs him to make a bed for them to sleep on, warning him 'you must pull the heather green, and make it soft for me'. Henry cannot refuse and must bed her, but on the morrow she turns out to be 'the fairest lady that ever was seen', stretched out beside him. This is an old Celtic *fabula*, an archetypal tale whose psychological interpretation can be explained in Jungian terms as the conquest (or integration) of the shadow. Until we embrace the dark side of the one we love, we are condemned to misperceptions and fruitless shadow play.

In magic, sprigs of heather may be employed to charm the nuptial bed, or better still, heather itself used as a bed on which to celebrate the act of love. The *úr* ogam, or a stave made from a twig of heather, may also be employed in spells of the love-magic variety. (This is most appropriate to an existing liaison that needs strengthening, whereas the previous ogam, *onn*, relates more directly to the chase.)

Spiritedness

Eadha (Aspen)

Names: *eadha, edha, eadhadh, eodha* (said EH-yuh) and also *edad, edhadh*. Botanical name: *Populus tremula*. Status: shrub: Sound: e

Elaborations on the Ogam Names
Horrible grief; test tree or Aspen.

Word Ogam of Morainn mac Moín
Aspen is distinguished man or wood,
a name for the trembling tree.

Word Ogam of Cú Chulainn
Aspen, kinsman to the birch, aspen.

Word Ogam of Óengus
Aspen: additional name for a friend.

Visualization

A shimmering aspen tree lit by moonlight, its leaves a raiment of gaping and grimacing faces.

Meaning

Eadha is the aspen or white poplar. As we shall see, this 'trembling' tree has associations with testing and the conquest of fear. It augurs an issue – vocational, romantic, financial, or spiritual – that you must confront and overcome. This is a sore trial which must be undergone; yet, on a positive note, you will emerge stronger and wiser for it.

Fear is a palpable physiological reaction: when we are terrified we literally tremble like the aspen tree quivering in the wind. Fear can paralyse the central nervous system and leave us immobilized and robbed of freedom of action. Our fear is often a greater adversary to us than the things we are afraid of; it can stunt our ability to live life to the fullest. Some people abide continually in this state, which is a debilitating condition.

Yet fear is also there for a reason. It pinpoints issues that we must respond to and address, however uncomfortable the process. The shadows which are so threatening actually carry a message in their bony fingers. As such, your fear can be your teacher, highlighting weaknesses and showing you where you need to strengthen yourself.

So it is that the conquest of fear involves accepting and embracing one's own personal darkness. This is an archetypal rite of passage that can be seen in the hero's quest in ancient sagas, or in the tale of the shaman who must journey into the frightening realms of the spirit world and return with the fruits of healing and wholeness for the wider community. Thus fear actually becomes a friend and ally, the 'additional name for a friend' of the *Word Ogam of Óengus*.

Reversed, *eadha* signifies being overwhelmed by the fears and shadows of the dark side of the imagination. While real terrors do exist, you are allowing them to assume a greater stature in your mind than they deserve. Remember, outer circumstances can only fully triumph over you when your spirit had been vanquished. Do not let this happen: become the master of your fear.

Keywords
Fear, testing, right of passage. Conquest of fear, 'feeling the fear and doing it anyway', befriending one's fears. Warrior spirit, spiritedness, self-confidence. Steadfastness, courage, resolution.

Reversed
Being overwhelmed by fear, need to master your fear.

Natural Characteristics

Aspen is the smallest member of the poplar family, a short lived species that begins to fail after sixty-odd years of growth. Poplars grow rapidly in their early years, however, attaining to heights of a hundred feet (sixty to seventy for aspen). They are lowland and valley-loving trees that crave moisture and often grow along river banks.

The Latin name of the aspen reveals one of its most significant features: it is *Populus tremula* – the trembling poplar. Aspen's long stalks and flattened, upright leaves means that it trembles at the slightest movement of wind; all the more so as this member of the poplar family haunts open spaces, such as fields, heaths, moorland, hills, and the wood's edge. This incessant movement has helped establish its aura as a tree and tree-letter connected to the world of the invisible.

Storylines

The theme of aspen's trembling leaves is widespread in Celtic lore. Mad Suibhné sings of it in his shamanistic ecstasy, where the aspen's trembling seems to augur battle:

> The aspen a-trembling;
> By turns I hear
> Its leaves a-racing –
> Meseems 'tis the foray!

The Word Ogams link aspen to testing and 'horrible grief', yet it is also noted as a 'distinguished man or tree', 'kinsman of the birch' and is associated with friendship. What does all this signify? First of all we need to look at the significance of aspen's trembling nature. Jacqueline Memory Paterson writes:

Aspen, the smallest member of the poplar family, is also known as the 'trembling', 'shaking' or 'quivering tree', for its leaves and branches move continuously upon the slightest of breezes. Because of its rustling leaves it is also called the 'whispering tree'. In ancient days the wind was regarded as a messenger of the gods and anything closely attuned to it, like the aspen, was considered sacred.[ciii]

Wind is, of course, a traditional symbol of spirit and the trembling of the aspen therefore implies the activity of spirits. It also represents the invisible realm being made visible, as the unseen influence of the wind creates rippling effects in the world of the seen. Aspen's trembling and quivering nature naturally associated it in the Celtic and classical worlds with fear and religious ecstasy.

In a tale from the Fenian Cycle, the great hero Osgar is likened to the aspen tree, in the same breath as a reference to the wind, signalling to us that aspen is acting as a meaningful marker within the story of a coming test of strength. Osgar must fight the High King of Ireland himself, in defence of the Fianna, and he indeed shows that great courage in the face of adversity that the Celts so admired.

> But as to Osgar himself, that began the day so swift and so strong, at the last he was like leaves on a strong wind, or like an aspen tree that is falling . . . When he saw the High King near him, he made for him like a wave breaking on the strand; and the king saw him coming, and shook his greedy spear, and made a cast of it, and it went through his body and brought him down to his right knee, and that was the first grief of the Fianna. But Osgar himself was no way daunted, but he made a cast of his spear of the nine spells that went into the High King at the meeting of his hair and the beard, and gave him his death . . . And then he himself fell like a king.[civ]

Osgar surmounts the trial of the aspen even in death. He represents the ideal of Celtic warrior society, by conquering his fear, being in 'no way daunted' despite terrible injury, and dying heroically. While the hero's death enjoyed by Osgar may not move our sympathies much today, we can recognize stoical endurance in his stance.

It is also important that in the Ogam sequence aspen comes before yew, which is the tree of death and immortality. It would seem that aspen's fearful aura stems in part from the fact that it represents the point where the veil between this world and the next is very thin; a frightful juncture for most people. Yet we are encouraged to face even this with courage and forbearance, as Osgar did. To pass the 'terrible test' of the aspen tree is to deserve the title of 'distinguished man' or woman alluded to in the *Word Ogam of Morainn mac Moín*, the mantle accorded to someone who can embrace death itself as a natural end to this cycle of earthly life.

Moreover, the *Word Ogam of Cú Chulainn*'s kenning, which calls aspen the 'kinsman to the birch', reminds us of the fact that death and birth were intimately linked in Celtic thought and that heroism was fuelled by the knowledge that after death one could look forward to the cauldron of rebirth in Tir na nÓg, the Land of Eternal Youth. Thus aspen comes to symbolize the conquering of fear appropriate to those who know they will be reborn in the Otherworld in another round of earthly experience. (As a classical parallel, the white poplar appears in the *Odyssey* as one of the Three Trees of Resurrection.)

Folklore and Magic

Aspen's use in the construction of shields has lent it magical associations as a ward against fears and dangers. Its close connection with the spirit world seems to have given it a role as a type of inoculant against supernatural menaces, similar to that of rowan. Apparently, it was especially used in this capacity in spells designed to cast out fear and negativity at Samhain, in order to begin the new year with a clean slate.

It is given a similar role in Bach Flower remedies, in which it is recommended 'for the healing of fears: fear of darkness, of death, of the religious, of secrets and unknown causes, and of fear itself'.[cv] Whether as a tincture, a magical stave, or used as an ogam in inscription, *eadha* has a clear magical function: as a ward against fear and to attract the qualities of courage and strength in the face of adversity. We can invoke it for the same purposes today, by carving *eadha* on an object or carrying a sprig of it, when anticipating fearful or threatening situations.

Transition

Idho (Yew)

Names: *idho, ioho* (said EE-yoh), also *idhadh, odha, idad, edhadh*. Botanical name: *Taxus bacca ta*. Status: peasant-tree.

Elaborations on the Ogam Names
[There is no extant elaboration for this tree-letter] *Word Ogam of Morainn mac Moín*
Yew is oldest of woods,
a name for a service-tree.
Word Ogam of Cú Chulainn
Yew equals essence of a sick man,
people or an age.
Word Ogam of Óengus
Yew equals abuse for an ancestor
or pleasing consent.

Visualization

A great yew tree stands in a dark grove, the gaping hollow of its trunk opening like a gateway.

Meaning

Idho, yew, is a tree of transition. It represents on the one hand things passing, ending and dying. One aspect of your life is fading away, ceasing to be. This is often a difficult or painful thing to accept. Yet *idho* also signifies that which is about to be reborn. It ushers in the new and draws our attention to the continuous cycle of endings and beginnings.

Yew traditionally stands as a gateway tree in Celtic thought. Its dark, hollow trunk marks it as an exit into the realm of the departed. Its bleak mouth draws in, swallows and consumes the things in your life which are withered and passing. There are many things which correspond spiritually to the archetype of death. A phase of your life, relationship, vocation, place of residence or some other matter is coming to an end. Yew houses the dead. This is a threatening thing to face, as we all become attached to the fixtures of our lives. However, without the old being cleared away, there would be no room for the new.

Viewed thus, the dark mouth of the yew takes on a new significance. It is not simply the menacing entrance to the underworld, but a gateway into another space, a portal to a new life. It takes you through and beyond whatever is ending in your life to the domain of that which is genuinely new. *Idho* thus links back with the first ogam (*beth*, birch, birth) in a typically Celtic theme of rebirth. To the Celts, nothing was final. When we look at Celtic knotwork, we see the lacertine pattern in which a single line passes under and over itself again and again, like the soul through its transformations and incarnations.

Reversed, *idho* can signify an actual death. Death is something none of us likes to think or talk about, and is especially taboo in modern culture. One of our greatest challenges it to transform this perspective. Death is threatening and beyond our comprehension: it involves anguish and suffering for those left behind. But since death is universal and inescapable, what might this great rite of passage be teaching us about our place in the natural order of things?

Keywords
Transitions, things ending, passing, dying, fading away, withering. An exit, a gateway, a grave, a sign of death. Transformation, renewal, rebirth. An opening, a new element approaching.

Reversed
Death, grief, pain, acceptance.

Natural Characteristics

Yew once inhabited the primordial coniferous forests of ancient Europe, prior to the triumph of the broadleaf. Apart from being a very ancient type of tree, it is also extremely long lived, the 'oldest of woods' in the words of the *Word Ogam of Morainn mac Moín*. There a number of yews around the British Isles that predate Christ, and the Fortingall Yew in Perthshire, Scotland, is said to be nine thousand years old!

Yew has poisonous seeds, was used in the construction of longbows and arrows, and has a long-standing association with death. Also significant here is the way in which a yew's trunk hollows out as the tree ages. These hollows, with their fluted openings, appear as symbolic gateways into the dark and chthonic realms, reflected in the fact that yews are often found in church yards. This and the fact that yew is evergreen lends it an ageless quality, an enduring association with immortality. Yet yew is also one of the first trees to flower in spring, symbolizing rebirth.

Storylines

Yew is beyond any shadow of doubt a tree identifiable with death, rebirth, and thus immortality. Its role in this connection is too well known and widely attested in European treelore to need much elaboration here. In the Graeco-Roman world it was connected to the funereal goddess Hecate, as echoed by Shakespeare when he places in his witches' cauldron

> . . . slips of yew
> Silver'd in the Moon's eclipse.[cvi]

Yew's function as a symbolic entry point to the land of the dead and the Otherworld beyond is illustrated in a great number of Celtic tales and folklore. With *eadha* (aspen, the preceding ogam) you can read how Finn and the Fianna must confront the Shapes (or spirits) they have offended in the Valley of the Yew Tree (that is, in the realm of the dead). Yew can barely be mentioned without death occurring in the same breath. In the Mythological Cycle, the goddess Aine, the daughter of the sea god Manannán, is revealed as a dangerous woman to offend. She not only has power to grant the gifts of life – healing, love, poetry, and music – but can also deal out death using a magical yew tree.

> And it was no safe thing to offend Aine, for she was very vengeful. Oiliol Oluim, a king of Ireland, killed her brother one time, and it is what she did, she made a great yew tree by enchantment beside the river Maigh in Luimnech, and she put a little man in it, playing sweet music on a harp. And Oilioll's son was passing the river with his step-brother, and they saw the tree and heard the sweet music from it. And first they quarrelled as to which of them would have the little harper, and then they quarrelled about the tree, and they asked a judgement from Oilioll, and he gave it for his own son. And it was the bad feeling about that judgement that led to the battle of Magh Mucruimhe, and Oilioll and his seven sons were killed there, and so Aine got her revenge.[cvii]

The little man within the hollow of the yew tree playing his harp may be a chthonic spirit, a survival from the 'evil' Fomóri or Fir Bolgs, who are even older than the Túatha dé Danaan. He leads the clan of Oilioll to their deaths, symbolically speaking, through the portal of the yew.

The immortality theme connected to yew is beautifully illustrated by a common Celtic *fabula* involving epic lovers. The most famous version of the legend involves Yseut and Tristan. After their deaths, they are buried side by side. Two yew trees are planted over their graves and magically entwine their branches in an immortal embrace. Enraged, Yseut's husband King Mark orders the trees cut down, but they regrow and after the third felling Mark admits defeat. The yew trees have signalled a love that lasts beyond the grave. A similar tale is told of the lovers Noísiu and Deirdré, whose tragedy occupies the eighth- or ninth-century *Longes mac Nusaig* (*The Exile of the Sons of Usnech*). Yew stakes are driven through the lovers' bodies to keep them apart, but instead they sprout and become trees whose tops embrace over Armagh Cathedral.[cviii]

Death was not the morbid matter to the Celts that it tends to be for us today. Nor did they imagine a grim and dour afterlife such as the gloomy Hades, Land of Shades, of Graeco-Roman religion. While warriors gained special favour in Tír na nÓg, the many coloured islands of the Land of the Ever Living appear to be open to all. Repatriation with loved ones, fun, feasting, play, and plenty await the dead in otherworldly locales replete with beautiful woods, sandy beaches, and luxurious duns. The belief in 'transmigration of souls' (reincarnation, essentially) also meant that death was by no means the end of the story, as far as earthly life was concerned.

Folklore and Magic

One of the 'Five Magical Trees of Ireland' felled by Christians was a yew. This 'stately bole' was the Tree of Ross, an ancient totemic entity praised as 'a firm and straight deity'.[cix] Yew's associations with the spirit world are revealed by the fact that yew staves were also used in druidic magic, including divination, as when the Druid Dallán uses 'wands of yew' carved with Ogam to divine the whereabouts of a missing woman.

Many churchyard yews are older than the church, suggesting that the early Christians capitalized on the yew cultus by building their structures next to these hoary trees. As Suibhné says in *Buile Shuibni* (*The Frenzy of Suibhné*): 'O yew-tree, little yew-tree/in churchyards thou art conspicuous.' Yew was so closely associated with the graveside that it later became customary to plant it churchyards, gaining it the title of 'cemetery tree', and demonstrating a continuity of symbolism which may stretch back to the most ancient of times.

While yew trees are great aids for mediating on acceptance of mortality, or intimations of immortality, especially when the yew is large and old enough to actually climb inside its hollow, *idho* is not to be invoked in magic, out of respect for its great and sovereign power.

The Four Treasures

And they brought from the four cities their four treasures: a Stone of Virtue from Falias, that was called the Lia Fál, the Stone of Destiny; and from Gorias they brought a sword; and from Finias, a Spear of Victory; and from Murias the fourth treasure. The Cauldron that no company ever went away from unsatisfied.

from *Cath Tánaiste Maige Tuired* (*The Second Battle of Moytura*)

Destiny

The Stone

Treasure: Lia Fál. City: Falias. Direction: North. Region: Ulster. Correspondence: Fate and destiny.
Why is a stone hard?
Why is a thorn sharp?
What is as hard as a stone
and as salty as salt?
        Taliesin[cx]

Visualization

A grey standing stone on a green hilltop presides over the surrounding landscape.

Meaning

Drawing this Treasure represents your destiny coming to the fore and taking you by the hand. Lia Fál is the Stone of Destiny brought from the city of Falias and, according to legend, installed on the hill of Tara in County Meath, Ireland. This stone reputedly cried aloud at the approach of a High King, in a myth similar to Arthur's having to draw the sword from the stone before taking his place as ruler of Camelot.

Whereas the Spear (see the Third Treasure) signifies your own creative will, which allows you a degree of control over your destiny, the Stone corresponds to the deepest, innermost purpose of your earthly existence. Every living being has a place and role to play within the larger cosmic design, and the appearance of the Stone in this reading is a sign that your own, unique fate-path is unfolding before you.

The Tara stone, as it was known, was placed at the mystical centre of Ireland, just as the oracular shrine of Delphi was considered the *omphalos* (navel) of ancient Greece. We can relate this in personal terms to the philosopher's stone that lies within us all: the source of insight and guidance that leads us unerringly towards our higher path.

The calling out of the Stone corresponds to the inner cry of recognition you experience when you harmonize with your true purpose. We still talk about a person's vocation as their 'calling', suggesting that one has been called to fulfil the law of one's being. Here, you answer the call and thereby discover the meaning of your life.

Reversed, the Stone of Destiny spells difficulty in the quest for meaning and purpose in life. Perhaps you are stumbling in the labyrinth, lost as if in catacombs of stone, drawn this way and that by conflicting forces. Stop dead still and take some time to listen quietly for the answer to your questions. There is a unique path for you waiting to be discovered, if only you search hard enough. Visualize a magical stone which whispers its secrets to your listening ears. What is it trying to say, and where might it be leading you?

Keywords
Destiny, your innermost purpose, your role in the cosmic design. One's fate-path, vocation or calling. Life's meaning.

Reversed
Difficulties in the quest; stumbling, being lost, conflicting forces. The need to find and follow guidance.

Storylines

The Lia Fál originated in the otherworldly city of Falias, which lay (symbolically speaking) in the northern quadrant. We should recall that in Celtic tradition the north was a mystical place connected to the Hyperboreans, otherworldly tribes from whom the Túatha dé Danaan themselves were descended. The root word *fál* means 'truth' or 'destiny', hence Falias and Lia Fál or the Stone of Destiny. From the realm of the old gods located in the north, therefore, comes the stone which betokens the fate of the land.

It may seems strange that, given this northwards orientation, the Stone is associated with the mystical centre of Ireland. Tara, after all, actually lies considerably south, in County Meath. Yet the direction of north was itself connected with the notion of the sacred centre, with the pole star (or Nail of the North) being regarded as a kind of still-point or pin around which the Wheel of the Cosmos revolves. Tara takes on a similar role in relation to the land: it is the axis around which the provinces of ancient Ireland constellate.

The notion of an *omphalos* at the mystical heart of the land is a common one. Delphi is famous as the navel of Greece, and oracular temples were consequently built there. Norse mythology has its sacred mountain at the centre, a function shared with the world tree, Yggdrasil. We can even draw a parallel with the massive Uluru (Ayers Rock) in Australia, which Aboriginal tribes regard as the rock of creation and central point towards which all their 'songlines' lead. In fact, most traditional cultures across the world share in this symbolism.

In Ireland, the Coronation Stone at Tara was immensely important, for it oversaw the crowning of kings. The legend which says

that the Tara Stone cries out at the approach of a High King is paralleled not only but the sword-in-the-stone theme of Arthurian
myth, but is related to Irish tales of heroes or rulers whose feet fit
perfectly into a set of mysterious footprints frozen in rock. But what
does this all mean? The underlying idea is simple: in each case the
land, the Earth itself, must identify and approve that one who is to
rule it. The ancient Earth powers thus bless the ruler and enter into
a sacral partnership with him, often symbolized by the king's marriage to an otherworldly maiden (the goddess of sovereignty).

Finally, this geomantic mapping of ancient Ireland into a
centre surrounded by four quarters is echoed in the design of the
game of *fidchell* or *brannumh* which figures so frequently in Celtic
myth, often translated as 'chess'. In this game, the king sits at the
centre of the board, assailed by forces which spring from the four
sides and represent the other four provinces. One Irish bardic
poem reads: 'The centre of the Plain of Fál is Tara's Castle,
delightful hill; out in the very centre of the plain, like a mark on
a party-coloured Brannumh board.'[cxi]

Board games were widely linked to divination in the ancient
world. Divination is, after all, a type of sacred game of fate, the
object being to wrest from the forces of chaos an ordered sense of
one's destiny and purpose in life. Thus we can link the Stone of
Destiny to a decisive moment in our own game of sacred play:
this is when our higher path and role is unfolded to us, as we
stand at the still point of our own inner centre and contemplate
the grander design.

Folklore and Magic

Irish legend regards the Tara stone (which has been moved slightly
from its original position to a nearby mound), as the real Lia Fál,
brought from Falias. It was once believed that the original Tara
Stone had been removed from Ireland and taken to Scotland, and
from thence to England. This was the Stone of Scone, brought by
Edward I from Scone to Westminster Abbey in 1296. In 1996 it
was returned to Scotland by the British government and deposit-
ed in Edinburgh Castle. However, archaeological evidence does
not support the Scottish hypothesis, so the current Tara Stone is
as close as we may get to the genuine article.

Stones in general have a deep resonance with Nature spirits

and the old gods. Although the stoneworks of Neolithic Europe (such as Newgrange, Stonehenge and Avebury) were built long before the Celts arrived in the British Isles, it is likely that the Druids employed them in some religious capacity, perhaps continuing certain rites from pre-Celtic peoples. In geomancy, stones are very grounding entities to have around us, and some practitioners of contemporary Druidry chose to construct their own more modest stone circles as sites of contemplation and seasonal ritual. In Wicca, the symbol of the encircled pentacle corresponds to the Element of Earth, and thus stones and the living soil.

Decisiveness

The Sword

Treasure: Sword of Nuada. City: Munster.
Direction: South. Region: Munster.
Correspondence: Discrimination.
I have been in a multitude of shapes
before attaining this fair form.
I have been a sword in the hand,
narrow, battle-notched . . .

Taliesin, *Cad Goddeu*[cxii]

Visualization

A shining sword hangs in the air, pointing downwards towards the Earth below.

Meaning

The Sword is both a weapon and an instrument of magical potency in Celtic myth. It is the sign of rulership, and as a treasured companion in battle it was often thought of as a living thing. We can relate this to our own warrior-selves, the aspect of our psyche concerned with defence, honour, fairness, and impartiality. Yet, on the shadow side, the Sword is also a token of battles and wounding.

The most famous sword of Celtic tradition is Excalibur, which Arthur pulls from the stone, thus proving his fitness for kingship. The sword here is clearly a symbol of leadership and strength, an embodiment of the decisive, no-nonsense nature of authority. So it is that power is like a sword: in the right hands it can uphold truth, in the wrong hands it is simply an instigator of conflict.

Whatever the power that lies in your hands, it is important to wield it with fairness and impartiality. To be able to discriminate (in the positive sense) with impartiality is important at this time. Drawing distinctions and separating out what is truly worthy from what is outmoded and useless is a vital process. But beware of taking up your sword without due cause.

Finally, the whole theme of wounding inevitably accompanies the Sword. Yet here we can see the regenerative dimension of wounds. Without a dismemberment of the parts of our lives, there would be no quest for wholeness and renewal. This Treasure differs from the *straif* ogam (whose thorns also correspond to the sword) in that it stresses this transformative aspect. Though painful, our wounds ultimately lead us to the waters of healing and renewal.

Reversed, you are living under the shadow of the sword. Is it you or another who is misusing their authority and power? The danger is that if you act blindly, you will feel the double edge of the sword you wield. Remember the old saying: 'live by the sword, die by the sword'. Alternatively, you may find yourself having to take up the sword to disentangle yourself from constricting circumstances. Cut the constricting knots and free yourself!

Keywords
Rulership, the warrior-self, strength. Also battles, wounding, conflict. Distinctions and separation.

Reversed
Misuse of power, acting blindly, the double edge.

Storylines

Núada Airgetám (of the Silver Hand) is one of the Great Goddess Dana's principal sons, and was once ruler of the Túatha dé Danaan. A kind of Gaelic Zeus, Nuada reminds us of the

Norse god Tiw or Tyr, who was a god of war and victory before
being usurped by Odin. Nuada was, similarly, a god of battles and
of battle victory, whom the Romans identified with Mars. He is a
figure of both strength and tragedy, however, for his reign was
quite literally cut short.

Like Tyr, Nuada was a god of fairness and justice, a noble ruler.
In *Cath Tánaiste Maige Tuired* (*The Second Battle of Moytura*), he
manages to obtain from the evil Fomóri an assurance that bat-
tles should always be fought with equal numbers on both sides.
This points to Nuada representing more than mere brute force:
he is an embodiment of the nobler aspects of the warrior ethos.
He bears the Sword that is a Treasure from the mystical city of
Finias.

There is a further parallel which allows us to identify Nuada
even more closely with Tyr: both fare badly in great mythological
battles, undergoing a similar sacrifice. In Norse mythology, Tyr
must place his right arm in the jaws of the terrible Fenris wolf as
a surety that the Aesir gods will not betray the beast's trust. In the
event, this trust is misplaced; Fenris snaps his jaws shut and Tyr
loses his hand. Nuada forfeits his in single combat with the fearful Fir Bolg champion, Sreng. This dark prince cracks Nuada's
shield in half and shears his arm off with one blow.

In both these mythological cycles we can see the classic tale
of a god of light and fair rule being eclipsed by the powers of
darkness, who consequently unseat him from his position of
power. For, owing to a custom which decreed that a blemished
man could never rule the land, Nuada ultimately loses his
kingship.

Yet there is a regenerative element to the tale, for Nuada benefits from the ministrations of the god of medicine, Díancecht.
Díancecht makes a silver hand for Nuada, which is so skilfully
crafted that it is as strong and supple as a real one, and though
this prosthetic graft does not initially take to Nuada's flesh,
Díancecht, his son Míach and his daughter Airmid, journey to
the castle in which Nuada rests to make the king whole again:

> As they came in, they heard the king groaning, for Nuada's wrist had
> festered where the silver had joined the arm of flesh. Miach asked
> where Nuada's own hand was, and they told him it had been buried

long ago. But he dug it up, and placed it to Nuada's stump; he uttered an incantation over it, saying: 'Sinew to sinew, and nerve to nerve be joined!' and in three days and nights the hand had renewed itself and fixed itself to the arm, so that Nuada was whole again.[cxiii]

This story is echoed in the later theme of the Grail King who, holed up in his castle in the wasteland, suffers from a wasting wound. The questing knight must find the King and ask him the crucial question, 'What ails thee?' before healing can take place.

Psychologically, there is a deep lesson in all this. Nuada is a warrior type who literally lives by the sword. Even though he also has noble qualities, the fact is that a sword cuts both ways and ultimately the bearer suffers wounds in the battlefield. This wound however, is transformative, for it leads to a new order. Despite his limb being restored, Nuada ultimately gives up the throne (which has been given back to him), offering it instead to the sun god Lugh. He wisely recognizes when to put the sword of rule to one side and allow another, brighter force to wield power.

Folklore and Magic

We have seen how swords in early Celtic society were regarded as living entities. Swords are used today in rituals by some Druidical orders, and they also figure in some of the stricter, more traditional orders of Ceremonial Magic. The tool in contemporary Paganism most closely resembling the sword is the *athame* (ritual knife) widely used by Wiccans to cast circles, though some groups also employ swords in some of their workings. The idea is that the blade as it passes through the air creates a special, sacred space within the circle: an area which is separated out from ordinary reality and sanctified.

I know a woman who had a powerful visionary experience in which a sword was gifted to her by the higher powers, with the admonition that she wield it responsibly. In those rare circumstances where she finds herself under attack or events conspire to undermine her security, she visualizes taking up this sword in her hands and cutting the problem or individual down to size, as it were. Thus, we can use magical tools without the need for actual, physical weapons.

Initiative

The Spear

Treasure: the Spear of Lugh. City: Gorias.
Direction: East. Region: Leinster.
Correspondence: Will and initiative.
I have cast my spear
into the camp of Eogan Indberg;
I do not know, famous its path,
whether my shot hit or missed.
    From *Serglige Con Culainn Inso Sis*
    (*The Wasting Sickness of Cu Chulainn*)[cxiv]

Visualization

A spear flies through the air, sparks flying from its tip like the rays
of the sun.

Meaning

The fiery Spear of Lugh, weapon of the Celtic sun god, represents
the directed will. It is a symbol of initiative, teaching that applying determination to circumstances helps make manifest your
dreams and goals. Like a spear speeding towards its target, your
focus takes you to the exact point you wish to reach.

Fire is an element of great energy and potency. It has both
creative and destructive potential, and must be handled with
wisdom and care. Human mastery of fire has, along with the
dangers, opened all sorts of possibilities for improving our lot
which otherwise would never have been possible.

In Celtic myth, Lugh possesses a magical spear which burns
with unbearable heat. It is so powerful that it sends itself speeding towards its target, smiting enemies which stand in its path.
This may be likened to the will and its fiery intensity. Rightly
wielded, such an instrument is invaluable; we need our will in
order to actually accomplish what we set out to achieve.

It probably won't escape your attention that the spear is a
phallic emblem, matching the ancient idea that the sun is the
head of a member whose dripping rays fertilize the Earth below.
Masculine, solar force dominates society today, yet such fiery

willpower and initiative when misdirected blazes destructively, threatening to destroy us all. Under direction of the higher self, however, the will actually *co-creates* rather than ravaging and laying waste. Use your will and its powers of manifestation wisely, and success will follow suit.

Reversed, we are made mindful of the fact that the Spear of Lugh was a dangerous weapon. It blazed with such heat that it needed to be bathed in nine cold baths (or, sometimes, the Dagda's Cauldron) in order to cool it sufficiently from its battle-lust. Similarly, the will can sometimes become your master, turning your higher self into a slave. Motivation and initiative are vital, but do not become a pawn to your needs and desires.

Keywords
The directed will, initiative, determination. Energy and potency, accomplishments, masculine force.

Reversed
Overweening ambition, battle-lust, enslavement.

Storylines

Lugh (Lleu, in Welsh mythology) is the Celtic sun god. In the Mythological Cycle he is described in these glowing terms: 'the brightness of his face was like the setting sun, so that they were not able to look at him because of his brightness.'[cxv] He lent his name to the great Fire Festival of Lughnasa (1 August, in the Old World) and is remembered in the name of the French city of Lyons, among others.

Lugh became chief of the gods by displaying mastery of many arts: he was a lore-master, healer, wizard, smith, harper, hero, and poet. There is a famous story of how Lugh gained entrance to the Realm of the Gods. He arrives at its entrance and proclaims his mastery as a *fidchell*-player, but the doorman answers laconically that they already have a chess player. And so Lugh boasts of his mastery as a harpist, but the doorman gives the same reply, and so on. Finally, Lugh asks the doorman if the gods have a hero who is master of all these arts, and the doorman grants him entrance, so that he may be tested.

Lugh's reign is a golden era in Irish mythology. He leads the Túatha dé Danaan to victory against their enemies the Fomóri, killing their king, Balor, by casting a stone from his sling into

Balor's baleful eye. But it is the Spear of Victory, forged for Lugh by Goibnui in the *Cath Tánaiste Maige Tuired* (*The Second Battle of Moytura*), which is the sun god's most prized possession

> He also had a magic spear, which, unlike the rod-sling, he had no need to wield himself; for it was alive, and thirsted so for blood that only by steeping its head in a sleeping draught of pounded poppy leaves could it be kept at rest. When battle was near, it was drawn out; then it roared, and struggled against its throngs; fire flashed from it; and, once slipped from the leash, it tore through and through the ranks of the enemy, never tired of slaying.[cxvi]

There is a wonderful description of the forging of spears in the Mythological Cycle which we can relate imaginatively to the creation of Lugh's fiery spear. It is described how before a battle the arms-makers of the Túatha dé Danaan would slave at their craft over enchanted weapons. At this time, Goibniu the Smith has special cause to vent his fury at the forge:

> And it was while Goibniu was making spear-heads for the battle of Magh Tuireadh, a charge was brought against his wife. And it was seen that this was heavy news to him, and that jealousy came on him. And it is what he did, there was a spear-shaft in his hand when he heard the story, Nes its name was; and he sang spells over the spear-shaft, that any one that was struck with that spear afterwards, it would burn him up like fire.[cxvii]

Lugh's spear was so ferocious in battle that it became known as the Spear of Victory. This weapon of the sun god was obviously part of an important theme in Celtic culture. Lugh's Welsh counterpart, Lleu Llaw Gyffes, requires the assistance of the magician-god Gwyddyon to trick the goddess Arianrhod, who has him imprisoned, into arming him with the weapons of manhood, including a spear. The solar hero Cú Chulainn's favourite instrument of war was also the spear.

Psychologically, the fiery spear that obeys no law but its own is a good symbol for a person's will and initiative. These are very powerful and useful forces, but like the Spear of Lugh, their heat and hunger for victory can also make them dangerous. Remember that Lugh's spear had to be cooled off in the Dagda's Cauldron when it was at rest. This symbolizes the balancing of outward, phallic heat and energy with the 'feminine' waters of the womblike cauldron.

Folklore and Magic

Spears and wands continued to carry magical associations well after the late Bronze Age warrior culture of Western Europe was eclipsed by the more civic Romans. You may be familiar with the legend from the twilight Celtic world of the Arthurian tradition, in which the Spear of the Grail (which was used to wound Christ in the side) became a sort of sacred emblem.

Spears do not, however, figure widely in modern magic. They are usually replaced by the wand, which is an object of power used in manifestation and transformation rituals. We can also visualize our will as a fiery spear being directed towards its target, without having to necessarily manufacture one. However, wands are marvellous and magical instruments. Modern Wiccan celebrations of Beltaine often employ the wand as a phallic symbol, which a young man (masquerading as the May King) dips into a ritual chalice held by a young woman (playing the part of the May Queen). This further underlies the symbolic identification of the spear or wand with the penis.

Abundance

The Cauldron

Treasure: Cauldron. City: Murias. Direction: West. Region: Connacht. Correspondence: Wealth, abundance, plenty.

I invoke the land of Eiru!
The shining, shining sea!
The fertile, fertile hill!
The wooded vale!
The river abundant, abundant in water!
The fishful, fishful lake!
    Toghairm na hÉireann (Amergin's Invocation
    of Ireland)

Visualization

A cauldron of bronze embellished with scenes of plenty, spilling over with the nuts, fruits, and grains of the Earth.

Meaning

This Treasure symbolizes abundance, for from the festooned Cauldron of the Dagda in Celtic legend spring all the gifts of earthly and otherworldly sustenance. Drawing the Cauldron augurs a time of plenty and freedom from want, when the cornucopia of Nature's bounty is being poured upon you.

On the most literal level, a cauldron is a large container which can hold a considerable volume within itself. It represents fullness, the wine of life coming to the top of your cup. On a deeper level, the cauldron is a magical vessel that catches the wealth that springs from the natural world. After all, everything we eat, drink, and imagine we own comes from the Earth itself.

The Celts saw worldly plenty as a spiritual gift. The fertile soil and the fish-flecked sea were expressions of the generosity of the gods of land and ocean. Treated in this way, and with respect for Nature's generosity, you have every right to seek after a fair measure of the Good Life.

Whether drawing the Cauldron relates to a one-off windfall, a boost to your finances, or a general phase of abundance, you should enjoy the fruits of plenty. With careful effort, you can consolidate your position so that all things necessary for survival are manifest according to your requirements. However, abundance is more than material plenty: it also represents a state of contentment and fulfilment.

Reversed, you are likely to be suffering from lack and deprivation. Perhaps the cupboard is bare or it is difficult to get by at the moment. This is a time to focus special effort on what you need, and how in practical terms you can go out and get it. People often survive on trust, a wing and a prayer, but as the saying goes 'the gods help those who help themselves'. Seek the waters of abundance to their source, for there you will find succour.

Keywords
Gifts, earthly and of the Otherworld. Cornucopia, fullness, gifts, generosity, a boon. Contentment, fulfilment.

Reversed
Lack, deprivation. The need to exert yourself.

Storylines

There are actually three great Cauldrons of Irish and Welsh Legend: the Cauldron of the Dagda, which grants absolute abundance; the Cauldron of Ceridwen, from which dead things are reborn; and the Cauldron of Anwynn (or the Master of the Abyss), which is a mysterious and magical vessel found in the underworld. The treasure that concerns us here is the first, which is a Cauldron of Abundance.

The Dagda was the supreme god in Irish mythology (though himself the son of Dana, the Mother of the Gods). He is affectionately referred to as 'the Good God'. His palace was at Bruig na Bóinde, or Newgrange, County Meath. This is the greatest of the dwellings of the *sidhe* (the Faery Folk) and a place of wild finery. As his residence here would suggest, the Dagda is an Earth god, which is quite a different identity to that of the sky fathers common in Indo-European myth. In his great cauldron 'everyone found food in proportion to his merits, and . . . none ever went away unsatisfied'. Known as the Undry, Dagda's cauldron provides limitless succour: meat and drink, fruits and grain and plenty.

There is a rollicking tale which depicts the relationship between the Dagda and unlimited plenty. In the *Cath Tánaiste Maige Tuired* (*The Second Battle of Moytura*), from the Mythological Cycle, the Túatha dé Danaan's adversaries, the Fomóri, receive the Dagda to their camp as an honoured ambassador. In reality, however, they plan to play a humiliating trick on him. They have prepared a great feast for the Dagda in a cauldron which he is honour-bound to eat.

They poured into their king's cauldron, which was as deep as five giants' fists, fourscore gallons of new milk, with meal and bacon in proportion. To this they added the whole carcasses of goats, sheep, and pigs; they boiled the mixture together, and poured it into a hole in the ground. 'Now,' said they, 'if you do not eat it all, we shall put you to death, for we will not have you go back to your own people and say that the Formors are inhospitable.' But they did not succeed in frightening the Dagda. He took his spoon, which was so large that two persons of our puny size might have reclined comfortably in the middle of it, dipped it into the porridge, and fished up halves of salted pork and quarters of bacon.

'If it tastes as good as it smells,' he said, 'it is good fare.' And so it proved; for he ate it all, and scraped up what remained at the bottom of the hole.[cxviii]

In some versions, the Dagda then gorges himself further by rising to the occasion with a young maiden sent by the Formors to tempt him. As you can see, he was commonly portrayed in the myths as a crude, uncouth god. He was often dressed in ill-fitting rags and soiled by his excesses.

However, we should not be fooled, for the Dagda is a master of many arts whose rustic facade actually points to his festive role as a fertility deity of early folk belief. His wife was Bóann, the goddess after whom the River Boyne itself is named, and he is also the god of *draiidecht* or Druidry. His great pot belly (a doublet for the cauldron itself) actually suggests a womb, pointing to the possibility that the Dagda was once a goddess figure of earlier beliefs. His appetite confirms his role as an embodiment of an abundance which can never be exhausted.

Folklore and Magic

In later folklore, the cauldron as a symbol of plenty was transformed into high farce. You may remember the children's story of a strange, rustic couple who own a bowl of porridge which never empties, or a sack of rice that never grows less, or a flagon of wine which can never be drained. In this we can hear the distant echoes of the Cauldron of Abundance. Indeed, the pot of gold at the end of the rainbow also strikes a chord here.

In modern Druidry, the mysteries of the Cauldron of Ceridwen are central to the rites of initiation, while many contemporary Pagan circles, including Wiccan covens, possess their own sacred cauldron, as well as a chalice, which is used as a ritualistic tool. In this context it is often dedicated to the Great Goddess, and regarded not only as a symbol of abundance but as an emblem of rebirth. There are many potential uses of such a magical instrument: in one festive Midwinter gathering I attended, a huge cast-iron cauldron was used as a pot out of which mulled wine was served.

III

Ogamcasting

Is it not the cauldron of the Master of the Abyss?
At its top are rings of pearls.
It does not boil the food of a coward,
That is not its role.

Preiddeu Annwyn (*The Spoils of the Abyss*)

Ogamcasting

Ogamcasting provides a complete system of casting and spreading the Ogam tree-letters, so that you will be able to practise for yourself this anciently rooted form of divination. Before turning to the practical techniques and methods, however, you will find a section on Celtic Divination. Here you can read about other traditional forms of Celtic divination, the wider 'arts of the wise' of which Ogam once formed an vital strand. An understanding of the importance of divination in Celtic society is valuable: after all, a whole Druidic class, the Ovates, were dedicated to the art. Viewed in this context, Ogam can be seen as one of range of traditional techniques designed to provide us with vital information about the flow of events in our lives, develop our powers of perception and psychic abilities, and establish a dialogue with the divine realms.

Next comes a section called the Ogam Revival, which gives a background to the contemporary rebirth of Ogam, providing some sense of context as to how and why Ogam has been reborn in our age. This will also help explain the otherwise baffling divergences between various commentators and their approaches to the tree-letters, thus avoiding confusion for those already familiar with, or interested in exploring, other systems of Ogam divination than the one set out in this book. The following section, Ogam Divination, provides a general orientation within this magical field of practice and experience.

We then move on to the Practical Work. Here you will learn the rituals of making, keeping, and using a set of Ogam divination-sticks. The simple procedures outlined will enable you to access with ease the wisdom of the Ogam. Finally, there are presented five spreads and castings, along with sample readings, which provide the basic models for divining with Ogam. Thus you can observe Ogamcasting methods as they work in practical, real-life situations. As I point out at this juncture, these methods are my own favourites from an almost infinite variety of possibilities, though each is tried and true. Practical experience will provide you with the tools to innovate your own approach, in the longer term.

Celtic Divination

In order to understand the underlying theory of Ogam divination, it is helpful to place it in the wider context of divination in the Celtic world and the world vision of which it is an integral part. Ogam is just one of many procedures designed to enhance the psychic faculties which the Celts attributed to human beings – such as clairvoyance, prescience, and prophetic ability. A brief sketch of some of the major methods alluded to in ancient sources also helps us to distinguish what is unique and appealing about Ogam.

There is, first of all, a crucial distinction to be drawn between two classes of activity which, though interrelated, are also quite distinct. This distinction is between 'prophetic' and 'divinatory' procedures.

Rites of Prophecy

Prophecy, in its broadest sense, may be said to involve *inner revelation*, often sought in the Celtic world through ritualistic practices. The most famous example of this kind of seership is probably the *tarbh feis* (bull-feast) mentioned in a number of sources. In this rite the Druid fasts and then drinks a broth made from (or eats chunks of) bull's flesh. Visions then well up in the subject's mind, oracular answers to questions posed. A variant on this ritual, known in Scotland as the *taghairm*, involved the seer being wrapped in a bull-hide for a night, during which dreams of an oracular nature arise. Obviously, this is a ritual form few people would wish to revive today!

A famous description of the *taghairm* appears in the *Mabinogion* tale *The Dream of Rhonabwy*, where the questing hero Rhonabwy arrives at dwelling with an ancient hall inhabited by a muttering hag. In this strange abode there is 'a yellow calf-skin on the floor; a main privilege was it to any one who should get upon that hide . . . ' And get on it Rhonabwy does, with miraculous results, for 'As soon as sleep came upon his eyes, it seemed to him that he was journeying . . . ' [cxix] Like a sort of shamanic magic carpet, the calf-skin bears him aloft on a long and extremely lucid vision.

This rite recalls for us the wider theme of dreams being

oracular in their own right. It is a vast subject, much elaborated from ancient Celtic epic to more recent fairytales, and well illustrated in another of the *Mabinogion's* stories, *The Dream of Maxen Wledig.* Maxen Wledig, supposed 'Emperor of Rome', is out hunting. But he falls into a mysterious sleep and dreams vividly of a strange and far-off island with a castle in its midst. In this somnambulant state he meets a 'comely maiden', endowed with the beauty typical of otherworldly women. He falls in love with her and visits her each night for a week. Finally awakening from this reverie, he decides to search her out in the flesh. Based on his recollection of the dream journey, she is eventually located and becomes his bride. The dream, in other words, not only proves prophetic but actually directs the action of the piece!

The domain of dream draws our attention to the unconscious mind as the seat of prophetic faculties. In Ireland, there was a triplicity of rituals known as the Three Illuminations: *teinm laega* (decoding by means of verse), *díchetul do chennaíb* (psychometric composition) and *imbas forosnai* (light of foresight). The first two Illuminations probably fall more under the category of divination proper. We can, however, certainly include as prophetic the *imbas forosnai.* This celebrated rite is described in *Cormac's Glossary* (from *The Yellow Book of Lecan*) in these terms:

> *Imbas Fosonai:* the inspiration of tradition, the knowledge that discovers whatever the poet wishes to know. It is done like this: the poet chews a piece of flesh from the red pig, or of cat or dog and so chewing puts it on the flagstone behind the door. He pronounces an invocation over it and offers it to his spirits. He calls his spirits to him and if they do not reveal the matter immediately he sings incantations over his two palms and calls the spirits again to keep his sleep undisturbed. Then he lays his palms over his cheeks and so falls asleep in this posture. He is watched to ensure that nothing interrupts him until the matter is revealed to him; this may be a minute or two or three, or as long as necessary. Patrick abolished this practice . . . [cxx]

The eating of animal flesh is reminiscent of the *tarbh feis;* in fact, the two are probably the same basic rite. Central to both is a process of shamanic trance and possible spirit-journeying, in which the Druid performs a rite designed to aid the process of contacting the spirits, thus obtaining from them the information sought. The *imbas forosnai* is also described in the ancient Irish epic, the *Taín Bó Cuilnge*, where the warrior-goddess Scáthach, who trained Cú Chulainn in arms, prophesies the hero's fate: 'Scathach spoke to him of his future and his end. She chanted to him through the imbas forasnai: the Light of Foresight'.[cxxi] There follows a series of verses which outline the whole of Cú Chulainn's fateful life in advance, reminding us of the Valkyrie Brunhild from Norse mythology, who in the celebrated *Volsunga Saga* instructs the hero Sigmund.

These are only a few strands from the fragmentary remains of techniques and practices of Celtic prophecy. But we can see their survival into more recent times in the general belief in Celtic countries that some individuals are possessed of *dá sheallach* (literally 'having two sights'), commonly referred to as the Second Sight or simply the Sight. The 'superstitious' belief that certain people possess a faculty which enables them to perceive in a way that transcends the five senses, still avowed by many to this day, has deep roots in ancient Celtic shamanic practice. Such faculties were anciently believed to be special, magical skills possesses by 'the people of many arts'. Yet the rites outlined above are designed to enhance such gifts, suggesting that they could be developed by anybody. Such ritual aids to prophecy are fascinating in themselves and relate tangentially to our study of Ogam divination, yet they are not acts of divination proper.

Divination Techniques

Divination can be defined as distinct from prophecy in that it involves the observation of *outside agencies* whose chance or random configurations (of events, shapes, patterns, etc.) are read as an omen or augury relating to current (or future) circumstances. Caitlín Matthews states the distinction somewhat negatively when she says that 'many forms of divination – those that use a series of symbolic analogues which do not involve trance – are not shamanic'.[cxxii] The 'symbolic analogues' she mentions are, crucially, the signs, whether they happen to be clouds, the flights of birds, cracks in mud, or Ogam sticks, which the diviner observes. Such 'signs' are symbolic in that they are considered to represent something other than themselves and are 'analogues' because they embody patterns within which we may discern the wider shape of events, including 'that which is to come'.

We may further divide divination into 'passive' and 'active' techniques: those which simply involve observing signs (such as watching clouds for auguries) are passive, while those which (like casting Ogamfews) require the casting or spreading of an actual system of symbolic objects or divinatory tokens (sticks, runes, cards, etc.) are active forms of divination.

There is a great mass of material regarding ancient Celtic divinatory techniques. Perhaps the first and foremost class involves pure observation of Nature and its forms. Of these, the most important are weather patterns and the activities of birds and animals. *Neldoracht* (cloud-watching) is frequently described in the Mythological Cycle of Irish literature and in many historical sources. This practice survived into the Christian era: the monks at Lindisfarne of the coast of Scotland, for instance, knew trouble was in the wind when they observed a dragon flying in the heavens (probably a cloud or other meteorological phenomenon), foretelling the approach of the Vikings in 793. The *Anglo-Saxon Chronicle* entry for that year infamously reads:

> In this year dire portents appeared over Northumbria and sorely frightened the people. They consisted of immense whirlwinds and flashes of lightning, and fiery dragons were seen flying in the air.[cxxiii]

These were dire signs indeed, judging by the subsequent sack of the monastery, but whether the augury is positive or negative, divination by observation of other natural phenomena – such as winds, tides, and solar, lunar and stellar phenomena – follows a similar observational principle.

Animals (including birds and fish) form a part of the natural world and as such are also obvious carriers of meanings and knowledge. We can note how to this day the strange behaviour of domestic animals can augur an earthquake or other natural disaster. For the Celts, who lived so close to the animal world, there was a vast body of lore assisting in the interpretation of many aspects of animal behaviour. This was strengthened by the totemic identities of various animals and their links to certain tribes. It is well known, for instance, that before going into battle against the Romans the famous Queen of the Iceni, Boudicca, released a hare onto the battlefield and its movements were watched with great trepidation. It seems likely that the hare was a tribal totem whose course would have been considered as an augury on the outcome of the battle (on this occasion the Romans lost the day).

It is likely that certain animals and birds were kept for the specific purpose of divination, and the divinatory lore surrounding birds was especially well developed. Diodorus Siculus makes a point of noting that the Druids predicted the future from the flight of birds. Favourites seem to have been the raven, wren, and crane, among others. Ravens, and the rook family in general, have long been regarded in the British Isles as particularly uncanny birds, and their aura of ill-luck – especially on the battlefield – is linked to the Celtic war goddess the Mórrígu, whose totem is the raven. In folklore, it is considered extremely unlucky if a flock of crows or ravens lands on your roof, auguring death in the family.

There is also a great deal of lore attached to the wren, sacred to the Druids and kept as a bird of augury. Its Welsh name is *dryw*, which was considered in the Middle Ages to derive from the same root as *Druid*: whether factual or not, this reflects a deeply seated belief in the connections between the Druids and the wren. The crane, as we will see, was also a sacred bird, in the classical as much as in the Celtic world; its long legs, beak, and delving habits establishing a symbolic association with wisdom. We can compare this with the Egyptian identification of the beak of the ibis with the pen of the scribe god Thoth.

Obviously, the possibilities of interpretation by Nature divination are endless. Regarding more *active* forms of divination, some Druidical rites appear to lie on the borderline. The grisly form of divination alleged in Roman accounts, where the Druids supposedly observed the death-throes of a sacrificial victim, would be active, since the diviner is actively seeking out a divine sign. In a similar category is scapulamancy, divination by the shoulder-blade (usually of an ox) which is heated in a fire. The bone is then checked to see how it has fissured, these cracks being interpreted as omens. A similar art was employed in ancient China, using the so-called tortoise-shell oracle of the Shang dynasty, with the unfortunate tortoise's shell being burnt on a bed of coals and scrutinized for patterns in the cracks. Here we get a sense of the archaic roots of divinatory techniques, where codification of oracular signs was in its primitive infancy. Later there evolved, one can speculate, the use of physical divinatory tokens of human design within a pre-established system (of staves, cards, etc.), of which Ogam is an example.

The problem is that so much of this was cloaked in secrecy that we are hard pressed to know the truth of matters esoteric which were practised so long ago. Overt references to actual rituals are quite rare. In the tracts of Irish Brehon law known as the *Senchas Már*, there is occasional mention of the Brehon judges making judgements on the basis of *crannchur* or the 'casting of the woods'. In cases of questionable guilt

> the lots are cast in this manner: three lots are put in, a lot for guiltiness, a lot for innocence, and a lot for the Trinity. This is enough to criminate or acquit them. If it be the lot of the Trinity that came out, it is to be put back each time until another lot comes out.[cxxiv]

The references to the Trinity alert us to the late nature of this material, though it doubtless reflects earlier practices, possibly once involving Ogam. There are also terms in Breton (*prenn-den*) and Cornish (*teulel pren*) which connote 'the throwing of inscribed pieces of wood'.

Much has been made of references in Welsh sources to *coelbreni* or 'omen-stick divination', alleged to have been used by Druids in a type of lot-casting ritual. An earlier generation of scholars, including figures such as Lewis Spence, tended to accept these sources unquestioningly, and some modern commentators have followed suit. However, the Peithynen (elucidator) – a sort of esoteric abacus supposed to have been employed in Druidic divination – is almost certainly a product of the fraudulent scholarship of that infamous swindler (or inspired innovator) of Celtic tradition, Iolo Morgannwg. Coelbreni thus falls into a dubious category.

It may of course be that Morgannwg himself drew on (and elaborated) elements of a far more ancient tradition, now forgotten, for divination by sticks is alluded to in Welsh poetry, most notably in the medieval cycle known as the *Poems of Taliesin*. As the great bard says:

> I am Taliesin,
> Chief of the Bards of the West,
> I am acquainted with every sprig
> In the cave of the Arch-diviner.[cxxv]

The 'sprigs' with which Taliesin is acquainted seem suggestive of Ogam wands and the grove of meanings which they signify. The reference to the 'cave of the Arch-diviner' reminds us of Druidic learning in caves and cells, and thus more tangentially of the Cauldron of the Welsh witch Ceridwen, found in the underworld. Yet such fragments brings us as close as we may come to direct references to Ogam divination in the extant sources.

Ogam Theory

We now turn briefly to the operative theory of Ogam divination. It is interesting to note that Ogam commentators do not generally appear as concerned with the theory of Ogam divination as do writers in the field of runecasting. This reminds me of the Chinese perspective on the *I Ching*, commonly known in the West as *The Book of Changes*. Although there is some theorizing, particularly at later dates, the Chinese sages do not seem to have felt the need to rationalize their understanding of how their great book of divination actually works. Simplicity is the essence of Taoist thought, and it is enough to observe that the procedures do actually work and are efficacious without having to dissect them!

> The Changes have no consciousness, no action; they are quiescent and do not move. But if they are stimulated, they penetrate all situations under heaven. If they were not the most divine thing on earth, how could they do this?[cxxvi]

There is, however, a perfect explanation which expresses in contemporary terms the principle underlying Ogam divination. The relevant term here is *synchronicity*. C. G. Jung introduced this word into circulation with his work *Synchronicity: an acausal connection principle* (1952). Synchronicity comes from two Greek roots: *chronos*, meaning time, and the root *sync*, meaning to happen in unison. Thus synchronicity refers to things which happen together in time. Jung defined it as 'meaningful coincidence', focusing on how apparently random elements could come together in a way that is meaningful and purposive. We have all experienced something along these lines, such as when we are just thinking of someone or something and they appear or come up in conversation. Often synchronicities suggest underlying patterns of a mysterious yet powerful nature. They point to a significance underlying events which transcends mere chance, as we understand it.

This is the same principle underpinning Ogam divination and, in fact, all forms of divination. When you cast an Ogam twig, pull a runestone from pouch, or draw a Tarot card from the deck, that twig or stone or card will relate to your circumstances in a most uncanny way. The 'common-sense' Western explanation would be that the person concerned simply imagines or projects the meaning onto the card. People who see hidden meaning in chance events are consequently labelled gullible or misguided, at best, in our culture. But this tells us more about the incorrigible biases of the Western intellect than it does about the nature of the universe or processes of divination. For in fact the act of divination draws on the principle of synchronicity, and by acknowledging the meanings which present themselves through the diviner's art, we are simply participating in the natural processes of the universe, as the Chinese sages understood so well.

How, in practical terms, do we take advantage of this miraculous law of synchronicity, and participate in the processes of Ogam divination? Once again, the answer is as simple as it is profound. The ogam-letters are inherently meaningful. Each resonates with practical and esoteric associations. All we need to do is employ a system or technique which liberates their meaningful qualities. This is achieved by laying out the ogams using a particular spread or casting. Each position in a spread covers a particular sphere of life (such as past, present and future) and by marrying the meaning of the ogam-letter with the position in which it falls, we find its unique significance for us. Astrology works in a similar way, by relating a planet and its meanings to the house in which it happens to be at a particular time.

Practical Work

Ogam encourages you to create your own set of Ogam twigs or similar tokens. In fact, there are many possible choices, and the whole process need not take longer than an afternoon. Below we will look at the creation of a personal ogam-set. Also explored are several rituals that focus our energies on various aspects of the process, and which make it all the more powerful and effective.

1 Making Your Ogam Sticks

As we have seen, Ogam was, according to the sources, traditionally carved on wands or rods for the purposes of divination. We can compare the two versions of the only concrete description of Ogam divination found in Irish epic. In the romance of *Tochmarc Étaín* (*The Wooing of Étaín*), the king is searching for his absconded wife. We read that 'At last, a Druid named Dallán learned, by means of ogams carved upon wands of yew, that she was hidden under Mider's *sidh* (earthen mound) of Bri Leith . . . '[cxxvii] In a second version of the tale it is a Druid named Codal who performs the divination: 'Codal of the Withered Breast took four rods of yew and wrote Oghams on them and through his enchantments he found out that Étaín was with Midhir in Brí Leith.'[cxxviii] The divergence in names may suggest that the identity of the Druid concerned is less important than the fact that it is a Druid who consults the Ogam, this being one in a range of 'enchantments' that Druids perform. Aside from the carving of ogams on wands or rods of yew, this account, like the veiled references in runic tradition, leaves much to the imagination.

Yet the principles of creating an ogam-set are simple and earthy for the modern day Ovate. It is best to actually gather a set of twigs taken (with respect, of course) from the trees themselves. Thus, you have a twig of oak marked with the *duir* tree-letter, a twig of alder marked with the *fearn*, a twig of willow marked *saille*, and so on. In reality however, this is not always possible, for some 'trees', such as vine and ivy, are not suitable, and besides, you may not have access to them all or may live in a part of the world where they do not readily grow. A simple alternative is to choose one wood, ash being the most traditional, and carve twenty ash twigs or wands with the Ogam tree-letters and the Four Treasures symbols. Alternatively, you could use wooden slips made from any tree or even sections of dowel.

You can also choose to mark your wands with a number of different instruments. A blade seems best, but you could even use a pen. I personally possess an ogam-set which consists of small, round, flat stones, much like those commonly used for Runes. Each is engraved with a tree-letter and they can be pulled from a pouch like runestones are. Some might object that this is not traditional, but then, there is no evidence that the Runes were used in this way either; in fact, Runes were probably also carved on ash twigs. And besides, Ogam too was once engraved on large stones for the purposes of boundary marking and memorials. Really, you can choose your own medium and method, so long as it feels meaningful and authentic.

You will find that the gathering of your twigs, stones, or other objects is itself a ritual, and there follows a set of ritual preparations, which are designed to empower or 'charge' the act of Ogam divination.

2 Opening the Crane-skin Bag

The 'Crane-skin of Secrets' is mentioned in a legend which can supply Ogam with a myth similar to that of Odin's acquisition of the Runes at the root of the World Tree. It also sets up a type of ritual model for the storage of Ogam in a special pouch or skin bag (in true shamanic fashion).

In Irish Mythology, the sea god Manannán mac Lir possessed a magical crane-bag, the Crane-Skin of Secrets. This was said to have been made from the skin of the heroine Aoife while she was in the totemic form of the crane. This medicine bag, 'a treasure of powers with many virtues', is considered by Robert Graves to have contained the Ogam alphabet. After Manannán, the sun god Lugh got hold of it, from whom it passed to the three sons of Cermait Honeymouth (that is, Ogma), and then back to Manannán. The crane-bag's secrets are thus shared around. Cranes are associated with the wisdom of the goddess and divination – their flight being interpreted, along with that of other birds, in divinatory rituals, as we have seen. In Geoffrey of Monmouth's *Vita Merlini* (*Life of Merlin*), it is described how several chiefs observe the flight of cranes in the air whose path took them 'in a curved line in the shape of certain letters'.[cxxix] If these 'letters' were Ogam, the hypothetical link between the crane and the Tree Alphabet would be strengthened.

In any case, this provides a mythological precedent for keeping Ogam cards or twigs ritually enclosed (when not in use) in a leather or cloth bag symbolically representing the Crane-skin of Secrets, just as the *I Ching* is traditionally bound or wrapped in yellow cow-hide in China. Once again, it is best to make your own bag (not, it should be added, at the expense of a crane!). Leather is best, though fine cloth is perfectly suitable.

Thus the authentic Ogam will consist of a bundle of twigs or other objects personally gathered and kept in your pouch, itself regarded as a shamanic tool or 'power object', to borrow from contemporary Amerindian terminology. You may also wish to somehow bless or consecrate your pouch, perhaps with words along the lines of the following.

> I dedicate this bag of secrets
> To the service of the gods
> To the good of all,
> By the crane of knowledge
> By the flight of the crane
> By the generosity of Aoife
> And the goodness of Manannán.

3 Charging and Invocations

There is also the issue of charging the ogams themselves. By charging, I am using a term from the magical tradition which refers to the consecration and empowering of talismans. Your ogams are talismans in their own right, and you may like to perform some sort of personal ritual to dedicate them to a particular purpose, such as self-knowledge, insight or healing. This could be achieved by focusing on the twig or stone in front of you (and, of course, its tree-letter) while stating out loud your intention to use your ogams for that particular role. Or, more simply, you may like to meditate on the meanings of each ogam in order, thereby following the turning wheel of the entire sequence – from *beth* (birth) to *idho* (death). Finally, you may wish to take your set to sacred places, places of power, such as mountaintops, deep woodland groves, stone circles, barrows and ancient wells. Whatever the land you live in, it will have its sacred fixtures. Seek these out and introduce them to your ogams.

We saw in Ogamlore how Ogam appears in the ancient sagas and later medieval sources as part of a ritual complex connected with solar gods. Ogma himself is a god of light, there are Word Ogams attributed to such semi-divine light-bearers as Óengus and Cú Chulainn, and the shaman-poets associated with trees of the sacred grove, such as Taliesin, 'Radiant Brow', are figures of light and enlightenment. We can, therefore, see Ogam as a tool of divine illumination, gifted to humankind by the 'shining poet', Ogma, as a system of insight and understanding. There are, as we also saw in Ogamlore, parallels across many cultures with gods who create or discover sacred alphabets or divination systems, such as Odin, Hermes, and Thoth. It makes perfect symbolic sense for such a deity to preside over the art of divination, traditionally considered a method of bringing hidden things to light.

Such legendary matter provides the basis for possible invocations or chants with which we can initiate divinatory proceedings. In contemporary Druidry, in particular, Ogam is credited with a sacral nature and its use is often embroidered with ritual. The following chant is designed to open and empower the act of Ogam divination.

> By stick and stone, and Ogam grove
> I call on Ogma Grianaineach
> The sun-faced bringer of wisdom!

> By stick and stone, and Ogam grove
> I call on the Well of Wisdom
> Found in the cave of Ceridwen!

> By Earth, Wind, Fire and Sea
> I sit within the turning wheel
> And drink from the Cup of Inspiration!

> By Earth, Wind, Fire and Sea
> I sit within the Ogam grove
> Clothed in the green robes of Druidry!

> By the word that was spoken
> Before the world began,
> Crane-Bag of Secrets, be open!

> By the word that was spoken
> Before the world began
> Awaken now these magic tokens!

As with any ritual, the point here is focus and intent, and the resonance the words and phrases carry from repetition across time and space. This is why traditional verse formulas are so often favoured, but you may wish to develop and offer your own invocation with words of special personal significance.

Spreads and Castings

As with Runes and other oracles, the possibilities for Ogam spreads and castings are endless. The five spreads which follow are drawn from a range of sources and are all, in my experience, extremely effective. My personal favourite is the Druid Spread, because of its mixture of psychological subtlety and sense of time-flow from the past into the future. However, even a simple spread, such as the first, the Three Weavers Spread, can be very illuminating. It is suitable for a quick, broad assessment of the overall flow of events, from past to present to future. The Wheel of the Year Spread is a solely predictive spread, based on placing tree-letters in the sequence of seasonal festivals which compose the ancient Wheel of the Year. This is useful for looking at the cycle connected to a major life event, such as pregnancy.

The Oracle of the Nine Mothers reproduces the simple structure of the Three Weavers Spread threefold. Three ogams are laid for each time phase (past, present, future). This is an excellent spread for scrutinizing the tendencies of your life situation along the arrow of time. I have already mentioned the Druid Spread: this spread has actually been imported from Tarot, illustrating the principle that you can easily adapt all manner of spreads and casting from outside sources. In fact, this is ultimately the way to arrive at what works best for you personally. Indeed, you may wish to evolve your own system, or improvise one according to the needs of the moment.

Finally, I have given an example of Free Ogamcasting. This is based on the most ancient form of divination, where one simply throws or casts Ogam twigs (or whatever counters you are using) onto an unmarked cloth. What is recommended here is that you interpret the ogams nearest to you as representing the past, the middle section as the present, and the furthermost as the branching possibilities of the future. Those which fall on the left-hand side represent the danger or shadow of the reading, while those which fall on the right-hand side represent the positive, progressive aspect. Meditate on this structure of meaning before casting the ogams onto your cloth. Please do note that such 'free' techniques of divination are actually the most challenging, for they require a high quotient of intuition in order to interpret the fall of the cards unaided by more defined positions. Nonetheless, with experience you may find this advanced technique grows on you.

In the five readings which follow my aim has been, as much as possible, to reflect the responses and perceptions of the people for whom the spreads or castings are being conducted. Of course, at first especially, you will probably be divining for yourself, which is in many ways ideal, so long as one does not wilfully distort the message of the oracle. You need not be a psychic and clairvoyant to divine, though practice will certainly enhance your intuition. Some people imagine that there is a taboo against performing a reading for oneself. Nothing could be further from the truth.

There is also a widespread misconception that when we do divine for another person, the diviner must act as a sort of prophet of people's circumstances. Personally, I feel that an oracle-reading should open a dialogue in which the diviner facilitates the querent's interpretation of the cards. Thus, rather than being a passive recipient of wisdom and advice, the person who consults becomes an active partner in the process, unravelling the message contained in the images and words of the oracle. Whereas the stereotypical fortune-teller panders to people's needs and compulsions regarding the future, the true diviner gently guides another person's own interpretation of the reading as it unfolds.

I: The Three Weavers' Spread

This simple spread is used in association with many oracle-reading systems and goes under various names. It relates directly to the past, present, and future. Please note, however, that I have added one position to this formula, making it in reality a four-fold spread.

The first tree-letter drawn defines the overall theme of the reading. You may wish here to *consciously choose an ogam* which represents this issue for you. Then the next three positions are laid out, sight unseen. Such a basic, introductory spread presents few problems. Though simple, it can be surprisingly effective in revealing the tendency in current events.

1

First Position: Overall theme

2   3   4

Second Position: Past   Third Position: Present   Fourth Position: Future

The Sample Reading

Reading: Jacqueline, a woman in her late twenties, was wondering about what is perhaps the most common of all subjects upon which oracles are consulted: love and romance. Her question: was a particular man appropriate for her as a lover, or should they instead remain merely friends. She felt the grip of attraction, yet something held her back; there was a threshold which she would not cross, and she was not certain why. The Three Weavers' Spread was employed, with a preceding tree-letter as the overall theme. The following was the result:

1: Present: Úr: ⫲

Úr (heather) fell in the position of the overall theme of the reading. Heather, we will recall, is a tree-letter of love and lovers, from the role of the plant in many traditional tales as the bed of passion's consummation. It is distinct from *onn* (gorse) in that gorse is an ogam of sexuality, whereas heather represents a more established mode of relationship. In the romance of *Tóruigheacht Dhiarmada Agus Ghrainne* (*The Pursuit of Diarmaid and Gráinne*) it provides a mattress on which the lovers become physically involved. And when the roistering lady in the folk-song 'Black Jack Davey' decants from a dull life with the squire, she exclaims:

Then I'll kick of my high-heeled shoes
all made of Spanish leather
and I'll put on my lowland brogues
and trip it o'er the heather.

Was it time, Jacqueline wondered, for her to kick off her boots?

2: Past: Ailm: +

Ailm (pine) is a tree-letter of elation and the Word Ogams connects it with the sound 'ahh', uttered in pain or ecstasy. It is associated with the wonder and terror of peak experiences. Jacqueline linked this few to her own erotic nature, and in particular to the enjoyment of sex. Yet at the present time she was, for some reason, holding back. Had she lost sight of the pleasure principle?

3: Present: Coll: ⅢⅢ

Jacqueline associated this ogam with a part-time course on herbalism she was sitting. She was working towards a long-term ambition to be a herbalist, and she saw her training as likenable to Finn's apprenticeship under the Druid Finegas, a time of study and reflection. (We will recall that in the myth, the lad Finn sits guilelessly on the banks on the Boyne, and as a result comes to taste of the flesh of the Salmon of Wisdom.) Her own esoteric interests also provided a sense of gradually dawning mystical enlightenment. Perhaps this was also a lesson in the value of allowing events to take their course, whatever way the tide might be flowing.

4: Future: Gort:

Gort (ivy) seemed to strike a jarring note for the prospects of the relationship at hand. Ivy is traditionally a tree-letter of tenacity, struggle and, potentially, constricting tendrils. Was this a confirmation of her misgivings, a warning against becoming embroiled in a potential love imbroglio? Jacqueline had had experiences which gave her a natural mistrust of men, and to her the words of the old folk-song 'a woman is a branchy tree, and man the clinging vine . . . ' were profoundly resonant. Yet perhaps she was also seeing a reflection of her own reluctance to get involved in a relationship in the reading. Independently minded, she relished her own time and space, and ivy seemed to her to represent all the shadow elements of romantic involvements. The counsel of this ogam seemed to be to take things slowly so as not to get to bogged down in emotional entanglements.

*

Overall, therefore, the reading augured some romantic possibility, yet counselled caution, directing Jacqueline's attention back to her own strengths and interests. *Ur*, connected as it is with love and romance, fits well as the overall theme, reflecting the nature of the question. However, while the present position could be promising, the future position warns of possible complications. Taken as a whole, she interpreted this to mean that the situation was not without potential, but that she needed to be careful to avoid the trap of having unrealistic expectations about the situation, especially in light of her own ambivalent state of mind!

II: The Wheel of the Year Spread

The Wheel of the Year is the seasonal cycle commonly celebrated in contemporary Paganism, especially its Celtic variants. The following readings involve overlaying the points of the Wheel of the Year with ogams, thus creating a divinatory analysis of an entire annual cycle. Two variants are here on offer: the Four Seasons Spread and the Eight Fold Wheel Spread. What this allows is for us to chart our progress through an entire year, with more of less detail, depending on whether you choose to use the Four Seasons or Eight Fold Wheel Spread.

The Four Seasons Spread

The Four Seasons Spread uses the four major seasonal points of the year. I have chosen the ancient Solstices and Equinoxes rather than the popular 'Fire Festivals' (see the additional points on the Eight Fold Wheel). These solar festivals are based on the proximity of the sun to the Earth, whereas the Fire festivals reflect the agricultural cycles celebrated by the Celts. However, those who wish to do so could easily substitute the Fire Festivals as the four points of the turning year. As always, do whichever you feel most comfortable with.

Either way, we simply lay out four ogams, starting with next festival from the day of the reading. This creates a seasonal fore-cast giving indications of the basic character of each of the four quarters ahead. (Remember, Ogamcasting should always be regarded as giving indications of trends rather than immutable predictions.) Alternatively, you might choose to place the first ogam on the marker for the Solstice or Equinox just passed, and allocate the following three to the spaces representing the next three seasons. That way, you can illuminate the issues of the recent past, which are sometimes just as obscure to us as the future! In the Four Seasons Spread which appears Southern Hemisphere dates are shown in parenthesis.

Summer Solstice
22 June (22 December)

Spring Equinox
22 March (22 September)

Autumn Equinox
22 September (22 March)

Winter Solstice
22 December (22 June)

Eight Fold Wheel Spread

Similar principles apply with the Eight Fold Wheel Spread as with the spread above. You simply lay eight ogams out, from the present moment till the end of a full annual cycle, or from *a point in the recent past* onwards (see below). This variant supplies more detail than the Four Seasons Spread and provides greater scope for turning the process back a season or two and therefore gaining insight into the events of the previous season. For example, it may be Midsummer, yet you lay the first ogam down for the Spring Equinox just past. This means that you can see the threads running through the past quarter: from Spring Equinox to Beltaine; into the quarter present (Summer Solstice); and on into the future with Lughnasa.

These two spreads – please note – are best used as a kind of chart against which to measure the unfolding of events and the challenges they bring. You will tend to find that the ogams laid out using these spreads correspond very closely to the unfolding of your life path. Yet ogams have many faces and do not always conform to our expectations, so don't be alarmed if a negative-seeming ogam appears in the future. It doesn't necessarily correspond to what your fears might tell you. Also, the point of Ogam and other forms of divination is to learn to work creatively and tranformationally with your future. A 'negative' omen gives you the opportunity to anticipate a difficulty and take action to avoid wrong turns in the future.

Summer Solstice
22 Jun (22 Dec)

Beltaine   Lughnasa
1 May (1 Nov)   1 Aug (1 Feb)

Spring Equinox   Autumn Equinox
22 Mar (22 Sep)   22 Sep (22 Mar)

Imbolc   Samhain
1 Feb (1 Aug)   1 Nov (1 May)

Winter Solstice
22 Dec (22 Jun)

The Sample Reading

The sample reading below was performed for Cathy, who some months before had discovered she was pregnant. This involved a considerable degree of soul-searching, for she and her partner already had two children and had been relishing the fact that they were now at school, thus freeing their time and energy for each other and outside interests. When she came for the reading, it was not hard to notice that her feelings about the pregnancy were in turmoil. Cathy consulted the Ogam at Beltaine, choosing to begin the spread four months before, at Midwinter: the time she had conceived.

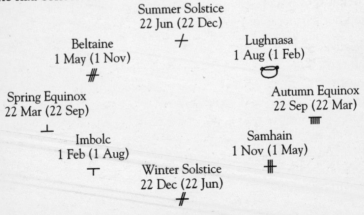

Summer Solstice
22 Jun (22 Dec)

Beltaine   Lughnasa
1 May (1 Nov)   1 Aug (1 Feb)

Spring Equinox   Autumn Equinox
22 Mar (22 Sep)   22 Sep (22 Mar)

Imbolc   Samhain
1 Feb (1 Aug)   1 Nov (1 May)

Winter Solstice
22 Dec (22 Jun)

Winter Solstice: ‡

Cathy had conceived at Midwinter. *Gort* (ivy) is generally reckoned a tree-letter of tenacity and survival. Cathy saw this as corresponding well to the depths of winter time, a dark quarter governed in nature by the stark hand of need. Yet she saw in the spiralling form of ivy an emblem of the life-force manifest in the conception of a child, thrusting itself into being, issuing forth of its own volition, whatever the plans of its parents.

Imbolc: ⊤

Imbolc was the period in which Cathy found herself to be pregnant. The tree-letter which fell in this position is *beth*, corresponding to birch. This is traditionally an ogam of birth and new beginnings – an accurate summing up of the recent past. The eruption of the new requires adjustment, especially in contemplating motherhood, with all it entails. The theme of 'birching' (ritually driving out the old to allow the new to take its place) matches the need to come to terms with this new turn of events.

Spring Equinox: ⊥

Húathe (hawthorn) is traditionally a tree-letter of trials and obstacles, by virtue of its role as a magical barrier and gateway tree to the Otherworld. Cathy saw in this a representation of her struggle to cross over into a state of acceptance regarding the changing circumstances of the time. Hawthorn's associations with defence and disputes over boundaries (we can recall the *aes* or 'satire' used by bards in which this tree is invoked against one's enemies) also suggested to her an unstated conflict between her and her partner over proceeding with the pregnancy.

Beltaine: ‖

With Beltaine, the reading reached the present. *nGétal* is, in my treatment, identified as the broom, an ogam of cleansing and purification. Cathy saw this as corresponding to the resolution of the inner and outer conflict over the unborn child. It was an emblem not only of her own renewed acceptance and focus on the future, but of the necessary re-establishment of concord with her husband. Would he come to accept the inevitable?

Summer Solstice: +

Muin (vine) at Midsummer seemed to Cathy to represent a counterpoint to *gort* at Midwinter. Both plants are sinuous climbers: the vine is nonetheless distinguished from ivy by being a fruit-bearing tree, with associations of harvest and pleasure. Cathy saw in this an image of the festive season ahead, a time flowing with favourable conditions and experiences, as the peak of the Wheel of the Year was reached; it also matched the mysteries of fermentation brewing within her own womb!

Lughnasa: The Cauldron ⊂⊃

One of the Four Treasures fell in this position; ironically, the Cauldron, which is a symbol of Abundance. Appearing at Lughnasa, which marked for Cathy the third trimester of her pregnancy, the Cauldron seemed an obvious symbol of her pregnant belly and its precious contents. Yet at the same time, the Cauldron represents the fulfilment of material needs. This seemed appropriate, as Cathy and her husband were enjoying a fulfilling, prosperous phase.

Autumn Equinox: ⊞⊞

This was the time at which the child was expected. The tree-letter falling in this place was *nuin* (ash), a tree connected to the legendary magician-god Gwyddyon, suggesting a boy rather than a girl – which proved to be as foretold. Gwyddyon is a figure who bears a wand of transformation and manifestation: Cathy saw this in the dual aspects of the child being manifest into reality and the accompanying transformations of family life which would inevitably ensue.

Samhain: ⊞⊞

The note upon which the reading closed was *úr* (heather) at the time of shadows: Samhain. Heather is traditionally a tree-letter of love and lovers. It forms the soft bed upon which lovers lie in many a traditional tale or ballad. Cathy linked this to her feelings of strength and security in her partnership with her husband. She had every confidence that their love would endure the ghosts, shadows, and doubts of Samhain (more popularly known as Halloween). Happily, this too has since proved to be the case.

III: The Oracle of the Nine Mothers

This spread is adapted from *The Celtic Oracle*, the Ogam divination handbook by Nigel Jackson and Nigel Pennick.[cxxx] It is composed by arranging the cards in three sets of triangles within a larger pyramid of nine positions, corresponding to the nine mothers or maidens of Celtic mythology who tend the Cauldron of Inspiration. The first triad, in the left-hand corner, represents the past. The second, higher triad, represents the present, and the final three cards, on the right-hand side, represent the future. Further details are provided below as to the exact significance of each position in this spread, as developed by my own work with this system.

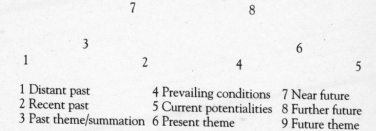

1 Distant past   4 Prevailing conditions   7 Near future
2 Recent past   5 Current potentialities   8 Further future
3 Past theme/summation   6 Present theme   9 Future theme

Each triad has a similar structure. The past is divided into distant past (1), recent past (2), and the theme or 'summation' of that phase of your life (3). We enter the present with certain prevailing conditions (4) and move forwards along certain lines of 'potentiality' (5) depending on our actions. This phase also has a ruling theme (6). Regarding 'that which is to come', we can look forward to the near future (7), the further future which unfolds from that (8), and finally, the overall theme of the future (9). This can be seen as the crown of the reading, as it highlights the point to which your progress currently tends, for better or worse.

The Sample Reading

Amos, a gifted sculptor, was questioning the relationship between his creativity and the state of his finances. Having trained as an apprentice in the jewellery trade many years before, he had been working freelance for several years making rings and talismans.

Although he managed to keep poverty at bay, he decided to consult the Ogam as to his financial prospects looking into the future, which, he admitted, seemed murky.

Amos was well respected in design circles, and was experiencing increasing coverage through exhibitions and in magazines. Alas, this had not translated into a corresponding increase in sales. Success seemed elusive, and the market unyielding, even for a man of considerable craft. He had, in his worst hours, contemplated a return to the manufacture of commercial jewellery for bread and butter money. Other propositions had crossed his path. Yet his heart rebelled against forsaking the Muse, and he hoped that the Nine Mothers might illuminate his dilemma.

9: ⊤⊤

7: ⊥⊥⊥⊥   8: ⊤⊤⊤

3: ╫╫   6: ⊤

1: ╫   2: ⊥⊥⊥   4: ╫╫╫   5: ╫

1–3: The Past: Gort ╫, Coll ⊥⊥⊥⊥ and Eadha ╫╫

1: *Gort* (ivy) is in the position of the distant past. We can recall that ivy is associated with tenacity and survival, which Amos interpreted to represent the entire phase of financial uncertainty and struggle. He felt that the whole basis of his current questioning revolved around issues of survival in a field of uncertain returns. The constrictive aspect of ivy was also appropriate as a symbol for the life-sapping effect of monetary worries.

2: *Coll* (hazel) comes next and is a tree-letter of wisdom and enlightenment. Interestingly enough, Amos had recently completed a ten-day retreat at a Buddhist monastery (though he was not a Buddhist) and he connected hazel, as a card of the 'nuts of wisdom', to the insights gained during this time of meditation. He also related *coll* to his attempts to arrive at a wise decision in life's forking pathways, an issue that had occupied him (despite himself) during meditation.

3: *Eadha* (aspen) is a tree-letter of fear and trembling, matching the mesmeric shimmering of the aspen's leaves. It falls here in the position of the overall theme of the past. How else could this be interpreted but as referring to fears or insecurity regarding the future, which had come to a head so recently? As a man reaching middle age, he seemed to be undergoing some rite of passage, questioning the foundations (and solidity) of his current life, and not without anguish. The real challenge of the trembling tree is, after all, the conquest of self-doubt.

4–6: The Present: Idho ⅢⅢ, Onn ✚, and Beth ⊤

4: *Idho* (yew) is a tree-letter of death and transition. Did this suggest that the fundamentals of his old life were suddenly breaking down and a new set of conditions about to emerge? Amos was willing to interpret yew as a symbol of some kind of closure and transition, without knowing exactly what it might signify. He had the feeling that something was 'in the wind': the future beckoning, the past to be cast out.

5: *Onn* (gorse) is a tree-letter of sexuality – especially connected to the female sex in all senses of the word – which, we may recall, contrasts with the more romantic character of *úr* (heather) as a ogam of love. To Amos, this represented affairs of the heart. Two years before the love of his life had left him, after a mutual altercation. He was seeing women again, but commitment was far from his mind. He was more interested in smelling the many sweet yellow flowers of *onn* than settling down on a bed of heather with one particular woman.

6: *Beth* (birch), like its opposite, *idho* (yew), presents something of an enigma. Birch is a tree of inceptions, new beginnings, and even birth. It could relate to projects and undertakings, or even childbirth. Falling in the overall theme position of the present, Amos saw several possibilities in the new phase which he sensed was emerging. His elder brother had recently offered to involve him in his business, which promised possible returns. A new breeze was blowing; there were possibilities in the wind.

7–9: The Future: Quert ⅢⅢⅢ, Nion ⅢⅢ, and Fearn Ⅲ

7: *Quert* (apple) is a tree-letter of youth, health and vitality. It is strength and virility, the 'force of a man'. At the time of the reading, summer was in the air, and with it the prospect of balmy days – and nights. A time, perhaps, to refresh mind and body, to drink elixir from whichever cup was offered. Not a time to constrict oneself with the knots of insecurity; at least, Amos let his interpretation of *quert* rest on this affirmation.

8: *Nion* (ash) is a tree-letter of transformation and manifestation connected to the Arch-enchanter of Welsh tradition, the magician Gwyddyon. The wand holds the power to change and create from the void the circumstances one desires. For *nuin* is a wishing wand which teaches this way of the wizard. Amos, as a servant of the Muse, was a believer. But could he sculpt a wand of manifestation to banish his financial troubles?

9: *Fearn* (alder) is a tree-letter which corresponds to the 'talking head' of the oracular god, Bran the Blessed. It is also connected by several Ogam interpreters with the 'Faery gifts' of artistic skill and creative expression. Amos saw in *fearn* the enduring strength of his dedication to his art and creativity. This tree-letter was perfect as an overall theme for the future; this 'crown of destiny', he felt, would remain his guiding star well into the future, whatever the future might hold.

In conclusion, the reading did not provide easy answers for Amos, but it gave sound counsel. Though the signs address the issues of survival and creativity, they reinforce the fact that the power over destiny lies partly in our own hands. The enduring images were of the wand and the 'talking head'. Amos saw in these both his commitment to his chosen art and the need to arrive at a means of manifesting more favourable circumstances through it. In this, he felt, lay the challenges ahead.

IV: The Druid Spread

This spread has been imported from the Tarot. As mentioned earlier, it is my personal favourite, by virtue of its marrying of psychological analysis and predictive elements. Its different positions interrelate in many ways. The upper three positions define the higher, symbolic value of past, present, and future experience, while the middle row illustrates a time-line of events from the past, into the present and future. The bottom row reveals the hidden influences, for better or worse, at work in a situation.

Another way of looking at this is that the left-hand 'cross' of staves is the past 'page' or 'chapter' in a person's life, the central column is the present, while the right-hand side is designed to show the nexus of future events, like a page about to unfold. In traditional Celtic terms, these areas (past, present, and future) can be seen as corresponding to the Maiden, Mother, and Crone aspects of the Triple Goddess.

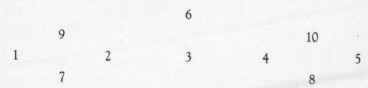

				6				
	9					10		
1		2		3		4		5
	7					8		

First position: Distant past
Second position: Recent past
Third position: Present
Fourth position: Near future
Fifth position: Further future
Sixth position: Overall theme
Seventh position: Blockages
Eighth position: Guides and helpers
Ninth position: Past theme
Tenth position: Future theme

Sample Reading

Emara was a painter in her late twenties. She ultimately hoped to live by her art, but a more pressing concern was that she felt lonely and unattractive. At times, to be alone in life may be counted a boon; matters are rather different when the solitude is enforced. The Druid Spread was the best layout for this question, by virtue of its combination of psychological profiling and future orientation. Yet oracles do not always answer exactly the question posed and, as we will see, in this case the Ogam directed Emara back to her own inner resources, rather than providing the promise of fulfilment in the external world.

First position: Distant past: ᚐ
Second position: Recent past: ᚉ
Third position: Present: ᚃ
Fourth position: Near future: ᚈ
Fifth position: Further future: ᚔ
Sixth position: Overall theme: ᚑ
Seventh position: Blockages: ᚏ
Eighth position: Guides and helpers: ᚎ
Ninth position: Past theme: ᚋ
Tenth position: Future theme: ᚌ

First Position: Distant Past: ᚐ

Ailm (pine/fir) commenced the reading. This is a tree-letter of elation, with wonder and terror in equal measure. It is also related in contemporary divination to gaining a higher perspective, an interpretation to which Emara felt attracted. As a painter, she felt themes of viewing and vision to be extremely important in her art and she sought to express these in her canvases. In personal terms, she felt that her outlook had become progressively more elevated in recent years.

Second Position: Recent Past: ⅢⅠ

Coll (hazel) is a tree-letter of enlightenment and learning, the 'cracking' of the Nuts of Wisdom. The story of Finn mac Cumhail's enlightenment on the banks of the Boyne struck Emara as relating to a sort of apprenticeship she had recently undergone. Her common or garden occupation had been waitressing, but a job at a vineyard had led to her being employed as manager under the tutelage of the vineyard owner. Part of her work involved studying viticulture, which she enjoyed and excelled in.

Third Position: Present: Ⅲ

Fearn (alder) is a tree-letter of oracular guidance and counsel, linked to the mythic theme of the talking head in Celtic culture. Emara's interpretation of this *few* falling in the present position was that the answer to her question lay within, and that she would have to seek for it in her own nature. She felt that she inclined toward the earthy and practical, and felt it hard to allow herself to express what she considered to be her more 'feminine' qualities. *Fearn* represented to her allowing this side of her personality to express itself.

Fourth Position: Near Future: ⅢⅠ

Tinne (holly) appearing in the near future, however, seemed to augur certain challenges. We can recall the image of the wild man figures of Celtic myth armed with clubs of holly and barring the progress of questing heroes. Emara was uncertain whether to interpret this as a psychological barrier to her goals (perhaps an animus figure arising from her own subconscious?) or as an objective trial that lay ahead. Was it related to a man or men in her life? Only time would tell. (Soon after, Emara experienced a passionate but stormy affair with a new man in her life, from which, however, she felt she learned valuable lessons.)

Fifth Position: Further Future: ⅢⅠⅠ

Idho (yew) in the further future suggests loss of some kind. Yew is, after all, the 'cemetery tree' of endings and leave-taking. Emara

sensed that some type of decisive ending or break with the past
lay ahead. Yet she also saw in the image of the yew's yawning
trunk a window of opportunity. The sundering of some element
in her life, she felt, was necessary so that a new one could come
to prevail. (About two years later, Emara in fact chose to make a
break with the past and move to a new city.)

Sixth Position: Overall Theme: ╫

Onn (gorse) as the overall theme of the reading was indeed
synchronistic. Gorse is the tree of sexuality in the Ogam codex
of signs, especially linked to that of female eros. It recalls such
figures of Celtic myth and legend as Adraste and Boudicca:
archetypes of female sexual liberation and independence. Emara
liked the image of the Lady of the Hare as an embodiment of
sexuality, expressed on its own terms. It appealed to her as an
powerful and affirming archetype.

Seventh Position: Blockages: ╫╫

Ruis (elder) fell in the position pertaining to blockages: the
elements of the subconscious or unconscious domain which
hinder us in our progress. Not only that, but this few is reversed.
Emara rejected the relevance of elder's associations of vengefulness and revenge. Instead, she saw in the persona of the Elder
Mother, vilified by patriarchal culture as an evil hag, a kind of
negative cultural construct of female identity. She saw her task as
reclaiming the positive, empowering aspect of this archetype,
thus 'unreversing' it, so to speak.

Eighth Position: Guides and Helpers: ╫╫

Straif (blackthorn) appears reversed in the position corresponding to the positive influences designated as 'guides and helpers'.
This forms a clear contrast to the previous position, which relates
to blockages. It is a tree-letter of strife and conflict, so Emara
at first wondered how this ogam could be of help to her. She
decided that her mild nature led her to habitually avoid conflict
and seek concord, often with the result that either her goodwill
was abused or she felt taken advantage of. She consequently read
this few as suggesting that she needed to be able to draw, symbolically speaking, on the swords and arrows of blackthorn fame to
defend and further her interests in the battle of life.

Ninth Position: Past Theme: ┼

Muin (vine) in the past theme position had a twofold significance for Emara. It obviously denoted her recent efforts at the vineyard – for which, of course, the vine is a perfect symbol – especially as she had been directly involved with grape cultivation in recent months. Complementary to this was the fact that her position had a bacchic aspect, with her being engaged in organizing and hosting group-bookings and parties. She enjoyed this light, festive atmosphere, as a counterpart to the more brooding side of her nature.

Tenth Position: Future Theme: ╫

Gort (ivy) as the future theme suggested further challenges ahead, though with the capacity to surmount them through the application of effort. Ivy, we can recall, is a tree-letter of tenacity and survival. This was germane for Emara because, much as she enjoyed her current work, she wished ultimately to achieve the goal of being a professional artist. Emara recognized in this ogam the practical challenges of survival in the world that confronted her, yet she felt that with tenacious effort she would one day achieve her goal.

Free Ogamcasting

This casting requires an ogam-set carved on twigs or small stones. The subject or querent holds these divinatory tokens in cupped hands, and after meditating on the subject of the reading, casts the ogams forward before him or her so that they flute outwards. The nearest stones are interpreted as representing the past (or at least the root of the current cycle of events), with the ogams fanning out into the branching possibilities of the future. Finally, the left-hand side of the casting is interpreted as representing the shadow-side of reality, while the right-hand side represents life's brighter points and the positive line to be pursued, as it were.

Sample Reading

Finn, a man in his late thirties, posed a classic query to the Ogam. Having been single for several years, since the end of a long-term relationship, he too was tired of being alone in life. He wondered when, and if, he would form another lasting (and meaningful) romance, and what he could do to aid the process. He intimated that he had no luck in love, yet it seemed to me that he was holding something back, unwilling to specify the underlying nature of the enquiry. He seemed burdened by hidden sorrows which ran deeper, perhaps, than the obvious problem. Finn posed this question to the Ogam, using Free Ogamcasting, and this was the result:

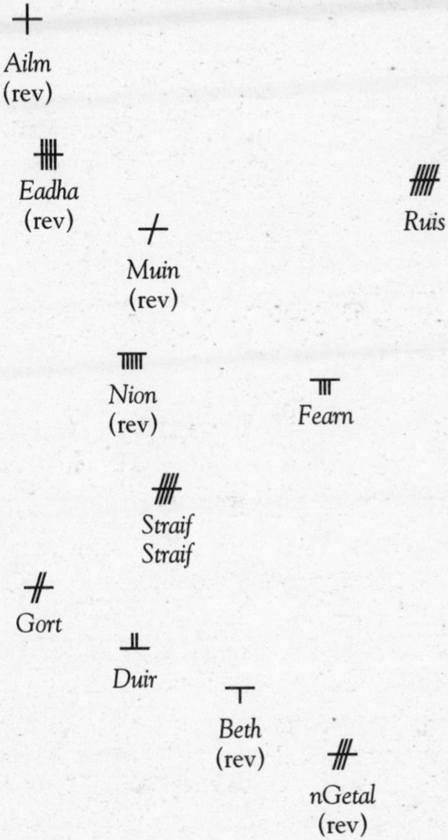

Ailm
(rev)

Eadha
(rev)

Muin
(rev)

Ruis

Nion
(rev)

Fearn

Straif
Straif

Gort

Duir

Beth
(rev)

nGetal
(rev)

The first thing to note with this reading is that the bulk of the ogams in the casting fanned out towards the left rather than the centre, with only one falling on the right. This symbolically casts long shadows over the majority of ogams which appear in the reading, pointing to various buried or submerged psychological factors which may be seen as the root cause of the current cycle in Finn's life. Finn was not blind to the symbolism of the left-leaning ogams, noting them with a wry grin.

Closest to Finn was *nGétal* (broom), an ogam of cleansing and healing connected with the role of the physician. This position at the 'bottom' of the reading should correspond to the distant past of the current circumstances. Finn choose to read the cleaning action (symbolized by the sweeping action of the besom) more as a 'root challenge' or formative issue of the reading, relating to the need to sweep out vestiges of the past and cleanse his perspective on romance.

Next the *beth* (birch) tree-letter appeared, slightly to the left and reversed. Birch is a tree of new beginnings, but its presence to the left of the casting and reversed suggested difficulties in initiating a new romance. To Finn it summarized the theme of his life at the time of the reading, and underlined the need to pursue the problem to its root causes in order to begin a new phase of increased possibilities.

Beside it, though further left, fell *duir* (oak), definitely upright. Oak is a tree-letter of solidity and strength, linked to the mythological figure of the oak king. Its identity in Ogam interpretation is widely seen as being masculine rather than feminine. To Finn this symbolized his strong sense of masculinity which was nonetheless enshadowed by the problems dogging his love life.

Further left still fell *gort* (ivy), a symbol of tenacity and ruthlessness in the natural world. Its proximity to oak further underlined the sense of constriction and weight upon Finn's shoulders, as if the upright bulk of the oak was bowed under the verdure of the ivy. This also related in his mind to financial difficulties which were pitching him into issues of survival rather than ease of existence, but I sensed that there were deeper, unresolved issues troubling him. Had he been the victim or perpetrator of some kind of disturbing abuse?

Above *gort*, *straif* (blackthorn) appeared. *Straif* is traditionally an ogam of strife and conflict, connected with themes of wounding. To Finn this appeared as a symbol of unresolved matters of the heart, rooted in the past and distant past. He wondered, without specifying the exact cause, whether these wounds had fully healed, pulling his attention back to the first ogam (*nGétal*), with its issues of cleansing and healing.

Left of *straif* is *nion* (ash), an ogam of transformation and manifestation. It was almost reversed, suggesting the challenges inherent in changing both internal and external conditions. Could it be, Finn wondered, that his difficulties in shifting his perspective towards the whole arena of romantic involvement (which he confessed a certain cynicism over) was reflected in his seeming inability to initiate a lasting, new romance?

Next, *muin* (vine) appeared, clearly reversed. The vine is generally regarded as a tree-letter of celebration, intoxication and divine ecstasy. This suggested several interpretations to Finn. Firstly, he had been somewhat depressed of late, brooding over past and present hurts. This made it hard for him to relax, let alone enjoy a mood of celebration. It could also signal an inability to harvest the fruits of life on offer; even a block in the flow of a more ecstatic mode of consciousness.

Still further left fell *eadha* (aspen), an ogam of fear and trembling. Finn linked this back to the last ogam, and the fact that he was nervous of being rebuffed. Did this surface emotion mask a deeper, more paralysing phobia that was rooted in past hurts and betrayals?

By itself, on an extreme left-handed limb, fell *ailm* (pine), a tree-letter of elation. Alas, it also appears reversed. To Finn this confirmed and contained the whole preceding set of ogams. His sense of wonder and ecstasy – the perspective symbolically granted from the tall branches of the pine – stood upended and dampened in the stolid ground of disappointment. Perhaps he had developed a phlegmatic disposition, a mood of resignation surrounding love and courtship which left little room for spontaneity and renewal.

Now we turn to the letters which fell to the centre and right of the reading.

Firmly in the centre was *fearn* (alder), a tree-letter of the word and communication, connected to the mythological figure of Bran the Blessed, the oracular chief of British Celtic tribes. As a gifted craftsman who sometimes gave talks and workshops, Finn could relate to his role his mundane and higher, spiritual role as a leader and educator. The appearance of alder in the centre of the reading seemed to be an affirmation of his sense of life-purpose.

Finally, slightly to the right and thus out of the shadows, in this system of casting, fell *ruis* (elder), seemingly at first a curious boon to receive. Elder is traditionally a tree-letter of regret, humiliation, shame and even revenge. In Celtic mythology it appears to symbolize the need to redress wrongs and balance accounts. Finn, however, put a positive spin on this, seeing it as an emblem of processing the lessons of the casting (or rather, the issues which it highlighted in his mind) and putting them behind him, 'laying the dead to rest', in his words.

Thus, he saw in the overall reading a reflection of the need to search out his romantic difficulties to their root emotional causes: to draw them out of the shadows before vanquishing them. The theme of cleansing raised in the first ogam is thus nicely complemented in the last, with the intervening tree-letters pointing to the issues to be resolved. Realization of an underlying bitterness or heaviness of vision that had crept into his personality provoked him to consider the need for counselling, though he was interested in something shamanic (perhaps Jungian analysis or psycho-synthesis) rather than conventional psycho-analysis. Work on his own negative, unconscious patterns was, he felt, the key to attracting happiness into his life.

*

With this reading, we have reached, in one sense, the close of our enquiry into *Ogam*; but in another sense, this is really the beginning, the point of departure. The readings above are only approximations of the wonderful art of Ogamcasting, which truly comes into its own with the creative fusion of the moment of divination, whether performed for yourself or others. It is hoped that the readings chronicled in the preceding pages will be of use in the practical – and intuitive – sphere of conducting divinations using Ogam. A book like the present one can provide intimations and suggestions, but as you progress you will find the roads best suited to your own journey, as they branch at every turn from the Path of Ogam.

The Ogam Revival

The rebirth of Ogam is quite a recent phenomenon, springing from the wider revival of divination systems in the West that has seen the Tarot, Runes, and *I Ching* adopted as popular oracles. It is also grounded in the resurgence of traditional Celtic story-telling, literature, music, art and dance. The Celtic legacy at times seems fleeting, intangible. Indeed, we associate things Celtic less with concrete remains than with a unique feeling – a sensation, a memory in the land, a lilt to music; the enchant-ment, the glamour, of a tale. Yet Celtica has resurfaced in various forms throughout the centuries, and in contemporary Europe (especially Ireland and Brittany), North America, Australia and New Zealand, the Celtic inheritance continuing to express itself. Furthermore, there is a deepening appreciation of the roots of the culture – the mystical and shamanic core of Druidry and the popular religion – and this is feeding into the more general revival of Paganism (and especially Celtic Paganism) today.

Of course, contemporary Druidry follows the spirit of the old traditions rather than attempting any dogmatic recreation, espe-cially as far as the 'Old Religion' of Celtic Europe goes: we are – it must be remembered – talking about a time period spanning several thousand years and a subcontinent crisscrossed by many different tribes and peoples. This is in fact why Ogam, and the early Irish lore it gives us access to, is of particular importance. Ireland was never Romanized, was Christianized only at a rela-tively late date, though comprehensively, and it was fortunate enough to escape the worst excesses of the Inquisition and witch burnings. The mythological heritage of the Emerald Isles is a cultural treasure trove and a unique window into the early tradi-tions of what is today the world's only independent Celtic state. Ogam, with its role as a receptacle of Celtic treelore, is therefore a key text not only of contemporary Druidry and the Western Mysteries, but of the wider rebirth of Paganism today.

The White Goddess

Ogam's reappearance in the field of popular interest was herald-ed with the publication of Robert Graves' famous study of

ancient poetry and religion, *The White Goddess*, in 1948.
Subtitled *A historical grammar of poetic myth*, the book was really
an expression of Graves' own personal mythology, interwoven
with a miasma of Irish, Welsh, Mediterranean and Near Eastern
material. Graves was profoundly learned in the classical tradition,
as his 1955 work *The Greek Myths* shows, and in *The White
Goddess* he sought parallels with Irish, Welsh, and classical
sources. He notes, for example, the resemblance of the oracular
god Bran to the Greek god Orpheus, which is a striking correspondence, though one which may suggest borrowings by the
Welsh from classical themes (the Romans had, after all, conquered much of Britain long before the medieval manuscripts
recorded the tales of the *Mabinogion*). Underlying many of
Graves' conjectures, furthermore, was the abiding image of the
White Goddess of the title, itself founded on the anthropological
fantasies of Margaret Murray. Yet although many of the observa-
tions and claims set forth in *The White Goddess* have not weathered recent developments in certain fields of scholarship well, its
insights into Ogam remain profound. We should also distinguish
between adventurous conjectures Graves made in what is, after
all, a scholastic quagmire, and the overall spirit of the work,
which distinguishes it as a classic of contemporary Celticism. The
Celtic tradition has always been fed and maintained by poets, and
Graves remains one of the greatest and most celebrated bards of
the twentieth century.

Essentially, Graves saw the Tree Alphabet as a codification of
natural lore relating to Druidry, Celtic religion, and the inspiration of the ancient poets. In two crucial chapters of *The White
Goddess*, he sets forth the meanings or associations of the
BethLuisNion letters, relating them to their fields of metaphor
and analogy in Celtic myth. Thus far we are on relatively firm
ground, though as we saw in Ogamlore, there has recently been a
tendency amongst some scholars to dispute the assumption that
trees formed the basis of the original Ogam. What is still more
controversial is Graves' claim to have discovered a hidden Tree
Calendar relating to the months of the Celtic lunar year in the
first thirteen of the Tree Alphabet letters. He writes: 'I noticed
almost at once that the consonants of this alphabet form a

calendar of seasonal tree magic'.[cxxxi] Subsequently, some authors have followed Graves' insights unreservedly and produced contemporary Celtic tree calendars and astrological systems based on his lunar Tree Calendar, while others have disputed his reckoning.

It is beyond the scope of this book to engage the complex arguments of the Tree Calendar. However, Graves' adjoining statement, that 'all the trees [of the Ogam alphabet] figure prominently in European folklore'[cxxxii] is undeniable. Despite the criticism levelled against his work in many quarters, the correspondences which Graves excavated from the fields of folklore and mythology are still a mine of valuable information. And although there were many other scholarly contributions of note, by writers such as Kaledon Naddair and Sean O'Boyle, Graves remains in some ways the father of modern Ogam divination. In the final analysis, his research has heavily influenced, for better or for worse, many subsequent interpreters.

Contemporary Commentators

Readers of this book may well find it useful to have a brief overview of the major contributors to contemporary Ogam divination. This is because there is quite a bit of divergence in the way different authors choose to interpret – or reconstruct the meanings of – the tree-letters. In the longer term, you may want to explore several different systems in order to enrich your understanding of Ogam, and this should prove a helpful and enlightening process. However, it can also result in confusion, for the paths followed by some of the authors in this field are somewhat difficult to reconcile with others. Having some overall understanding of where each is coming from can save a lot of time and frustration.

The first attempt to retrieve Ogam as a popular oracle was Colin and Liz Murray's *The Celtic Tree Oracle: a system of divination*, published in 1988. Although important and deservedly well known, not all aspects of the Murrays' approach have been accepted by subsequent authors. The Murrays followed Graves' notion of the Tree Calendar, but their primary focus was the divinatory significations of the twenty ogams of the BethLuisFearn Tree Alphabet and *forfeda* (five extra letters). They state that 'the use of this alphabet was symbolic and . . . each letter had a host of ideas and thoughts centred around it relating to Celtic cosmology and philosophy.'[cxxxiii] Seeing the ogams as 'keys that open a door to a parallel world of knowledge, meanings and associations',[cxxxiv] the Murrays presented their Tree Oracle as a set of cards in a wooden box with a green cloth segmented for the practice of divination. Their commentaries on each card give both its mythological or folkloric meaning, along with a description of each tree and set of divinatory meanings.

In 1992 *The Celtic Oracle: a complete guide to using the cards* by Nigel Pennick, with cards illustrated by Nigel Jackson, appeared. Also a boxed set accompanied by an interpretative booklet, this work involves a somewhat different approach to Ogam. Pennick, who describes the script as a 'shamanic mystery language',[cxxxv] focuses on each ogam as a primarily mythological symbol. Thus the *luis* few (rowan) becomes the Lady of the Unicorn, *coll* (hazel) is the Nuts of Wisdom, and *straif* (blackthorn) the Increaser of Secrets. Some of these mythological correspondences stem from the Word Ogams, but the authors also read across to the other Ogam alphabets discussed in Ogamlore (Colour Ogam, Fortress Ogam, etc.) and this produces a set of associations alongside for each tree-letter, including its ruling deity, bird, herb, colour, and uses. As we have seen, such direct linkages are interesting but questionable, and this approach has been criticized, most notably by Steve Blamires (see below). Nonetheless, this is a very charming and workable system of divination, beautifully illustrated.

The commentary in *The Celtic Oracle* is a severely shortened version of the authors' original manuscript, which was released five years later as *The New Celtic Oracle* (1997). This volume is much more detailed in its treatment of the mythological correspondences.

Edred Thorsson, familiar to many from his books on the Runes, entered the fray in 1994 with *The Book of Ogam: the Celtic tree oracle*. This work is not accompanied by a set of cards, though his text does contain illustrations by Anne Marie Hoppe. Thorsson counsels, quite reasonably, the creation of one's own collection of Ogam twigs. He expresses impatience with much of the previous material on offer, with its 'acceptance or invention of "poetic truths"', including Graves' work. He comments: 'Graves is useful as a collection of lore about the individual fews, or "trees", but the system and history he proposes for it is nontraditional.'cxxxvi

Now, Thorsson observes that 'the ogham system is first and foremost a system of classification of things in a cosmological order' that aided the bards and Druids in the memorization of their lore, used 'for the organisation of all disciplines of thought.'cxxxvii He also recognizes the basis of the various scripts (Tree Ogam, Dog Ogam, Woman Ogam, etc.) as lying in the phonetic sequence of the Ogam letters, from which spring the many lists given in medieval manuscripts. This, so far, is all well and good. Yet in his actual presentation of the divinatory meanings of each Ogamfew, Thorsson bases his body of correspondences around these root sounds or letters. *Coll* (hazel) for example is linked to the divinities and heroes Cian mac Cainte (father of the sun god Lugh), Caillach (a type of malevolent hag) and Cú Chulainn because they share the consonant /c/.

It does indeed seem likely that this is how the bards of old used the root sounds to collate lists of various kinds, but for the purposes of divination it creates great difficulties. *Coll*, for instance, has a clear mythological tale attached to it in the story of Finn mac Cumhail, who tastes the salmon of wisdom which has eaten the nuts of the magical hazel tree, or with Cormac, who has the hazels themselves revealed to him by the sea-god Manannán mac Lir. Thorsson mentions Finn and he agrees that this tree-letter signifies knowledge, especially of an otherworldly kind. Yet he also links *coll* to the mythological or legendary figures of Cian, Caillach, and Cú Chulainn, none of which are especially relevant to the mythology of the hazel! In fact, this approach seems to me to be quite misleading – at least for the purposes of divination.

Richard Webster's *Omens, Oghams and Oracles: divination in the druidic tradition* (1995) presents the reader with a system of Ogam alongside several other types of Celtic divination. Of Ogam he writes: 'the letters were symbolic, with each letter indicating a wide variety of ideas relating to Celtic philosophy'.[cxxxviii] He too regards Ogam as a 'complete cosmological system', also employed in divination.

> Each ogham relates primarily to a tree, which is then in turn related to a colour, animal and tree month . . . . The Celts had a wide variety of items that could be connected with each ogham, allowing a single tree to act as a mnemonic [memory aid] for a large number of apparently unconnected objects.[cxxxix]

Though Webster follows Jackson and Pennick by giving the colour and animal correspondences, his commentary generally follows the folkloric and mythological associations of the trees themselves. The chief strength of Webster's work is to show Ogam in the context of various other traditional divinatory techniques. He also adheres to Robert Graves' Tree Calendar.

Celtic Tree Mysteries: secrets of the ogham (1997) by Steve Blamires makes the unorthodox claim that the Tree Alphabet is older than Ogam, though in fact, as we saw in Ogamlore, scholars of the alphabet are generally moving in the reverse direction. Focusing on the trees themselves as receptacles of symbolism, Blamires criticizes writers who create bodies of 'magical' correspondences for ogams based on the Book of Ballymote, dismissing the lists of 'other Ogams' as late and corrupt. He does, however, reproduce the Word Ogams along with his texts as keys to the meaning of the tree-letters, discussing the qualities of the trees on three levels: physical, mental, and spiritual. In fact, Blamires' work is more concerned with the magical, esoteric, and ecological aspects of the trees than their divinatory function. He notes that he does not find Ogam to be 'very helpful in answering questions relating to the mundane world',[cxxxx] but kindly provides a table of divinatory meanings in an appendix.

These are the main offerings on Ogam interpretation to date, though there are also the magical workbooks of solo practitioners, contemporary Druidic orders, and countless other Pagan groups. A number of such offerings have recently been launched into cyberspace, contributing to the World Wide Web of commentary that surrounds the old Tree Alphabet's mysterious fews. There are also a number of books on treelore which have appeared recently, such as Jacqueline Memory Paterson's *Tree Wisdom* (1996), which are concerned with the mythology and folklore connected to the trees, though not necessarily with Ogam itself. You may wish to explore these many sources in order to enrich your understanding of the Tree Alphabet in the longer term, though the websites in particular should be treated with caution, as they contain a lot of hearsay masquerading as fact.

Pronunciation Guide

This section is designed to provide a basic pronunciation guide to some of the more important, commonly used, or difficult Irish and Welsh names and terms found in this oracle.

The existence of different pronunciations of Irish words (due to divergences of Old, Middle and Modern Irish, and dialectal differences), compounded by the presence of varying scholarly systems of notation, make it very much a starting point rather than final destination! Please also note that, unlike English, some Gaelic words do not have a stressed syllable. Finally, some of the quotations in this book, such as those from Lady Gregory's *Irish Myths and Sagas*, employ variant spellings and the quoted passages may lack accentation.

Amergin	AH-mer-gin
Annwyn	ANN-oon
Aoife	EEF-eh
Balor	BAH-lor
Beltaine	BAL-tinna
Birog	BIRR-ogue
Brí Leith	bree lay
Bricriu	BRICK-roo
Bruig na Bóinde	broy na BONE-yeh
Caoilte	KWEEL-teh
Cathbad	KATH-vhad
Ceridwen, Keridwen	keer-ID-win
Cian	KEE-an
Conan	KONE-an
Cormac	KOR-mac
Crimnall	KRIV-all
Cú Chulainn	KO-hull-in

Dagda	DAG-da
Deirdré	DER-dru (the u is hardly said)
Díancecht	DEE-an keck't/ DEE-an haht
Diarmaid O'Duibhne	DEER-mid o DIE-neh
Dindsenchus	din-SHEN-cus
Dubhros	DUV-ros
Emain	EV-in
Étaín	AID-een
Falias	FA-lee-as
Fenian	FINN-ee-an
Fianna	FEE-an-ah
Finn mac Cumhail	Fin mac Cool
Fir Bolg	fir bolg
flesc	flayshk
Fomór, Fomóri, Formórian	FOE-mor, FOE-mor-ee, FOE-mor-ee-yn
geiss, geasa (plural)	gesh, GAS-ah
Goibniu	GYB-noo/ GWIV-neh
Gorias	GOR-ee-as
Gráinne	GRAUN-ya
Lia Fál	LEE-ah FAW-il
Lugh	LOO
Macha	MAK-a
Maeldúin	male-DOON
Mag Tured	moy-TOOR-a
Manannán mac Lir	MAN-ah nin mac LEER
Matholwch	MATH-o-law
Maxen Wledig	MAX-in OO-le-dig
Medb	mayv
Mider, Midhir	MID-ir/MID-yar
Milesian	Mil-EASE-yan
Mórrígu	MORR-ig-oo
Murias	MOOR-ee-as
Níamh	NEE-av
Noísiu	NEESH-eh
Óengus Og	AEN-gus OG
Ogam, Ogham	OH-am
Ogma	OG-ma
Oisín	ush-EEN
Olwen	oh-WEEN

Rónán	ROE-nan
Samhain	SOW-in/SOW-een ('sow' as in female pig)
Scáthach	SCOU-ha/ SKAW-thach
Searbhán Lochlannach	SAR-an LOCH-an
sidhé	shee
Suibné	SWEE-nee
taebomnae	tay-bo-nay
Taín Bó Cuilnge	TOYN-bo HOO-ling-eh
Tara	TOW-er (to rhyme with 'power')
Tir na nÓg	teer na n-ogue
Túatha dé Danaan	TOO-ha day DAN-an
Usnech	OOSH-na
Yspadden Penkawr	ee-pa-DHAN pen-KWER

Bibliography

Anderson, William and Hicks, Clive, *The Green Man: archetype of our oneness with the earth* (London: HarperCollins, 1990)

Barron, W. R. J. (ed. and trans.), *Sir Gawain and the Green Knight* (Manchester: Manchester University Press, 1974)

Blamires, Steve, *Celtic Tree Mysteries: Secrets of the Ogham* (St. Paul, Minn.: Llewellyn, 1997)

Brewer, D. S., *Malory: The Morte D'arthur*, York Medieval Texts (London: Edward Arnold, 1996)

Cable, James (trans.), *The Death of King Arthur* (London: Penguin Books, 1976; 1971)

Calder, George (ed. and trans.), *Auraicept na N-Eces* (Edinburgh: John Grant, 1917)

Carpenter, Edward, *The Origins of Pagan and Christian Beliefs* (London: Senate, 1996; originally published as *Pagan & Christian Beliefs*, London: George Allen & Unwin, 1920)

Chrétien de Troyes, *Arthurian Romances*, trans. D. D. R. Owen (London: Dent, 1987)

Cowan, Tom, *Fire in the Head: shamanism and the Celtic spirit* (San Francisco: HarperSan Francisco, 1993)

Daniels, Peter T. and Bright, William, 'Ogham', in *The World's Writing Systems* (New York: Oxford University Press, 1996)

Dillon, Miles, *The Cycles of the Kings* (Dublin: Four Courts Press, 1994)
— *Early Irish Literature* (Dublin: Four Courts Press, 1994)

Dooley, Ann and Roe, Harry, *Tales of the Elders of Ireland: a new translation of Acallam na Senorach by Ann Dooley and Harry Roe* (Oxford: Oxford University Press, 1999)

Gantz, Jeffrey (trans.), *Early Irish Myths and Sagas* (London: Penguin Books, 1981)
— *The Mabinogion* (London: Penguin Books, 1976)

Goodenough, Simon, *Celtic Mythology* (London: Tiger, 1997)

Graves, Robert, *The White Goddess*, 1986 (originally published London: Faber & Faber, 1986; 1961)

Gregory, [Augusta,] Lady, *Irish Myths and Legends* (Philadelphia, Pa. and London: Courage, 1998; originally published as *Gods and Fighting Men*, London: John Murray, 1904)

Guest, Charlotte (trans.), *The Mabingion* (London: Folio Society, 1980)

Hough, Graham, *The Mystery Religion of W. B. Yeats* (Sussex: Harvester Press, 1984)

Hutton, Ronald, *The Pagan Religions of the Ancient British Isles* (Oxford: Blackwell, 1991)

— *The Triumph of the Moon: a study of modern pagan witchcraft* (Oxford: Oxford University Press, 1999)

Jones, Leslie Ellen, *Druid, Shaman, Priest: metaphors of Celtic Paganism* (Middlesex: Hisarlik Press, 1998)

Jones, Prudence and Pennick, Nigel, *A History of Pagan Europe* (London: Routledge, 1997; 1995)

Kinsella, Thomas (trans.), *The Tain: Translated from the Irish Epic Tain Bó Cuilnge* (Dublin: Dolmen Press, 1970)

Knott, Eleanor & Murphy, Gerard, *Early Irish Literature* (London: Routledge & Kegan Paul, 1966)

Koch, John and Carey, John, *The Celtic Heroic Age: literary sources for ancient Celtic Europe and early Ireland and Wales* (Massachusetts: Celtic Studies Publications, 1997)

Layard, John, *The Lady of the Hare: being a study in the healing power of dreams*, London: Faber & Faber, 1944

McManus, Damian, *A Guide to Ogam* (Maynooth: An Sagart, 1991)

Markale, Jean, *Celtic Civilization*, trans. Christine Hauch (London: Gordon and Cremonesi, 1978; originally published as *Les celtes et la civilisation celtique*, Paris : Payot, 1976)

— *Merlin: Priest of Nature*, trans. Belle N. Burke (Rochester, Vt.: Inner Traditions International, 1995; originally published as *Merlin l'Enchanteur*, Paris: Éditions Retz, 1981)

Mason, Eugene (trans.), *Wace and Layamon's Arthurian Chronicles* (London: Dent, 1986; 1962)

Matarasso, Pauline (trans.), *The Quest of the Holy Grail* (London: Penguin Books, 1986; 1969)

Matthews, Caitlín, *The Celtic Book of the Dead: a guide to your voyage in the Celtic otherworld* (London: Aquarian/Thorsons, 1992)

— and John, *The Encyclopedia of Celtic Wisdom* (Shaftesbury: Element, 1994)

Matthews, John, (ed.), *The Bardic Source Book: inspirational legacy and teachings of the ancient Celts* (London: Blandford, 1998)
— *A Celtic Reader: selections from Celtic legend, scholarship and story* (London: Aquarian/Thorsons, 1991)
— *The Celtic Shaman: a handbook* (Shaftesbury: Element, 1991)
— *The Druid Source Book: from earliest times to the present day* (London: Blandford, 1997)
— *King Arthur and the Grail Quest* (London: Blandford, 1994)
— *Taliesin: Shamanism and the bardic mysteries in Britain and Ireland* (London: Aquarian, 1991)
Mór, Caiseal, *The Song of the Earth* (Sydney: Arrow, 1996)
Murphy, G., *The Ossianic Lore and Romantic Tales of Medieval Ireland* (Cork: Mercier Press for the Cultural Relations Committee, 1971; originally published Dublin: Sign of the Three Candles, 1955)
Mytum, Harold, *The Origins of Early Christian Ireland* (London: Routledge, 1992)

O Croinin, Daibhi, *Early Medieval Ireland: 400–1200* (London: Longman, 1995)

Paterson, Jacqueline Memory, *Tree Wisdom: the definitive guidebook to the myth, folklore and healing power of trees* (London: Thorsons, 1996)

Rolleston, T. W., *Myths and Legends of the Celtic Race* (London: Senate, 1994)
Ross, Anne, *Everyday Life of the Pagan Celts* (London: Batsford, 1970)

Spence, Lewis, *The Magical Arts in Celtic Britain* (Durango, Co.: Longwood Academic, 1995; originally published London; New York: Rider, 1945)
Squire, Charles, *Celtic Myth and Legend, Poetry and Romance* (London: Gresham, 1939)
Stewart, R. J. (ed.), *The Book of Merlin, insights from the First Merlin Conference, London, June 1986* (London: Blandford, 1987)
Suilleabhain, S. O., *Storytelling in Irish Tradition* (Cork: Mercier Press for the Cultural Relations Committee, 1973)

Tallant, Robert, *Mardi Gras* (Gretna, La.: Pelican, 1976)
Thorsson, Edred, *The Book of Ogam: the Celtic tree oracle* (St Paul, Mn.: Llewellyn, 1992)
Tolkien, J. R. R., *Tree and Leaf* (London: Unwin-Hyman, 1988; 1964)
Tolstoy, Nikolai, *The Quest for Merlin* (London: Coronet: 1985)

Wells, Peter S., *The Barbarians Speak: how the conquered peoples shaped Roman Europe* (Princeton: Princeton University Press, 1999)

Wilhelm, Richard and Baynes, Cary, *The I Ching or Book of Changes*, Bollinger Series XIX (Princeton: Princeton University Press, 1980; 1950)

Wilson, David M. (ed.), *The Northern World: the History and Heritage of Northern Europe* (New York: Harry N. Abrams, 1980)

Zaczek, Iain, *Chronicles of the Celts* (London: Hodder and Stoughton, 1997)

— *Ireland: Land of the Celts* (London: Collins and Brown, 2000)

References

Introduction

i Squire, *Celtic Myth and Legend*, p. 151–2.

I: Ogamlore

ii Quoted in Markale, *Celtic Civilisation*, p. 225.

iii Wilhelm/Baynes (trans.), *The I Ching or Book of Changes*, pp. 328–9.

iv Quoted in Markale, *Celtic Civilisation*, p. 257.

v Gregory, *Irish Myths and Sagas*, p. 110.

vi Cited in Matthews, *The Encyclopedia of Celtic Wisdom*, p. 50.

vii Cited in Matthews, *The Encyclopedia of Celtic Wisdom*, p. 49–50.

viii Quoted in Markale, *Celtic Civilisation*, p. 64.

ix Gregory, *Irish Myths and Legends*, p. 27.

x Gregory, *Irish Myths and Legends*, p. 120.

xi Quoted in Markale, *Celtic Civilisation*, p. 50.

xii Strabo, *Geographica*, IV, 4, 197–8, trans. W. Dinan, cited in Matthews, *The Druid Source Book*, p. 18.

xiii Diodorus Siculus, *Histories*, V, 28 and 31, trans. T. D. Kendrick, cited in Matthews, *The Druid Source Book*, p. 18.

xiv Carr-Gomm, Foreword in Matthews, *The Druid Source Book*, p. 5.

xv Carr-Gomm, Foreword in Matthews, *The Druid Source Book*, p. 5–6.

xvi Tacitus, *Annals*, XIV, 30, trans. A. J. Church and T. D. Broadribb, cited in Matthews, *The Druid Source Book*, p. 23.

xvii Gregory, *Irish Myths and Legends*, p. 41.

xviii O'Curry, 'Druids and Druidism in Ancient Ireland', in Matthews, *A Celtic Reader*, p. 21.

xix Vopiscus, *Numerianus*, XI, trans. T. D. Kendrick, cited Matthews, *The Druid Source Book*, p. 24.

xx Pomponius Mela, *De Situ Orbis*, III, 2, 18 and 19, trans. T. D. Kendrick, in Matthews, *The Druid Source Book*, p. 20.

xxi Matthews, *Taliesin*, p. 281.

xxii Matthews, *Taliesin*, p. 294.

xxiii Cited in the Introduction, Matthews, *The Bardic Source Book*, p. 12.

xxiv Cited in the Introduction, Matthews, *The Bardic Source Book*, pp. 12–13.

xxv Chadwick, *Scottish Gaelic Studies*, IV, 1935; 97. Cited in Dillon, *Early Irish Literature*, p. 36 footnote 10.

xxvi Cited in the Introduction, John Matthews, *The Bardic Source Book*, p. 13.

xxvii   Matthews, *The Celtic Tradition*, p. 49.
xxviii   Matthews, *The Celtic Tradition*, p. 49.
 xxix   Markale, *Celtic Civilisation*, p. 109.
  xxx   Dillon, *Early Irish Literature*, p. 1.
 xxxi   Gregory, *Irish Myths and Legends*, p. 165.
xxxii   Cited in Markale, *Merlin*, p. 115.
xxxiii   Quoted in Markale, *Merlin*, pp. 47–8.
xxxiv   Trans. J. G. O'Keefe (ed. and trans.) in *The Adventures of Suibhne Geilt*, D. Nutt (London, 1913), quoted in Matthews, *The Encyclopedia of Celtic Wisdom*, p. 177.
xxxv   Markale, *Merlin*, p. 91. See chapter five, 'Sacred Incest'.
xxxvi   Troyes, *Arthurian Romances*, p. 286.
xxxvii   Adapted from *The Mabinogi of Taliesin*, Idrison, *The Cambrian and Caledonian Quarterly*, 1835; cited in Matthews, *The Bardic Source Book*, pp. 81–7.
xxxviii Markale, *Celtic Civilisation*, pp. 239–40.

II: Ogamfews

xxxix   Tolkien, *Tree and Leaf*, p. 98.
   xl   Gregory, *Irish Myths and Legends*, p. 322.
  xli   Gregory, *Irish Myths and Legends*, p. 326.
 xlii   Markale, *Celtic Civilisation*, p. 249.
xliii   Gregory, *Irish Myths and Legends*, p. 103.
 xliv   Gregory, *Irish Myths and Legends*, p. 343.
  xlv   Gregory, *Irish Myths and Legends*, p. 98.
 xlvi   Markale, *Celtic Civilisation*, p. 239.
xlvii   *The Myvyrian Archaeology of Wales*, cited in Markale, *Celtic Civilisation*, p. 76.
xlviii   *The Myvyrian Archaeology of Wales*, cited in Markale, *Celtic Civilisation*, p. 76.
 xlix   Guest, *The Mabinogion*, p. 45.
    l   Porteous, *The Lore of the Forest*, p. 177.
   li   Blamires, *Celtic Tree Mysteries*, p. 91.
  lii   Matthews, *The Celtic Book of the Dead*, p. 28.
 liii   Gregory, *Irish Myths and Legends*, p. 130.
  liv   Graves, *The White Goddess*, p. 174.
   lv   Guest, *The Mabinogion*, p. 71.
  lvi   Matthews and Matthews, *The Encyclopedia of Celtic Wisdom*, p. 60.
 lvii   Guest, *Mabinogion*, p. 115.
lviii   Markale, *Celtic Civilisation*, p. 247.
  lix   Gregory, *Irish Myths and Legends*, p. 70.
   lx   Gregory, *Irish Myths and Legends*, p. 122.
  lxi   Gregory, *Irish Myths and Legends*, pp. 125 and 128. The King of the Land of the Ever-Living Ones (Manannan) later tells Cormac that 'the man you saw kindling the fire . . . is a young lord that is more liberal than he can afford, and everyone else is served while he is

getting the feast ready, and everyone else profiting by it . . . ' This would seem to relate to the institution of sacral kingship, which from early times was regarded as a role of service and sacrifice.

lxii   Markale, *Celtic Civilisation*, p. 190.

lxiii   Pliny, *Historia Naturalis*, XVI, 249, trans. T. D. Kendrick, cited in Matthews, *The Druid Source Book,* p. 21.

lxiv   W. R. J. Barron (trans.), *Sir Gawain and the Green Knight*, p. 47.

lxv   Gregory, *Irish Myths and Legends*, p. 114.

lxvi   Gregory, *Irish Myths and Legends*, p. 241.

lxvii   Gregory, *Irish Myths and Legends*, p. 165.

lxviii Gregory, *Irish Myths and Legends*, p. 27.

lxix   Porteous, *The Lore of the Forest*, p. 49.

lxx   Gregory, *Irish Myths and Legends*, p. 52.

lxxi   Malory, *The Morte D'arthur*, trans. D. B. Brewer, p. 147.

lxxii   Matthews, *The Celtic Book of the Dead*, p. 27.

lxxiii Gregory, *Irish Myths and Legends*, p. 120.

lxxiv   Gregory, *Irish Myths and Legends*, p. 124.

lxxv   The Ogham Tract, reproduced in Matthews, *The Encyclopedia of Celtic Wisdom*, p. 51.

lxxvi   Matthews, *Taliesin*, p. 311.

lxxvii Harris, *The Ascent of Olympus*, quoted in Porteous, *The Lore of the Forest*, p. 161.

lxxviii J. G. O'Keefe (ed. and trans.) *The Adventures of Suibhne Geilt*, quoted in Matthews, *The Encyclopedia of Celtic Wisdom*, p. 177.

lxxix   Murphy, trans., *Duanaire Finn*, quoted in Blamires, *Celtic Tree Mysteries*, p. 155.

lxxx   J. G. O'Keefe (ed. and trans.) in *The Adventures of Suibhne Geilt*, quoted in Matthews, *The Encyclopedia of Celtic Wisdom*, p. 17.

lxxxi   This is a traditional song, most notably rendered by the English folk rock band Pentacle in modern times.

lxxxii McManus, 'Ogham', in *The World's Writing Systems*, p. 341.

lxxxiii Blamires, *Celtic Tree Mysteries*, p. 160.

lxxxiv Markale, *Celtic Civilisation*, p. 245.

lxxxv   Gregory, *Irish Myths and Legends*, p. 36.

lxxxvi Gregory, *Irish Myths and Legends*, p. 30.

lxxxvii Gregory, *Irish Myths and Legends*, p. 183.

lxxxviii Gregory, *Irish Myths and Legends*, p. 255.

lxxxix Cecile O'Rahilly, *Tain Bo Cuailgne*, cited in Blamires, *Celtic Tree Mysteries*, p. 167.

xc   Gregory, *Irish Myths and Legends*, pp. 162–3.

xci   Gregory, *Irish Myths and Legends*, p. 193.

xcii   Spence, *The Magic Arts in Celtic Britain*, p. 28.

xciii   Gregory, *Irish Myths and Legends*, p. 283.

xciv   Gregory, *Irish Myths and Legends*, p. 284.

xcv   Paterson, *Tree Wisdom*, p. 279.

xcvi   Guest, *The Mabinogion*, p. 148.

xcvii   Troyes, *Arthurian Romances*, p. 286.

    xcviii Troyes, *Arthurian Romances*, p. 287.
     xcix Gregory, *Irish Myths and Legends*, p. 294.
        c Gregory, *Irish Myths and Legends*, p. 406.
       ci Gregory, *Irish Myths and Legends*, p. 230.
      cii Gregory, *Irish Myths and Legends*, p. 355–6.
     ciii Paterson, *Tree Wisdom*, p. 299.
      civ Gregory, *Irish Myths and Legends*, p. 395.
       cv Paterson, *Tree Wisdom*, p. 301.
      cvi Quoted in Graves, *The White Goddess*, p. 194.
     cvii Gregory, *Irish Myths and Legends*, p. 99.
    cviii Graves, *The White Goddess*, p. 194.
      cix Graves, *The White Goddess*, p. 194.
       cx Matthews, *Taliesin*, p. 289.
      cxi Quoted in Jackson and Pennick, *New Celtic Oracle*, p. 182.
     cxii See Markale, *Celtic Civilisation*, pp. 238–43.
    cxiii Squire, *Celtic Myth and Legend, Poetry and Romance*, p. 81.
     cxiv Gantz, 'The Wasting Sickness of Cu Chulainn' from *Early Irish Myths and Sagas*, p. 173.
      cxv Guest, *Irish Myths and Legends*, p. 43.
     cxvi Squire, *Celtic Myths and Legends*, p. 63.
    cxvii Guest, *Irish Myths and Legends*, p. 73.
   cxviii Squire, *Celtic Myths and Legends*, p. 108.

III. Ogamcasting

     cxix Guest, *The Mabinogion*, p. 131–2.
      cxx Matthews, *The Encyclopedia of Celtic Wisdom*, p. 248.
     cxxi Kinsella (trans.), *The Tain*, p. 34.
    cxxii Matthews, *The Encyclopedia of Celtic Wisdom*, p. 240.
   cxxiii Crossley-Holland, *The Norse Myths*, p. xvi.
    cxxiv Matthews, *The Celtic Tradition*, p. 44.
     cxxv Spence, *The Magical Arts in Celtic Britain*, p. 107.
    cxxvi Wilhelm/Baynes (trans.), *The I Ching or Book of Changes*, p. 315.
   cxxvii Squire, *Celtic Myth and Legend*, p. 151–2.
  cxxviii Gregory, *Irish Myths and Sagas*, p. 110.
    cxxix Jackson and Pennick, *The New Celtic Oracle*, p. 37.
     cxxx Jackson and Pennick, *The Celtic Oracle*, p. 94.
    cxxxi Graves, *The White Goddess*, p. 165.
   cxxxii Graves, *The White Goddess*, p. 165.
  cxxxiii Murray, *The Celtic Tree Oracle*, p. 8.
   cxxxiv Murray, *The Celtic Tree Oracle*, p. 13
    cxxxv Jackson and Pennick, *The Celtic Oracle*, p. 7.
   cxxxvi Thorsson, *The Book of Ogam*, p. xi.
  cxxxvii Thorsson, *The Book of Ogam*, pp. 13–14.
 cxxxviii Webster, *Omens, Oghams and Oracles*, p. 60.
   cxxxix Webster, *Omens, Oghams and Oracles*, p. 63.
    cxxxx Blamires, *Celtic Tree Mysteries*, p. 251.

Index of the Tree-Letters

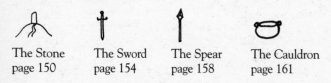